The Politics of Preference

The Politics of Preference

Democratic Institutions and Affirmative Action in the United States and India

Sunita Parikh

Ann Arbor

THE UNIVERSITY OF MICHIGAN PRESS

2000   1999   1998   1997   4   3   2   1

A CIP catalog record for this book is available from the British Library

Library of Congress Cataloging-in-Publication Data

Parikh, Sunita, 1959–
    The politics of preference : democratic institutions and
affirmative action in the United States and India / Sunita Parikh.
        p.   cm.
    Includes bibliographical references (p.   ) and index.
    ISBN 0-472-10745-3 (cloth : acid-free paper)
    1. Race discrimination—Government policy—United States—History.
2. Minorities—Government policy—United States—History.
3. Affirmative action programs—Government policy—United States—
History.   4. United States—Politics and government—1945–1989.
5. United States—Politics and government—1989–   6. Race
discrimination—Government policy—India—History.   7. Minorities—
Government policy—India—History.   8. Affirmative action programs—
Government policy—India—History.   9. India—Politics and
government—1857–1919.   10. India—Politics and
government—1919–1947.   11. India—Politics and government—1947–
I. Title.
HT1523.P27   1996
305.8'00973—dc20   96-25176
                                                             CIP

For My Parents
In Memory of
Chandulal P. Parikh and Bhanu K. Parikh

Acknowledgments

I began this project nearly ten years ago as a dissertation proposal because I was interested in understanding why similar solutions to social problems arise in ethnically heterogenous polities that are otherwise quite different. In the middle 1980s, affirmative action was a moribund topic in the United States but full of life and controversy in India. Today it is practically a settled issue in India and an extremely lively one in the United States. In both countries, however, we know much more about the conventional wisdom that justifies or attacks affirmative action than we do about its political history. This book is designed to provide that knowledge.

In the ten years I have worked on affirmative action, I have racked up many debts. My dissertation committee did its best to help me produce a strong thesis, and my ultimate lack of satisfaction with it was due to my limitations, not theirs. Susanne Rudolph has been a strong and supportive mentor since my college days, and her standards for case research have remained with me even after her direct influence ended. Theda Skocpol showed me that truly comparative work is not only possible but crucial. William Julius Wilson provided steady encouragement when I doubted the wisdom of pursuing a controversial topic, as much through his example as his words. Russell Hardin helped me to bring some of the standards of positive theory to a comparative historical analysis and pointed me toward the direction I eventually adopted in the book.

The University of Chicago has always provided a singular environment for learning. The Department of Political Science has managed to house almost as many theoretical approaches as faculty members, which means that students frequently become confused, but they also learn a wide array of methods to tackle a research question. I gathered very different ideas from Lloyd Rudolph, Duncan Snidal, and Jon Elster, but I am indebted to all three. Wilder House, under the direction of Theda Skocpol and then David Laitin, provided a research environment that cut across disciplines, hierarchies, and ideologies and forced me to think critically; the rapport that the inhabitants developed has produced a huge crop of excellent junior (and now senior) scholars. You know who you are.

At Columbia I have been fortunate to have had wonderful junior colleagues who took an interest in my work, including Edward Mansfield, David Spiro, Gregory Gause, Sharyn O'Halloran, and David Epstein. Robert Shapiro, Ira Katnelson, and Scott Adler read drafts of the manuscript and offered valuable suggestions. Chuck Cameron in particular has showed great patience and support over the last six years. He has helped me learn positive theory and rational choice, read numerous drafts of chapters and papers, and never despaired (at least outwardly) at my repeated inability to find the Nash equilibria in a simple matrix. Outside Columbia, John Ferejohn, Andy Rutten, Bruce Bueno de Mesquita, and Barry Weingast encouraged me to combine comparative and rational-choice methods; I benefited greatly from all our conversations.

Three foundations have been instrumental in making the realization of this project possible. The Rockefeller Foundation provided dissertation support when few other sources were available due to the controversial nature of the work. The Spencer Foundation, under the presidency of the late Lawrence Cremin, provided an almost perfect work environment in which I learned about education, affirmative action, and much more. The Harry Frank Guggenheim Foundation is supporting a project on political violence that has turned out to bear directly on the issue of preference policies. The Hoover Institution graciously provided office space and other resources for me as a Visiting Scholar in 1992 and as a National Fellow in 1995–96.

In India, many people were generous with their time, attention, and resources. In addition to those cited as interviewees, several other scholars, politicians, and civil servants in Gujarat and Karnataka provided information that helped shape this book. Andre Beteille encouraged me to undertake the comparison when few others were enthusiastic, and he shared his own comparative work in progress to help me along. Achyut Yagnik in Ahmedabad has been a friend, mentor, and invaluable resource, and he and his colleagues at SETU have taken wonderful care of me for over a decade. In Bangalore, Narendar Pani and Jamuna Rao have generously shared with me their knowledge, research, and connections. From England, James Manor graciously provided introductions and contacts. My aunts, uncle, cousins, nieces, and nephews have supplied room and board, transportation, research contacts, and frequent reality checks.

A few people deserve special mention. Roger Noll read every draft of the manuscript, and his critiques made me strive to improve it as much as I could. Edwin Amenta read the dissertation and early drafts of the manuscript, endured endless conversations, and provided support. Robyn Noll never read a word but gave me encouragement, lunches, and dinner parties whenever I needed them. Mari Terzaghi spent many hours providing the support, criticism, and above all insight that made me stay on track. Alfred Darnell has been my best friend for the last fifteen years, and his intellectual companionship has featured everything from conceptual discussions to charts and graphs. I suppose I could have done it without them, but I am glad I didn't have to make the attempt. The flaws that remain, despite their best efforts, are mine.

This book is dedicated to four people. My mother, Nellie Bass, kindled my interest in politics and social issues at an early age and encouraged me to choose academics as a career when most thought I was misguided. My father, Arvind Parikh, has given me support and understanding to a remarkable degree. My grandfather would not have known what the term *role model* meant, but that's what he was for his family. He packed more into any given year than most of us manage in a decade, and he set impossibly high standards, many of which he achieved. My aunt's strength and humanity were wedded to an unquenchable desire for learning and adventure that she passed on to her daughters, nieces, and grandchildren. I think both would have enjoyed the spirit of this book.

Contents

CHAPTER 1

Introduction

In comparative politics, studies that attempt to explain the development of similar political phenomena across different countries are less common than the subdiscipline's title suggests. Even when the object of research is explicitly comparative rather than limited to a single nation, it is still frequently subject to one of the many forms of balkanization from which comparative politics suffers. Developed and developing countries are analyzed separately. Economic factors coexist uneasily, if at all, with cultural variables in many research agendas. Methodological approaches are usually trichotomized, with scholars choosing among a few detailed qualitative case studies, large quantitative data sets across a range of countries, or formal models that are developed with little empirical support. In some cases these decisions are justified. If one is studying the development of social policies, for example, it makes sense to limit the universe to developed countries, primarily in Western Europe and North America. If the historical time frame is long, especially for developing countries, it is often next to impossible to obtain reliable quantitative data. But the rationales behind many of these choices are less convincing. Empirically, individuals frequently hold cultural and material interests at the same time, and there is no analytical reason why they should not do so in theory. Many policies and political processes that are of interest to scholars and lay observers occur across developed and developing countries. And there are no logical reasons why methods cannot be synthesized to overcome weaknesses that are present in each and to provide greater explanatory leverage than any single methodological approach.

These limitations became particularly apparent to me when I set out to compare the countries and issues addressed in this book. I wanted to understand why affirmative action was developed and adopted in the United States and India, and why it has endured even after becoming controversial and unpopular in both places. But existing approaches to comparative politics provided no guides as to how such an analysis might be undertaken. This book represents my efforts to transcend traditional boundaries and expand the range of research that is conducted. It has three goals. The first goal is substantive: to explain why ascriptive policies like affirmative action that focus on groups, especially minority groups, endure in democratic countries that emphasize the primacy of the individual and that reward electoral majorities more frequently than minorities. The second goal is methodological: to enlarge comparative analysis to include comparisons that have hitherto been treated with skepticism or excluded in social-science research. The third goal is theoretical: to provide a new framework by which to analyze the politics of the policymaking process.

Affirmative action is a worthy subject of analysis for a number of reasons.[1] First, it is a major social policy in the United States and India, but its emergence and development have not been carefully studied. This neglect is in contrast to other important social policies, such as social security (Cates 1983; Quadagno 1988; Derthick 1979; Skocpol and Ikenberry 1983), employment policy (Weir 1992; Slessarev 1988), and welfare (Danziger and Weinberg 1986; Ellwood 1988). There is no dearth of books on affirmative action, but these tend to focus on the legitimacy of the concept or the policy, and the perspectives range from the scholarly and philosophical to the personal and polemical (Goldman 1979; Bennett and Eastland 1979; Glazer 1987; Fullinwider 1980; Carter 1991; Steele 1991; Ezorski 1991). While such foci are appropriate and welcome in a debate that raises issues fundamental to our political culture, they are insufficient. Even more problematic is the near-total ignorance of the empirical context in which politicians initiated and expanded a set of policies that have come to antagonize important parts of the nontargeted population.

This paradox arises because of the structures and incentives created by democratic political institutions. A current assessment of affirmative action in the United States would conclude that it is a highly controversial policy about which both political parties and the American public feel at best ambivalence and at worst hostility (Schuman, Steeh, and Bobo 1985; Page and Shapiro 1992). In India, the expansion of reservation policies in recent years has led to riots and contributed to the fall of governments (Yagnik and Bhatt 1984; Kohli 1990; Bouton and Oldenburg 1993). But these were not always the dominant attitudes and behaviors. Affirmative action was introduced quietly and without much opposition in the United States by a Democratic president and expanded by Republican and Democratic presidents and Democratic legislatures, and it was legitimized in India by its most revered and beloved leader, Mahatma Gandhi. How the policy traveled from these auspicious beginnings to its current predicament can best be understood by exploring the changing political conditions under which it was introduced, expanded, and then challenged. The same electoral incentives that made affirmative action an appealing policy eventually undermined its effectiveness because the political coalitions that parties created were transformed over time.

Beyond gaining a better substantive understanding of affirmative-action policies and politics in the United States and India, this study offers a fruitful way to think about "ethnic" policies more generally. In addition to falling within the category of social policies, affirmative action also can be legitimately classified with policies that target recipients on the basis of their ascriptive characteristics. After years of scholarly neglect, the world-wide resurgence of political mobilization around ascriptive identities such as religion, race, and nationality has led to a renewed interest in under-standing these phenomena. Affirmative action is one of the most impor-tant of these ascriptive policies, and understanding the political conditions under which such policies emerge, as well as the type of support and oppo-sition they arouse, has the potential to shed light on ethnic politics and policies in other contexts. The fact that a policy is based on an ascriptive characteristic signals only the salience of that characteristic in society, not what the salience is; that is, just because a policy is "ethnic" does not mean that ethnic attachment fully explains its adoption. In democratic political systems, reelection is a paramount concern for politicians. Ethnic policies offer a way to capture preexisting vote blocs, which is more appealing than developing policies that require the formation of new vote blocs. By ana-lyzing the political, ideological, and cultural factors surrounding affirma-tive action in two very different cases, we may be able to unpack the rela-tive importance of ascriptive identities versus political interests.

If we agree that the topic is an important one worthy of study, then the United States and India are two countries that should be considered if the subject is the development and implementation of ascriptive policies in democratic polities. They are large, heterogeneous societies in which pre-viously excluded groups were granted benefits by the majorities that had historically oppressed them. In each case, majorities used the democratic process to develop policies that provided these group not just equality, but also preferences in the areas of employment and education. Why did this happen?

I argue that this counterintuitive outcome came about because of two conditions: the requirements of democratic politics and the heterogeneous nature of U.S. and Indian society. Democratic politics requires politicians and political parties to attract enough votes to get elected. This is most eas-ily done by mobilizing groups of voters with common interests because they are already sorted (whether consciously or not) into groups. In an ethnically heterogeneous society, ethnic markers are likely to be especially salient. In a homogeneous society, by contrast, where groups are marked by different cleavages, other types of policies may emerge; for example,

Britain was historically homogeneous ethnically, but it was divided by class, and policies centering around class were developed. The particular type of ascriptive policy that is formulated is likely to vary according to a number of contextual factors. In the United States and India, affirmative action arose in part because of the blatant exclusion and oppression of specific minorities, particularly blacks and untouchables, and the dissonance between these practices and stated principles of equality. In both countries, proponents of affirmative action have invoked the idea of compensation for past wrongs as justification (Ezorsky 1991; Srinivas 1986).

If these countries were within the accepted scope of comparative analysis, then a historically rich, qualitative comparative case study method would be an obvious choice to guide the explanation. But using the United States and India as cases in a comparison violates several tenets of comparative analysis (Przeworski and Teune 1982; Ragin 1987; Skocpol and Somers 1980). One is an advanced industrial country, the other a developing country. Their cultures and histories are vastly different. And the policies are not identical. But these dissimilarities are less important than the characteristics described above that the two countries share: democratic political institutions and societal heterogeneity. If these two factors are indeed the primary reasons for the development of affirmative action, then the other variations across factors need not be an obstacle.

Such an approach is inconsistent with the historical richness and multicausal complexity of qualitative comparative analysis, but it is in keeping with the expectations of rational choice and formal theory. This approach emphasizes strategic behavior on the part of actors and assumes that this behavior is consistent across countries, time, and issue areas (Elster 1989; Ferejohn 1991; Kreps 1990; Alt and Shepsle 1990). The rich historical and cultural context that comparative analysis requires drops out, since rational choice relies on factors that are independent of context or that incorporate context into the assumptions. In the cases under study here, if democratic institutions are present to structure incentives for politicians, then policies will be developed that target the desired groups of voters. In any heterogeneous democracy, regardless of other characteristics, this relationship should hold. The United States and India provide a fairly stringent test for formal theory. If, as its proponents argue, formal theory should apply across many different types of cases and issues, then it should work in countries that are dissimilar on dimensions that comparative scholars generally consider crucial.

However, even if a rational-choice approach can explain the adoption of ascriptive policies in the United States and India, it will leave important questions unanswered. Just as comparative analysis suffers from limitations due to its assumptions, formal theory's assumptions preclude the analysis of issues that are of substantive interest in these cases. The method can account for why certain classes of policies might be adopted, but it cannot distinguish among policies within those classes (Kreps 1990). So the question of why affirmative action, rather than some other ascriptive policy, was chosen cannot be addressed. The preferences of abstract actors in strategic situations can be assumed, but the preferences of real actors in specific historical periods and across time cannot be. And the timing of policy initiation and adoption, which is so carefully explored in qualitative comparative studies, is assumed or ignored by rational-choice scholars.

To understand the development and endurance of affirmative-action policies in the United States and India requires an approach that isolates key common variables in the cases and is also able to demonstrate convincingly that other variables often considered critical are in fact unimportant. But it also must take into account the importance of specific contexts in order to show why these policy choices and not others were made and why these decisions were taken at specific times. I present such a method after providing an overview of the cases and a more detailed justification for their selection, as well as an explanation of the specific strengths and drawbacks of the two approaches on which the method builds, comparative historical analysis and rational choice.

Selection of Cases

The selection of the United States and India as cases is difficult to justify according to accepted standards of comparative analysis. The policies developed in each country were not identical, and the ways in which they expanded display critical differences. The countries are also different along many dimensions that might be considered important in explaining the emergence and endurance of affirmative action. However, if policies are conceptualized as strategic choices made by political actors to appeal to voters, then the factors that are similar across the two countries are striking and relevant. I hypothesize that ascriptive policies are popular in heterogeneous societies like the United States and India because they tap into issues that are of high salience to existing vote blocs. Affirmative action is an appealing choice within this category because it goes beyond formal equality to provide preferences for groups whose treatment by the majority has been particularly egregious. Over time, the electoral appeal that affirmative action could provide has resulted in its expansion to other groups, and over time its very success has also given rise to calls for its abolition. In both the U.S. and Indian cases the factors hypothesized as important—democratic institutions, politicians seeking to appeal to voters, and previously excluded constituencies—have been present.

In the United States, affirmative-action policies developed as a bureaucratic response to meet the political goal of increasing black representation in employment, first through preferences in government contracts and eventually through programs in all government-funded enterprises. In India, quotas for untouchables and later for low-caste groups known as "other backward classes" (OBCs) were established by political leaders first as a signal of their attentiveness to issues of inequality and later as appeals to politically salient groups. While the circumstances surrounding the introduction and extension of affirmative action were quite different in the two countries, they were driven by similar political needs.

In the United States, affirmative action came about slowly and without much publicity. Its origins lie in the early years of the Kennedy administration. In the 1960 presidential campaign civil rights had been an important issue for both Kennedy and Nixon (Sundquist 1968; Graham 1990; Carmines and Stimson 1989). But while Kennedy won the presidency, the Democratic party lost seats in both houses of Congress, and the programmatic majority needed to pass civil-rights legislation seemed unattainable. Rather than initiating a battle with Congress, Kennedy and his advisors chose to address civil rights by strengthening existing committees and programs within the executive branch. The President's Committee on Equal Employment Opportunity, chaired by Vice President Johnson and stocked with cabinet officials, developed programs that would signal to the civil-rights constituency that the administration was attentive to equality issues. These programs initially consisted of voluntary plans in which contracting companies explained and documented how they would increase minority representation in their hiring practices. The reports were filed at the companies' discretion, but they laid the foundation for the compliance-reporting procedures that eventually became mandatory and that constituted the basis of affirmative-action goals and timetables.[2] These early programs were welcomed by the groups they targeted, but they were not seen as a substitute for civil-rights legislation. Affirmative action in the form of employment guarantees was a goal of segments of the civil-rights movement, especially in the north, but it was not a primary component of the platform put forth by those controlling the movement's agenda (Graham 1990).

In the Johnson administration black and liberal voters were an even more important constituency, and the expansion of affirmative action reflected this importance. After the passage of the Civil Rights Act of 1964 and the establishment of the Equal Employment Opportunity Commission, compliance reporting was relocated to the Office of Federal Contract Compliance (OFCC) in the Department of Labor. The OFCC was able to avoid potential negative congressional scrutiny because the committee in charge of its oversight was the equally liberal House Education and Labor Committee. Working quietly through administrative procedures, the OFCC developed increasingly stronger guidelines that converted the compliance review process from a voluntary to a compulsory one with specific rather than vague requirements.[3] In this process the government was actually aided by contractors, who had realized that if they were forced to file affirmative-action programs in order to win federal contracts, then they would be better off with detailed instructions (Graham 1990). In time, these details began to take on the look of precise quotas, even though they were called goals and timetables.

Government support for affirmative action peaked during the 1970s and was buttressed by favorable Supreme Court decisions. Perhaps most surprisingly, during the first Nixon administration affirmative-action programs were not only defended against attacks by opponents, their scope and intensity were expanded. This outcome seems irrational in light of Nixon's 1968 election campaign, which emphasized a "southern strategy" that directly appealed to whites disaffected by the unrest of the 1960s and unhappy with civil-rights and antipoverty legislation. But it is worth remembering that liberal northern Republicans constituted a major proportion of Nixon's agency appointees, and affirmative-action programs were not well understood by the American public.[4] By the end of 1972, affirmative-action plans covered all government employment at the federal, state, and local levels as well as educational institutions receiving government funds. The election of Jimmy Carter as president continued the expansion of affirmative action, with the African-American constituency becoming increasingly important as southern voters proved themselves willing to desert the Democratic party even when it ran a native son as its presidential candidate. In 1977 one of the Carter presidency's early successes was legislation stipulating that 10 percent of all federal government construction contracts were to be set aside for minority contractors (*Congressional Quarterly [CQ] Almanac* 1977). This law was noteworthy because it represented the first acceptance of a specific numerical target by the two elected branches of government. Throughout the 1970s opponents challenged the expansion of affirmative action in the courts, but the Supreme Court consistently upheld most of the policy's provisions.

In the 1980s the overall political landscape was transformed in ways that had crucial ramifications for affirmative-action policy in particular. As the American public learned more about the policy in the 1970s, it liked affirmative action less, and preference programs were seen by detractors as symptomatic of the excesses and misdirection of the post-1964 civil-rights agenda (Bennett and Eastland 1979; Glazer 1987). The conservative wing of the Republican party responded to these emerging attitudes by virtually abandoning appeals to African-Americans in favor of direct appeals to northern working-class and southern white voters, especially men, in which they promised to curtail civil-rights enforcement and eliminate preferences such as affirmative action.

Accordingly, after winning the 1980 presidential election Ronald Reagan set out to roll back twenty years of forward progress on affirmative action, and to a large extent he was successful. During his two terms the Justice Department curtailed its civil-rights enforcement, switched to the opposing side on affirmative-action court cases, and severely limited implementation of affirmative-action programs within the government and in the private sector where the government had influence (Amaker 1988). Reagan could not abolish affirmative-action and civil-rights enforcement completely, in part because his administration's positions were too extreme for those congressional Republicans who needed to garner at least part of the African-American vote to be reelected. And despite Reagan's enormous personal popularity, Democratic dominance of the House through both his terms and the Senate through the second half ensured that he would have to compromise. But thanks to his efforts, as well as to the continuation of much of this policy by Reagan's successor, George Bush (*CQ Almanac* 1988, 1990, 1991), by the end of three terms of Republican presidential administration, affirmative-action policy occupied a position that was considerably weaker than during its high-water mark of the 1970s.

The story of U.S. affirmative action spans thirty years and is located primarily at the federal level. By contrast, analogous policies in India began nearly a century ago, spanned colonialism and independence, and featured important developments at the national and state levels.[5] Preferential treatment for minority groups began with Muslims as the targeted group under British colonial rule at the beginning of the twentieth century. In the decades that followed, the right to separate electoral representation was offered to other groups as well, including Sikhs, Christians, Anglo-Indians, and untouchables. The largest and most organized opposition to British rule, the Indian National Congress, was against these policies and attempted to discourage other groups from accepting them, but it met with limited success. Muslims refused to give up separate electorates and compromise with the Congress (Government of Britain 1932). But while the Congress could afford to lose Muslim support and still maintain its standing as the dominant indigenous political movement, British acknowledgment of its position as the leading political group would be less certain if it could not keep untouchables within its fold. Therefore, Congress leaders had a strong incentive to counter the British offer of separate electorates with similar protection within the Congress fold. In 1932 they came to an agreement with the untouchable leadership that guaranteed the latter their own political representation within the Congress (Tendulkar 1952). At the same time, regional Congress elites acquiesced in policies that gave low-caste Hindus in southern Indian states special preferences in regional political representation, government employment, and education to counter the charge that they were Brahmin-dominated and insensitive to the needs of low-caste Indians (Irschick 1969).

Given the antipathy of the Congress party, and especially Nehru, to reservations in political representation, it would not have been surprising if they had been eliminated when India attained independence in 1947. But instead, the principle and practice of reservations were enshrined in the constitution, and during the 1950s and 1960s the policy was extended to public employment and higher education (Galanter 1984). In southern Indian states, reservations were continued in these areas for OBCs as well as for untouchables. This arrangement was politically both satisfactory and stable. It affirmed Congress's commitment to untouchables, and it did not alienate caste Hindus because the positions reserved for targeted groups were few and their ability to take advantage of them uneven. In the south, the numbers of positions reserved for targeted groups were much bigger, but the number of high-caste Hindus was very small (4 percent), so few votes were lost by the Congress.

After the 1971 elections, this accommodation broke down, and reservations were extended to situations in which they produced considerable conflict. The death of Jawaharlal Nehru in 1964 and the unexpectedly quick death of his chosen successor in 1966 had led to a power struggle as different factions within the Congress party fought for supremacy. The party eventually splintered in 1969, and with each new party needing to work to attract existing vote blocs and mobilize new ones, preferences became an attractive programmatic appeal. Among the most assiduous in promoting them was the Congress-I party of Indira Gandhi. When she swept to power in 1971, she brought with her allies that extended reservations to OBCs in the north, much to the dismay of the many high-caste Hindus there.

The 1977 elections resulted in the defeat of the Congress-I and the accession to power of the new Janata party government. Janata might have been expected to roll back or at least halt the expansion of reservation policies, since its base was among high- and middle-caste Hindus who were opposed to reservations. But the party was looking to expand its electoral coalition and drive a wedge into Indira Gandhi's power base, and so it continued to introduce reservations in north Indian states and to appoint a commission to consider OBC reservations at the central government level. In 1979 Janata was defeated by the resurgent Congress-I, but Indira Gandhi, who returned to power, continued to support reservations.

Indira Gandhi was able to maintain an unlikely political coalition of high-caste Hindus, low castes, untouchables, and other minorities because of her name, her personality, and her political power. But since her death this balance has proved to be much more difficult to achieve. The consequence has been that most parties pay at least lip service to the idea of affirmative action in order to woo the large low-caste vote blocs, but a serious adherence to the policy antagonizes nontargeted groups. Parties in the north or at the center who try to extend the implementation of affirmative action to OBCs in practice, not just principle, usually find themselves presiding over riots that hasten the fall of their governments (Yagnik and Bhatt 1984). But they cannot completely abandon the policy because then large blocs of low-caste voters would in turn abandon them.

In both the United States and India, affirmative action emerged and endured as a policy because it provided a way to appeal to existing and new groups who were electorally important. The contexts in which the policies were devised and implemented varied considerably. But the structure of incentives for the actors making the policy choices were the same. Affirmative action was introduced because it was able to solidify and expand electoral coalitions; it could bring in new vote blocs without jeopardizing existing ones. As the policy became better known, it became more disliked by nontargeted groups, and it was no longer an appeal with no downsides and clear upsides. The early coalition could no longer be assumed. But by this point, affirmative action was also a major symbol of a party or politician's commitment to those minorities' concerns, and it was difficult to roll back or eliminate programs without losing these groups' support.

Strengths and Weaknesses in Existing Methods

Comparative historical analysis has been utilized in the study and explanation of social phenomena for decades, but it has become more widely used and its techniques have become more sophisticated and refined in the last fifteen years (Heclo 1974; Shefter 1977; Skocpol 1979; Katznelson 1981; Skowronek 1983). Rational-choice methods have also become more commonly used, especially in the study of American politics, over about the same period. These research strategies represent clear advances over traditional studies of public policy, which tended to be devoid of theory, highly descriptive, and too firmly rooted in the cases being described to provide generalizability (Pressman and Wildavsky 1984; Bardach 1977; Kaufman 1960). Despite their advantages, however, neither approach has resulted in a general theory of the process of policymaking across countries, policies, and time. Rational-choice methods provide such generalizable theories, but they are too abstract to be able to explain how substantive aspects of policies developed. They are best at demonstrating how actors' preferences structure choices and outcomes, and they can predict which actors are likely to win. But in so doing, they assume the contexts in which preferences and choices are made, which leaves those interested in understanding specific empirical outcomes dissatisfied. By contrast, comparative historical analysis is extremely effective at explaining why policies take the particular shape they do, but the studies are so grounded in the details of their cases that the most that can usually be generalized from them are patterns of policy development that are conditional upon historical, cultural, and structural factors. This is not necessarily seen as a disadvantage by the method's adherents, however (Skocpol 1984; Steinmo, Thelen, and Longstreth 1992).

It might be said that the two methods start from opposite sides of the spectrum to explain the same phenomena. Comparative historical scholars emphasize macrosocial factors across time to explain how policies develop, and unless people are extremely powerful or well situated, the importance of individuals actors is secondary. Rational-choice adherents, on the other hand, assume away or ignore historical, cultural, and socioeconomic-context variables to concentrate on the specific choices that individuals make. In comparative historical analysis individuals' preferences and strategies are always seen through the lens of the social process that both creates and constrains them. For example, Hugh Heclo's influential book (1974) focuses on bureaucrats, but their choices are always made within severe structural constraints. In addition, bureaucrats are not seen as self-interested. In rational choice, preferences are assumed and strategies are determined according to an assumed or highly simplified context. Both of these foci are often able to produce powerful results, but they also impose costly limitations.

Comparative Historical Analysis

As with single-case studies, the emphasis that qualitative comparative historical analysis places on contextual factors produces research that provides readers with a richly textured understanding of the multiple conditions under which policies emerge as socially important options, win places on the political agenda, and then become entrenched after passage. Historical patterns, social conditions, economic factors, and political configurations are all woven into a detailed exposition of the cases to explain policy development. In the best research, the reader comes away with a subtle and nuanced understanding of the policy process, and the narrative is good history in that it evokes the atmosphere of a period and makes what could be a dry exposition of variables come alive. Lynn Hunt (1984) and Theda Skocpol (1994) both accomplish this, although they study very different phenomena.

However, while the ability to include multiple causal factors is an advantage, the complexity that brings the analysis closer to the social reality being studied also impedes its extension to the explanation of other social realities. For example, scholars have argued that the development of social policies during the New Deal was brought about by the conjuncture of a sense of crisis brought about by the depression, the presence of a Democratic president with an overwhelming Democratic majority in Congress, and the existence at the state level of policy options formulated by experts (Amenta and Skocpol 1988). Does this mean that we can expect social policies to be developed only when these three conditions are present? Moreover, is one factor more important than the other? For example, can we have a lesser sense of crisis as long as we have the political and informational factors in place? The development of War on Poverty policies would suggest that we can, but nothing in the comparative method predicts it because the method does not rank the factors, either relatively or absolutely.

In order to extend this theory to other countries it would be necessary to develop analogues for the political variable, since other countries have different political systems. But we have no real guides as to how we might do that. The greatest strength of comparative historical analysis lies in its ability to provide richness and detail in the explication of social phenomena, especially as they develop and change over time. But this richness and detail has two weaknesses. The first, as Ragin points out, is that "the limited variety of cases imposes a necessary indeterminacy. Thus, the investigator must support his or her chosen explanation by citing surrounding circumstances and, more generally, by interpreting cases" (1987). This weakness can be minimized, as Amenta shows (1991). By using a variety of methodological approaches, in his case a multiplicity of comparative strategies as well as limited but effective quantitative analysis, the factors he cites as causal variables are made more convincing. But the second weakness is more difficult to overcome. Multiple conjunctural causation may indeed explain the cases being analyzed, but it is unlikely to result in theories that can be generalized to other contexts, since identical conjunctures are rarely evident across cases. At best they provide blueprints for the use of comparative historical analysis in other instances.

Creating comparisons, either across cases or within a single case, increases the potential for generalizable results, since factors have to be present in more than one case for them to be considered relevant in explaining outcomes, and this comparative leverage elevates the method over standard individual case studies. Careful selection of cases to be compared further increases the potential for contributions to theory by allowing more factors to be controlled and thus limiting the number that contribute to the outcome. As Charles Ragin has observed, comparative case studies attempt to "approximate experimental rigor by identifying comparable instances of a phenomenon of interest and then analyzing the theoretically important similarities and differences between them" (1987, 31). Within the comparative analytical framework there are two methods that have been developed: the similar-systems approach and the different-systems approach (Ragin 1987; Przeworski and Teune 1982).

In the similar-systems approach, cases are selected because they have numerous historical, social, and other contextual variables in common. These variables are then held constant, and the contextual variables that differ across the cases are analyzed with the expectation that they will explain differences in the outcome to be explained. For example, in the study of social policies, the United States and Britain are considered to be appropriate cases for comparison because they share numerous cultural and political traditions but their social policies diverge (Weir and Skocpol 1985; Amenta and Skocpol 1988). The key aspect of similar-systems analysis is that the factors to be held constant must be enough alike that they cannot reasonably be thought to contribute to the variations in outcomes to be explained.

The different-systems approach chooses cases that share few factors in common but are of interest because despite their differences they have similar social outcomes. In this approach the factors across which the cases differ are ignored and those few in which they are similar are analyzed with the expectation that they account for the similar outcome that is being explained. This method is less frequently used than similar-systems comparisons, but it would be appropriate, for example, if the explanandum is agrarian rebellion and the cases chosen are Peru and Vietnam (Paige 1975). The key aspect of the approach is that the variables and the outcomes considered to be the same are in fact sufficiently similar that they can be treated as alike.

Given that the variables do not have to be quantified or measured, these requirements would not seem to be too constraining. But because they set standards for comparisons, they exclude certain comparisons just as they include others. Generally speaking, comparisons are drawn from within the subsets of developed or developing countries, but not across them. Sometimes this is a result of the question being asked; social policies, for example, are found almost exclusively in developed countries. And in different-systems analyses, it is rare to find instances of the same phenomena happening across developed and developing countries. But when phenomena occur in cases that are outside the normal range, the comparative method is unable to provide a framework of analysis.

This inadequacy is particularly apparent in the affirmative-action case. The United States and India are not sufficiently alike for a similar-systems comparison; that is, it is difficult to argue that most historical and cultural variables are similar enough to be held constant. Certainly there are characteristics common to both countries that are relevant when studying affirmative action: democracy, federalism, legal traditions based on British common law, and ethnically heterogenous populations. But there are many differences, for example, caste versus egalitarian ideologies, group versus individual identity, colonial versus independent histories, and some of these are likely to have influenced the development of affirmative-action policy according to the rules of comparative historical analysis.

The different-systems approach would appear to be more promising, since it is based on different societies' experience with common social phenomena. But the U.S. and Indian policies cannot reasonably be considered to be sufficiently alike to permit the use of this method. For example, in the United States affirmative action is found in both the public and private sectors, whereas in India it is almost exclusively found in the public sector. U.S. affirmative action is carried out through vague-sounding "goals and timetables," whereas in India laws stipulate precise percentages in employment and higher education that must be set aside for targeted groups. It is difficult to argue that these differences do not stem from historical and cultural differences in the countries, and a different-systems analysis is unlikely to adequately capture these relationships.

As I noted above, every method has limitations, and the comparative method certainly should not be condemned because it cannot handle every possible comparison. But the comparison of affirmative action in the United States and India is one that shares many of the characteristics with case-based comparisons that fit the method. These are major policies in two of the world's important democracies. Their analysis falls squarely within what Ragin terms "one of the distinctive goals of comparative social science . . . to interpret significant historical outcomes" (1987, 11). Therefore, it is worth exploring whether there are conditions under which this unusual comparison can be made.

Rational-Choice Methods

If it is correct to say that rational-choice methods approach the study of policy from the opposite end of the spectrum from comparative historical analysis, then it would not be surprising to find that its strengths and weaknesses lie in opposite directions as well. Rational choice is effective at providing simple generalizable theories that do not depend on the specifics of a particular case. It is able to isolate a few key variables to explain policy development and relegate the rest to the background. The major focus of analysis is the strategic behavior of individuals, and the method assumes that individuals act rationally and purposefully in ways that further their interests. Since the unit of analysis is the individual, rational-choice scholars assume that social phenomena can be explained by aggregating individual behavior to the social level; society as a whole is rarely a unit of analysis. Social-context variables such as history and culture may be explored, but the method does not require such exploration. Social outcomes such as policies are therefore explained as the result of individuals rationally pursuing their own interests, rather than as the result of the conjuncture of specific political, historical, or cultural forces.

Individuals are shaped and constrained by institutional and structural factors just as in comparative analysis, but there are two crucial differences. First, contexts are not treated as independent influences. Instead, they are subsumed into the preferences of individuals, with the assumption that these preferences accurately reflect and embody the contexts in which they are developed. Second, in rational-choice analysis, institutions and structures are considered to be the product of individuals' choices, not preexisting constraints on them. In contrast with comparative historical perspectives, rational-choice scholars would predict that institutions that constrain actors against their interests will be eliminated for more favorable ones.

Since rational-choice theories attribute greater explanatory weight to individual behavior than to structural conditions, and since individual motivations are believed to be consistent across contexts, there are few limitations on the types of cases that can be compared. In a rational-choice analysis, the United States and India comprise a perfectly acceptable comparison. Contexts and institutions vary, but individual behavior can be assumed to be consistent across the cases, since in both the relevant actors are politicians who seek policies to garner votes and bureaucrats who seek policies to strengthen their agencies and their policy influence.

Analysis using rational-choice methods has made significant contributions to our understanding of politics and policies, especially for the United States. The contributions of positive theory to a more refined knowledge of how interests are aggregated within government and how laws and institutions reflect the interests both of politicians and their constituents have been immense (Weingast and Marshall 1988; McCubbins, Noll, and Weingast 1987, 1989; Cox and McCubbins 1993; Krehbiel 1991; Eskridge and Frickey 1988; Eskridge 1990; Gely and Spiller 1990). Rational-choice approaches have provided explanations for the institutional and policy choices that are more theoretically rigorous and more substantively convincing than previous research. And the growing application of these methods to other countries with different political systems has been encouraging (Laver and Shepsle 1990; Laver and Schofield 1990; Tsebelis 1990; Rosenbluth 1989). Research to date suggests that individuals behave similarly across different institutional and cultural contexts.

Nevertheless, weaknesses remain that undermine rational choice's claim to provide the best explanation for social actions and outcomes. Among the most important of these weaknesses are those arising from the assumptions used and its effectiveness at explaining real-world outcomes over time. As with the comparative historical approach, it would be unfair to criticize rational choice for failing to take into account factors that it expressly rules out. However, while the assumptions made in accordance with the method are acceptable from an analytical point of view, some of them make it more difficult to answer questions that are of interest even to scholars working within the rational-choice perspective. Two assumptions in particular illustrate this problem: taking the policy space as fixed when studying the politics of policy formation; and the assumption that preferences are stable.

The assumption that actors' preferences are stable and consistent is one of the basic axioms of rational-choice methods, and indeed of economistic approaches more generally (Kreps 1990; Rasmusen 1989; Binmore 1992; Gibbons 1992). Of course this assumption is not based on an actual belief that preferences never change and never contradict each other. Rather, the treatment of preferences as stable reduces the number of potential causes and it does not in many cases appear to distort the explanations achieved. Unfortunately, while these compromises can be justified in relatively stable political settings and across short periods of time, they are more difficult to defend in more volatile political situations and across long historical periods (North 1981; Ferejohn 1991). For example, in the United States over the period analyzed in this book, whites appeared to change their attitudes regarding equal rights for blacks. It may be that preferences changed across time in response to new information and new situations, or it is unlikely but theoretically possible that many individuals in the nineteenth century had no preferences about race relations and equality, but then their counterparts in the twentieth century developed them. Either way, we cannot use the preferences exhibited by actors in one setting to predict those in the other. It is worth emphasizing, given the debates that have arisen on the subject of preferences, that I am not arguing that any assumptions about preferences are automatically suspect. Rather, I am maintaining that in certain analyses—especially those with a circumscribed time frame—assumptions about preferences may be quite appropriate, but in others the same assumptions will create problems in the analysis and may lead to an inaccurate explanation.

A second key assumption, that the choice of one policy over competing ones can be taken at face value, raises a slightly different issue. In many rational-choice studies of policymaking, the question of why a specific policy option arose in the first place is either ignored or attributed to the triumph of the interests represented by that policy. But there are many interests jostling for attention at any given time, especially within the political arena, and the victory of one over another is rarely due to political factors alone. Without a more textured view of where policies come from, it is difficult to predict why a particular policy gets onto the agenda rather than others. For example, why did the Kennedy administration settle on preference policy development emphasizing employment guarantees at the executive-branch level as the alternative when they concluded that congressional legislation for civil rights was too difficult?

An added problem with an assumed policy space is that it is difficult to choose from between several outcomes within that space that are equally possible in theory. Just as the assumption of a policy space precludes analysis of why that particular policy space comes to be occupied, the existence of many possible solutions to a single game makes it difficult to know why any particular solution becomes the one selected (Kreps 1990, chap. 5). The presence of multiple equilibria is a feature of game-theoretic models, and rational-choice scholars have developed methods of narrowing down the likely candidates through the use of concepts such as conventions, norms, and other institutions. But in abstract models these solutions are often stipulated rather than investigated empirically. And as such, they are of limited utility in this case, where we are interested in understanding why affirmative action in particular was selected as the appropriate policy in United States and India.

In order to analyze the issue and cases under consideration here, I propose an approach that combines aspects of both of these methods to provide theoretical rigor and generalizability with sufficient contextual richness to generate substantive insights as well. I begin with the rational-choice assumption that while contexts vary to create different preferences and strategies, individuals behave in consistent, rational ways across these contexts. Moreover, I assume that individuals, not historical forces or social movements or crises, act either singly or together to bring about social outcomes. These latter conditions shape the preferences and strategies of individuals, but historical conjunctures and social movements do not pass legislation; politicians do. In these cases, the outcomes are public policies, which are passed and implemented by governments, and therefore the key actors are elected and appointed political actors. Finally, I accept the rational-choice assumption that only a few key variables need to recur across cases to explain policy outcomes. In this instance, the variables are democratic political institutions and heterogeneous societal groups, which the two cases share.

While these assumptions are necessary to explain how affirmative-action policies were passed and implemented, they are not sufficient. Rational-choice methods depict policy outcomes as the result of negotiations and bargains among actors, but they rarely explain the empirical circumstances behind policy adoption. To understand the historical, cultural, and social context that influenced policy development it is necessary to employ the methods of comparative historical analysis. Careful empirical research explains why affirmative action was seen as an appropriate policy choice, why it appeared on the political landscape when it did, and why politicians chose to appeal to social groups that had historically been ignored or systematically excluded from electoral coalitions. In the previous paragraph I asserted that political actors pass and implement policies. But rational choice cannot explain why they make specific choices, except to say that they are preferred. Comparative historical analysis, on the other hand, can help to explain where these preferences come from. Together with rational choice, it can contribute to the development of a method that joins theoretical rigor with empirical richness.

Explaining Affirmative Action: A New Approach

Ideally, a comparative analysis should combine rich and detailed case studies that explain the specifics of social outcomes with a theoretically rigorous analysis that can be used to predict analogous social outcomes in other settings. Affirmative action in the United States and India offers the opportunity to explore whether a new approach can accomplish both of these goals. How can we offer substantively satisfying explanations of affirmative action in such different countries while still providing a theory that explains more than these two cases?

The solution employed here is to begin with the framework of rational-choice methodology, which models the behavior of strategic actors and allows me to compare cases that are outside the range of accepted comparative historical analysis. However, if I treat the preferences as exogenously determined, then I will miss much of the context in which policies are developed, as well as the reasons why politicians choose certain policies over others. Therefore, preferences and contexts are neither assumed nor treated as exogenous to the analysis; they are determined through examination of empirical data from both primary and secondary sources. The resulting approach is one that shares features with both methods but differs from each.[6] While there is extensive primary data that is frequently presented in the narrative format used in comparative historical research, the historical material is not as comprehensive as in that research, and it limits itself to fewer variables, since the theory here is more parsimonious. Analogously, the theory and modeling is less elegant and sophisticated than that used in more abstract rational-choice research, because it is constrained by the empirical realities of the case. Fewer factors are assumed, and the lower level of abstraction is accompanied by a higher level of empirical complexity.

To summarize, the theory being developed here selects as few independent variables as possible, but then it embeds these variables within the contexts in which they occur. Thus, preferences, strategies, and outcomes are parsimoniously explained, but they are not abstract concepts. Instead they are given meaning by the environment that creates them.

Affirmative Action as Strategic Choice in Context

Following rational-choice methods, the study assumes that actors are purposive and goal-oriented and that they seek to achieve their preferences. However, unlike most rational-choice analyses, these preferences are not assumed. They are determined through the examination of empirical evidence, and their behavior is then modeled according to the precepts of rational choice. An empirically sensitive approach is thus combined with rational-actor models to produce the assumption that while the preferences (and therefore goals) of actors may vary in different countries or different historical periods, all individuals regardless of their cultural makeup seek ways to fulfill their desires and achieve their goals.

Before proceeding, it is important to differentiate preferences about outcomes from preferences about policies. Politicians everywhere seek to be elected or reelected. But they may have different preferences over the policies they develop or support in order to attract votes. These preferences about policies can be strategic (e.g., wanting to get acceptable electoral coalitions) or ideological (personally preferring affirmative action over the absence of such policies).

The assumption that actors choose behavior that will help them to achieve their goals has the potential to produce an almost infinite range of preferences and goals, depending on how much the cultural context varies. But in the two cases being studied here, there is a fair degree of convergence in preferences. This convergence occurs because in the study of politics, and especially the politics of policymaking, there are commonalities across contexts. Almost all actors in the political arena seek to capture at least a share of political resources, including power, influence, money, and policies that address their particular interests. The way that these resources are allocated and fought over varies across political systems, and the means by which individuals and groups gain benefits will also vary, but their desire to do so varies much less. Thus, in the United States and India, it may be argued that the historical and cultural conditions under which affirmative-action policy developed were divergent, but the political reasons behind its development were similar.

Research from a rational-choice perspective has assumed, usually correctly, that legislators in the U.S. Congress value reelection highly (because that is a precondition for achieving any other goals), and that they seek to ensure reelection by pleasing their constituency through constituency service, delivery of resources to their district, and satisfactory voting records (Mayhew 1974; Fiorina 1977). In parliamentary systems, politicians have similar incentives, but parties play a larger role because they have more power institutionally and they exercise more control over their members. Therefore, it is important when looking at parliamentary systems to examine party preferences and strategies (Laver and Schofield 1990).

Elected officials with larger and more diverse constituencies and more power than individual legislators, such as parties in India and the president in the United States, use policies and programs to attract blocs of voters beyond the constituencies of individual legislators. Although some policies are narrowly targeted, the more commonly favored policies have high salience, target a unified vote bloc, and avoid offending nontargeted voters. Affirmative action possessed all three characteristics when it was initiated and then implemented in both the United States and India, and even after it became controversial it retained the first two.[7]

The view that policies serve the strategic interests of elected officials is hardly a new one; it has been hypothesized in work on the U.S. Congress and in the study of political economy. But it has not often been applied to comparative analyses of policy development and implementation. Comparative studies have tended to focus on the ways that policies are formulated and then put onto the political agenda; consequently, these studies concentrate on the experts who develop them and the interest groups that interact with elected officials to convince the latter to pass policy legislation (Amenta et al. 1987; Amenta and Skocpol 1988). But these approaches neglect the question of why elected actors bow to interest-group pressure, and if they do, why they select certain policies over others.

By beginning with the assumption that, like legislators, parties and leaders need to be elected in order to pursue other goals, we can theorize about how they achieve that end. And by assuming that these actors have to put specific electoral coalitions together in order to win, we can begin to make predictions about which vote blocs might successfully fit together and which policies are likely to appeal to those vote blocs. This approach is more specific than the argument that policies are designed to appeal to the electorate generally; rather, it focuses on prospective winning electoral coalitions and the policies that will appeal to them. In addition, the approach allows for the adoption of policies that do not originate in the demands of interest groups, and it suggests a rationale for why actors might introduce policies before being forced to do so by demand groups outside government (Riker 1986).

By seeing policies as programmatic appeals that help sell parties and leaders seeking election to vote blocs, we assume that certain types of strategic behavior exist regardless of institutional or cultural context. The United States and India may not be similar or different along the dimensions required by the standard comparative methods, but in both countries policies are passed and implemented by elected officials who need to be responsive to the constituencies who elected them.

The strategies and actions of relevant actors are described in words, but in keeping with the tenets of positive theory, they are also modeled formally. Models are developed at those times when a major event has occurred in the policy process. The purpose of these models is to isolate and emphasize the specific actors that take part in each policy "game" and to show how and why these games result in new policy outcomes. The models all begin from the same basic set of assumptions discussed above that govern rational-choice analyses of behavior, but the types of models used vary somewhat. This variation occurs because every interaction is not the same. For example, in the U.S. case, the actors play a symmetric game, one in which every player is essentially equal. But in India during the independence movement, the British could impose their will unilaterally on the Indian players, which created an asymmetric situation. The games vary, but these are variations of type and context rather than ones that affect the comparability of the actions and outcomes.

With the exception of one game that models negotiations among the British Raj and Indian political groups during the independence movement, all the models fall within the general category of spatial theories of voting (Enelow and Hinich 1984, 1990). In the simplest forms of these models, symmetric actors with complete knowledge of each other's preferences move sequentially, and the policy outcome is determined by the relative preferences of the actors and the order in which they move. This approach was developed for the U.S. separation-of-powers context and captures nicely the games played over affirmative action in the United States. In the parliamentary system that characterizes India, policy outcomes in majority governments are affected less by formal institutions than by coalitional conflicts within one actor, the political party. To model these policy outcomes, I borrow from research that uses the median-voter theorem and focuses on outcomes produced by political coalitions (Laver and Shepsle 1990; O'Halloran 1994). Finally, during the independence movement in India actors had asymmetric levels of power, so a three-person serial game with imperfect information is used (Kreps 1990). The characteristics and assumptions of each of these models are explained in greater depth in later chapters.

These models are not identical, but they fall within the same general methodological approach: the formalization of actors' preferences and strategies and the outcomes that result from their interactions. The models all assume strategic behavior, but since the types of behavior, possible strategies, and relative positions of the actors vary, the models vary to take these differences into account. These variations are comparable to differences in types of qualitative data: interview data are often combined with data from written primary sources such as archives and newspapers to provide evidence for a hypothesis.

Just as there are different types of models within the general category of strategic formal theory, the assumption that policy choices across different cases spring from the same incentives does not mean that the policies themselves will be the same. The specific form that the policies will take will depend on the characteristics of the electorate as well as the historical and cultural contexts of the specific case. In addition, the structure of the political institutions will have an important influence. All the actors seek reelection, but they do not seek identical political offices in identical political systems. For example, we might expect that in a separation-of-powers system, the losing electoral coalition will still have voice, so it may be able to negotiate compromises in the winning coalition's policy. In a parliamentary system, by contrast, the losers have less voice, and we might expect to see stronger policies.

To summarize, this approach hypothesizes that in democratic political systems, policies are an instrument that elected political actors adopt to gain votes and, similarly, appointed politicians promote in order to consolidate and expand their professional positions and spheres of influence. The latter are not elected by voters, but they too have constituencies that they must satisfy. It may also be the case that both sets of actors have ideological or moral interests in the policies as well, but these can only be fulfilled if they continue to occupy their professional positions, so self-interest in the form of reelection is assumed to be prior. The policies that are adopted are chosen because they attract or retain specific groups within the political actors' coalitions. Ascriptive policies are likely to be adopted in countries with heterogeneous social groups who are in the process of mobilizing, because ascriptive characteristics are highly salient.

This perspective helps to make sense of the affirmative-action cases in the following way. Affirmative action, which was chosen as a policy for similar historical and cultural reasons in the United States and India, was introduced by presidents and parties as a way of attracting the votes of the groups that it targeted. Black votes were important to the Democratic and initially also the Republican parties, and affirmative action was a method of signaling party commitment to that electorate. Similarly, the Indian National Congress and later the Congress party needed to attract untouchables and then OBCs in order to solidify or expand their electoral coalitions, and preferences were a salient signal. As the policies became more controversial, the extent to which they were embraced by elected politicians varied according to the electoral coalitions the parties were trying to put together. The Republican party of Ronald Reagan essentially abandoned appeals to African-Americans and focused its attention on opponents of affirmative action; therefore, it was in the party's interest not only to back off positive implementation but even to reverse existing policy. In India, the controversy over reservations has meant that parties that can afford to have soft support from low-caste Hindus play down preferences as an option, while parties that depend on that support push preferences even in the face of potential social conflict.

This argument is simple and sounds intuitively compelling. But it also seems a bit thin and self-evident. Of course politicians select policies that will appeal to potential voters. But why some policies over others? And who develops the policies and forces them on to the government's agenda? In the case of affirmative action, the question again arises, why choose such a potentially controversial policy? Did no one notice that it contained elements that went beyond civil rights, that it institutionalized preferences, and that it privileged groups over individuals? In both countries, politicians made choices within particular contexts. We can make sense of their choices only if we understand these contexts, which leads us back to comparative historical methods.

The comparative historical approach directs us to examine policy formulation using a long historical view and paying special attention to social and cultural factors. In the United States, since affirmative action was targeted first and most prominently at African-Americans, this means exploring the way that race relations in American society and the role of race in politics contributed to placing affirmative action on the policy agenda. In India, affirmative action was first targeted at untouchables, so it means investigating the role of untouchability and the reasons behind caste Hindus' decision to provide preferences for a previously excluded group. In both countries the targeted groups were initially excluded from equal political treatment, but by the mid–twentieth century their political fortunes began to improve.

In addition to the backgrounds and characteristics of the targeted groups, it is useful to look at the historical record in order to understand why and how majority attitudes changed. Blacks and untouchables were always striving to improve their positions, but only in the twentieth century did they become successful. This success could be attributable to causes internal or external to the groups, or both, but empirical research is necessary to determine the answer.

In light of the antagonism that exists toward affirmative-action policies today in both countries, the question of why such policies were considered acceptable is worthy of investigation. The emphasis on the primacy of the individual in the United States and the codification of individual rights within the Indian constitution contradict the policy's emphasis on group attributes. Careful historical analysis is the effective way to explain this apparent paradox. Similarly, since affirmative-action policies have been the focus of government attention and enforcement, it is worth examining the conditions under which government action is considered appropriate in this realm. In the United States there has traditionally been tension over the proper scope of state intervention, especially in issues considered social rather than political. In India, reservations were introduced under a colonial government, but their legitimacy outlasted that of the British Raj. Qualitative research can help uncover the circumstances that made these unlikely circumstances possible.

I suggested above that rational choice and comparative historical analysis approach the study of the same phenomena from opposed ends of a spectrum. Rational choice concentrates on individual strategic behavior to achieve preferred outcomes, while comparative historical analysis concentrates on the complex interplay of historical, social, and cultural factors to explain social change. Each acknowledges that the other's focus is of some importance, but neither pays it much attention. How might they be reconciled so that they can both contribute to a theoretical explanation? Here, I reconcile them by according them different roles within the framework. In explaining the particular choices made when formulating and then implementing policies, I concentrate on the behavior of politicians. But I spend time establishing the context in which their policy preferences arose and in which their strategic behavior take place. Affirmative-action policy arose as a possible option because of the complex interplay of factors that comparative historical analysis directs us to identify and explain. But as the analysis will show, the adoption of specific policies at particular points in time occurred because of specific politicians' preferences, bargains, and winning strategies.

Four assumptions can be drawn from this approach. First, *policy histories are punctuated equilibria.* Policies can change significantly over time, but within a discrete period preferences and institutions are essentially stable. In the United States, affirmative action's policy history can be broken into three periods: the Kennedy-Johnson period of formulation and initial expansion; the Nixon-Carter period of further expansion and consolidation; and the Reagan-Bush period of retrenchment and reversal. India's experience can be similarly divided: the British colonial period in which reservations were introduced and accepted for scheduled castes and south Indian OBCs; the period of Congress party dominance, when reservations for these groups were expanded and entrenched; and the post-Congress breakup, when party competition was accompanied by policy expansion to nonsouthern OBCs. Within each policy regime, institutions and preferences are consistent, but across them there are critical variations.

Second, *if institutions and preferences are stable, then they can be modeled formally.* If actors, preferences, and institutions are in equilibrium within a particular period, then the policy outcomes they produce can be studied using formal models that capture the key elements of the process and provide a causal framework with predictive capacities. In the United States, within the first two periods elected officials appealed to minority-vote blocs through the expansion of affirmative action. By the third period there was opposition to affirmative action, and politicians used policy retrenchment as a way to appeal to them. In India, the attractiveness of reservations as a policy varied across the periods; in the second period the Congress party's dominance of the political landscape allowed them to offer reservations only in those regions and to those groups for which they would be acceptable, but by the third period party competition led parties to support reservations even when that support created social conflict because the targeted vote blocs were too important to abandon. Although institutions, actors, and preferences varied across periods, within each period actors' preferences and the institutions in which they operated were stable.

Third, *major changes can be explained through analysis of the contexts in which they are embedded.* Just as formal models allow periods of stable institutions and preferences to be analyzed to develop a causal framework, comparative historical analysis provides a method by which the shift from one set of equilibrium institutions to the next can be understood. Why, in the United States, would one Republican president expand affirmative action and a second contract it? Why would colonial rule in India be succeeded by a one-party dominant democracy, which is then succeeded in turn by party competition? These questions can only be answered by exploring the context in which these changes took place and investigating the reasons behind the specific outcomes we want to explain.

Fourth and finally, *in a comparative study the proper units of analysis are models, not countries.* As a recent book on qualitative methodology points out, all analyses, whether qualitative, quantitative, or formal, abstract from empirical reality (Keohane, King, and Verba 1994). Therefore, the critical question to be answered is, can these abstractions be fruitfully compared? Comparative historical analysis provides such models in its similar-systems and different-systems approaches, but perhaps because the approaches emphasize thickly descriptive narratives, an elision is often made from considering them as cases to seeing the cases as the countries themselves. This is a mistake. In considering whether to compare the United States and India, the important point is whether the essential elements abstracted into the model can explain the outcomes in which we are interested. For affirmative action, I argue that it can.

The models being compared in this analysis are models of political actors making strategic choices within particular contexts. In both the United States and India, the heterogeneous nature of the societies combined with the incentives created by democratic political systems to create demands for and offers of affirmative action as a policy choice by these actors. Cultural, historical, and institutional differences led to differences in the specific contours of the policies adopted in each country, but the primary reasons behind their adoption were similar. In the early stages of policy development these programs were relatively unproblematic because the nontargeted majority was little affected by them. But as the programs became more extensive and competition over jobs and college admissions became more intense, previously acquiescent groups grew hostile to the policies and undermined the stability of the electoral coalitions that had been created. The result in both countries has been controversy and conflict, with parties and politicians scrambling to placate opponents without losing supporters completely.

Overview of the Book

Studies of social change in general, and policy development in particular, usually have to strike a balance between explaining aspects of the larger environment that contribute to the policy process and the specific conditions under which particular policy choices are made. Rational choice usually emphasizes individual decisions at the time of policy adoption and neglects more indirect effects, while comparative analysis emphasizes the multiplicity of factors that place policies on the political agenda and then extrapolates from these to explain individual decisions. The explanatory framework used in this research attempts to strike a more even balance between these two extremes by analyzing both the macrosocial context from which future policies emerge and the micro-level individual negotiations that produce specific policies.

The remainder of the book is divided into two main parts and a concluding chapter. The first part, comprising chapters 2 and 3, presents the historical and cultural context in which affirmative-action policy came to be formulated and adopted as a policy option in the United States and India. Among the questions to be examined in this study are why specific policies are selected and why certain responses to social and political needs come onto the political agenda. In these chapters I address this question by reviewing the historical and cultural background of race and caste relations in the United States and India and the acceptable role of the state in shaping and eventually transforming these relations. I explore the context in which later policy formulation and implementation are embedded. This specification of context helps explain why certain policies arise as possibilities rather than others, why interest groups find them salient, and why those who are not directly affected by them consider the policies to be acceptable. Comparative historical analysis suggests that in order to explain a phenomenon it is important to understand the characteristics that comprise it and determine where the antecedents to these characteristics might be.

In rational-choice terms, these chapters illuminate why the specific policy space of affirmative action came to be chosen, why the groups they targeted comprised preexisting vote blocs, and why the policies would be acceptable to nontargeted groups as well.

There are several characteristics that distinguish the policy. First, the policies imply compensation for the groups they target, since they go beyond formal legal equality. Second, the types of policies being studied here are government initiated, so they presuppose the right of the government to intervene in this arena. Third, they target some social groups and not others, so they assume a special position for those groups in this policy area. And finally, they involve privileging traditionally excluded minorities over the majorities that excluded them, a paradox that needs to be explained. In these two chapters I explore the factors that make these characteristics of the policy both possible and attractive. I show how historical, cultural, and socioeconomic factors combined to create a favorable context for the emergence of affirmative action, and I delineate the efforts of the groups that became targeted by the policy to force their concerns onto the political agenda.

The context in which social phenomena such as policies occur comprise opportunities, constraints, and boundaries. Historical, ideological, and cultural factors create the opportunity for certain types of policies to be developed. At the same time, however, factors can impose constraints on the possible shape that policies can take, because historical events or ideological beliefs will make certain choices very difficult or costly. Some choices are ruled out less consciously, and we might think of these limits as boundaries rather than constraints. Here I use the term *boundary* to signify a type of unconscious constraint, where historical, social, or cultural factors have made certain options unthinkable or, to borrow a phrase from cricket, beyond the boundary.

Chapter 2 establishes the feasible sets for affirmative-action policies by focusing on the ideological importance of race, caste, theories of individualism and equality, and the proper role of the state in the United States and India. Chapter 3 explores the political factors that led to changes in majority attitudes toward blacks and untouchables, the political conditions and patterns of mobilization that spurred the development of affirmative action, and the policies that preceded and laid the foundations for affirmative-action policies.

The second part of the book analyzes the development of affirmative action in the two countries using the theoretical framework introduced above. The U.S. and Indian cases are divided into two chapters each. Chapter 4 discusses the rise of affirmative-action policy in the United States during the administrations of John F. Kennedy, Lyndon Johnson, and Richard Nixon. While policies were initially established and developed through presidential and bureaucratic initiatives, Congress and the Supreme Court were also key participants in this expansion. Chapter 5 discusses the final expansion of affirmative action during the late 1970s and then focuses on the retrenchments in affirmative action during the presidencies of Ronald Reagan and George Bush and the reasons behind this policy shift. As in the earlier period, initiative usually rests in the administration, but they only achieve their goals with the collaboration of all or part of Congress and the Supreme Court.

Chapter 6 addresses the introduction of preferences in India under British rule and during the first two decades of Indian independence. Reservations were introduced and adopted as a policy choice during the colonial period despite the reluctance of the Indian National Congress, but they were then legitimated in the constitution and expanded after independence when the Congress party controlled the government. Chapter 7 focuses on the expansion of reservation policies after the Congress party split to OBCs in northern and western Indian states and at the central-government level, despite increasing opposition from high and middle castes. Finally, chapter 8 concludes the book by evaluating the theoretical and substantive findings of the study and discussing the implications of this policy analysis for the current debate over affirmative-action policy in both countries.

CHAPTER 2

The Context of Affirmative-Action
Policy Development

In this chapter I set out the conditions under which affirmative action became an attractive policy choice, both for social groups and for politicians seeking electoral support. The argument that the conditions of democratic politics create incentives for political actors to develop or respond to demands for policies accounts for the emergence of policies in general, but it cannot explain the emergence and development of specific policies. In other words, why are some policies chosen rather than others, and in this case, why were affirmative-action policies seen as the appropriate choice? This is where the orientation and techniques of comparative historical social science become important, because they focus our attention on the conditions that give rise to particular policies in specific situations. Political actors will, of course, select policies that are the most likely to prove acceptable to potential voters, but these choices are shaped by their knowledge of the demographic, historical, and cultural attributes of the population.

The United States and India are very different countries, so it is not surprising that the contexts in which policies were developed diverge considerably. But they also share one crucial similarity: ethnically heterogeneous populations in which one group has historically been denied basic political and social rights. In the United States African-Americans were first enslaved and then systematically excluded from political participation and equal socioeconomic opportunities until well into the twentieth century. In India the caste system created a social hierarchy within the majority Hindu population that limited opportunities for those groups low in the caste hierarchy and completely excluded groups known as untouchables, who were considered outside the caste system until the early twentieth century. Given these historical contexts, it is easy to see why affirmative action would be perceived as an appropriate policy if previously excluded groups began to be targeted by political actors, either for normative or pragmatic reasons.

It is important to remember, however, that this analysis seeks to explain not only the adoption of affirmative-action policies by politicians, but also the retention of these policies in the face of growing popular opposition. As this chapter shows, there were historical conditions and ideological concepts that provided compelling rationales for both of these polar developments. In the United States, the enshrinement in the Declaration of Independence and the Constitution of the ideals of equality and equal opportunity for all individuals conflicted with the practice of slavery and then discrimination to create what Gunnar Myrdal called "the American Dilemma" (1944). This dilemma, which had influenced politics since the United States became independent from Britain, provided the grounds on which proponents of civil rights could argue that African-Americans were entitled to equal treatment under the law, and its effects were cited to support activist policies such as preferences and compensation for past wrongs.

But the importance of equality of opportunity was difficult to separate from the liberal emphasis on the individual, which was at least as deeply entrenched an ideological concept as that of equality and equal opportunity. While social groups were protected in both reality and in law, the recurrent emphasis on the individual as the primary unit of politics meant that affirmative action, which selected individuals using the criterion of group membership, was vulnerable to the criticism that it violated a crucial tenet of American political philosophy by rewarding groups at the expense of individuals. This argument has frequently been invoked by critics of affirmative action, and it has proved to be rhetorically and substantively effective.

Finally, the role of the state in the American polity occupies an uneasy position. On the one hand there exists a profound mistrust of state intervention in supposedly nonpolitical arenas. On the other hand, however, the state has, by omission and commission, used its power to reward some social interests over others throughout the history of the republic. Therefore, affirmative action as a state-mandated policy can draw support from ideological concepts of the acceptable sphere of state intervention, but it can be criticized just as strongly.

The one circumstance in which the power of the U.S. state has consistently increased has been during times of crisis. Abraham Lincoln was accorded wide powers during the Civil War, and Franklin Roosevelt was able to expand significantly both the power and the reach of the state during the Great Depression. During the 1960s, the civil-rights movement created, if not a sense of crisis, at least a sense of urgency, which opened up a space in which state intervention was seen as permissible by a majority of the American public. This "permission" enabled the passage of the Civil Rights and Voting Rights Acts, but it also created opportunities for more gradual and subtle policies such as affirmative action. However, as the sense of urgency lessened, so too did the rationale for state intervention.

In India, the primacy of equality and equal opportunity found its analogy in an opposite institution, the caste structure. The ideology of caste as a religious and social organizing principle legitimated the unequal treatment of low castes and untouchables. But the colonization of India by the British challenged the supremacy of caste ideology in two ways: first, it gave prominence to the ideals (although not the practice) of liberalism, individualism, and equality; and second, British rule undermined the high-caste argument that those who were at the top of the political and social hierarchy somehow deserved to be there.

These challenges became especially important when Indians, led by the Indian National Congress, aggressively began to confront British dominance and demand a voice in governing their own country. The British, with an eye toward divide-and-rule strategies that would ensure their dominance and undermine potential unity within the Indian opposition, encouraged Indians to participate by organizing according to ascriptive identities. The Indian National Congress, however, argued that Indians were not irrevocably divided by primordial identities and argued that the individual was the proper political unit, not religious, caste, or regional communities. The debate over participation and representation thus took on an ironic twist, as the supposedly hierarchical and traditional Indians argued for individualism and equality, while the ostensibly modern, egalitarian British argued for unequal treatment based on primordial group identities.

Both long-standing and more recent political ideologies offered support for but also undermined the legitimacy of affirmative-action policies. Caste ideology reinforced the dominance of group over individual identities, which gave support to the group-based orientation of the policy, but privileging low castes and especially untouchables went against fundamental tenets of caste doctrine. Similarly, the newer but increasingly powerful philosophies of individualism and equality presented ideological problems for affirmative action, but the growing commitment to equality of opportunity made the historical oppression of low castes and untouchables more problematic and gave credence to interventions to improve their conditions. As in the United States, when the majority groups began to acknowledge the injustice of their treatment of untouchables, the appeal of policies that redressed the resulting inequalities increased.

These strategies of intervention were supported by Indian conceptions of the role of the state. In contrast to its U.S. counterpart, the Indian state has historically been accorded wide-ranging powers by society. While the state is always supposed to be accountable and responsible to society, it has been expected to intervene in social and political matters, and this expectation has held across ancient, colonial, and modern independent states. During the independence movement the state's role was assumed by the British Raj but contested by the Indian National Congress. The Congress's leadership of the struggle for independence, as well as the enormous personal popularity of Gandhi, Nehru, and other Congress leaders, made the postindependence Congress party synonymous with the state. This convergence, along with the recognized need to spur economic and social development, gave the state wide-ranging powers to initiate and expand policies, among which was affirmative action.

However, this expansive state role has begun to encounter some resistance, at a time when the democratic character of the state is not in question. Indeed, the exigencies of democratic politics have contributed to unease with the use of state power to develop and extend affirmative-action policies. When the Congress party dominated the Indian political landscape and enjoyed almost unquestioned legitimacy, its policy choices were generally accepted as necessary and appropriate. But when the Congress party split and political power fragmented among competing splinter groups, the difference between the institution of the state and the party that governed it became more apparent and more problematic. One result is that today policies are scrutinized to determine whether they are designed to serve broad social interests or narrow partisan ones, and those that appear to serve the latter are considered with much more suspicion. Thus, while the state is still accorded wide-ranging powers, parties do not always benefit from this potential influence, and in the affirmative-action policy arena the division is increasingly pronounced.

I explore these factors in more detail in order to understand the conditions under which affirmative action became an attractive policy choice, both for social groups and for politicians seeking electoral support. I look at the role of race, caste, and intergroup relations; ideals of equality and individualism; and the role of the state. I do not argue that these factors are connected in a direct causal way with the rise of policies, because they provide both support and constraints. Nonetheless, they created what rational-choice scholars have called the "feasible set" (Elster 1989; Darnell 1995), that is, the environment in which specific policies become possible and even attractive.

United States

Liberalism, Individual Rights, and Equality

Liberalism has frequently been considered to be an inextricable part of American political culture. In his analysis of American liberalism, Hartz remarks that liberalism is so deeply entrenched in American society and thought that it is not even called liberalism, but "the American way of life" (1955, 11). American liberalism encompasses many aspects of social and political culture, and among the most important is the significance it accords the individual and the concept of social equality. According to Hartz, "the master assumption of American political thought, the assumption from which all of the American attitudes discussed in this essay flow [is] atomistic social freedom" (1955, 26). Freedom to pursue individual goals and limitations upon the demands society and government may make are central to the U.S. political and social compact, and American myths from the frontier to Horatio Alger have affirmed these values.

How did individualism become such a central part of the political culture? Hartz locates the strength of Lockean liberalism in the absence of a feudal tradition: "Its liberalism is what Santayana called, referring to American democracy, a 'natural' phenomenon" (1955, 5). Comparing the liberalism that arose from the American Revolution with those of the French and English Revolutions, Hartz argues that the latter has a philosophy acquired through "an internal experience of social diversity and social conflict" (1955, 14), while the former is unchallenged and absolute.

Critics of Hartz's emphasis on Lockean liberalism and his assertion that American liberalism is "natural" have pointed to the intense ideological conflict that accompanied the founding of the republic (Bailyn 1967; Pocock 1975). Representative government was not created in a vacuum; instead, it emerged from American revulsion against the corruption of the British political system. In refuting the position of Locke as "patron saint of American values," Pocock argues that the founding constituted "an ambivalent and contradictory moment within a dialectic of virtue and corruption, familiar to sophisticated minds of the eighteenth century" (1975, 546–47). In this interpretation, American politics was essentially conservative because it involved the restoration of governmental virtue after the corruptions of parliamentary England.

Despite their differences with Hartz over the role of ideology and the centrality of Locke's political theories in the formation of the republic, however, historians of republicanism agree that there was a critical shift in the view of the individual as citizen. Classical theory's construction of the individual "as civic and active being, directly participant in the *res publica* according to his measure" was replaced by "a theory in which he appears as conscious chiefly of his interest and takes part in government in order to press for its realization" (Pocock 1975, 523). Moreover, in this new politics there arose a conception, termed by Wood the "romantic view" (1969, 606), that "individuals in America were the entire society: there could be nothing else—no orders, no lords, no distinctions" (607).

This view of the American polity as divided by interests rather than classes was resisted by conservative republicans, who believed that the representative system favored by the Federalists "relied too heavily on an energetic government driven by men's passion for fame, and insufficiently on virtuous tendencies in society itself" (Hanson 1985, 80). These conservative republicans were able to control the presidency from 1800 to the late 1820s and implement their anticommercial, elite-oriented policies. But with the election of Andrew Jackson in 1828, politics was transformed by a movement that "effectively unleashed the energies of acquisitive individualism that had been increasingly frustrated by the constraints of mercantile policies" (Hanson 1985, 126–27). Jackson, in both person and policy, came to represent the virtue of the laborer and yeoman farmer, whose work was approved as productive. Accumulation by these citizens, who "worked hard, saved, and invested their money in productive (as distinct from speculative) ventures," was seen as contributing to the national interest as well. Thus, Jacksonian citizens who pursued their self-interest fused public and private interests "into a dynamic moral force for expansion" (Hanson 1985, 129).

The absence of corporate conflict rooted in feudalism, which meant inter alia the absence of classes, redefined the political and cultural debate from one in which corporate groups had interests to one in which there were no a priori groups, only individual citizens. Tocqueville drew attention to this phenomenon in his comparison of aristocratic and democratic social relations:

> Each class in an aristocratic society, being clearly and permanently limited, forms, in a sense, a little fatherland for all its members, to which they are attached by more obvious and more precious ties than those linking them to the fatherland itself. . . . In democratic ages, on the contrary, the duties of each to all are much clearer but devoted service to any individual much rarer. . . . As each class catches up with the next and gets mixed with it, its members do not care about one another and treat one another as strangers. Aristocracy links everybody, from peasant to king, in one long chain. Democracy breaks the chain and frees each link. (1969, 507–8)

In this historical context, the individual triumphed over the collectivity in law and theory as the primary social unit. American did not abandon corporate groups and communities, but they transformed them into voluntary associations whose goals were to serve individual interests that could not be accomplished by individuals working alone. Tocqueville commented that associations were necessary in democratic societies because no citizen "is in a position to force his fellows to help him. They would all therefore find themselves helpless if they did not learn to help each other voluntarily" (1969, 514). But these groups do not reproduce themselves automatically, like corporate groups in feudal societies, and therefore they must depend on voluntary attachments by each succeeding generation.

The significance of individualism was thus established from before the Revolutionary period and is sustained in the constitutional articulation of natural rights. Communities based on shared interests were not prohibited, and indeed they were encouraged by the absence of traditional ties. However, they never acquired standing independent of that accorded voluntarily by their members. As a result, associations, interest groups, and community organizations are as prevalent as they were in Tocqueville's time, if not more so, and the interests of groups have been accorded standing in law, but they have rarely trumped the social, political, and constitutional legitimacy that individual rights enjoy.

The American passion for association that Tocqueville discovered in his travels creates genuine communities, but communitarian impulses cannot disguise the fact that in American culture, freedom means "freedom *from*—from people who have economic power over you, from people who try to limit what you can do or say" (Bellah et al. 1985, 25). The settling of North America was fraught with danger, and it encouraged ties between neighbors, but the absence of a feudal tradition meant that these relations remained voluntary. And the abundant land and natural resources that the continent had to offer rewarded individual initiative and provided strong arguments for an individualist frame of reference.

The primacy of the individual in American culture is almost impossible to separate from a second fundamental concept, the right of all citizens to social and political equality. The axiom that it is "self-evident, that all men are created equal," is as closely identified with the United States as the institution of democratic politics. Gordon Wood argues that "Equality was in fact the most radical and most powerful ideological force let loose in the Revolution. . . . Once invoked, the idea of equality could not be stopped, and it tore through American society with awesome power (1991, 232). American political thinkers drew on the English republican tradition and the emphasis in Lockean liberalism on the equal role of each citizen in the establishment of the political state to construct an ideal of a society in which all citizens were free and equal, and these arguments provided much of the intellectual and political justification for the colonial rebellion against the British Crown.

The notion of equality advanced in the colonies was based on the eighteenth-century liberal concept that all men were equal in society and before the law. Americans' focus on legal and political equality originated in the dissatisfaction of the colonists with British policies, with Americans arguing that they deserved to be treated in the same way as British subjects in England.

> From the beginning of the colonial argument, the American case rested on the assumption that Britain's colonial subjects had rights and privileges identical with those at home. But when Americans began to grasp the fact that the British, whom they regarded not as their masters but as fellow subjects, were systematically treating them as unequals, they recognized the corollary that differences did exist between the colonies and the home country in fact if not in constitutional status. This difference of fact gave rise to the need for assertions of equality. (Pole 1978, 14)

While the focus was usually on inequities in the application of common law, such as trials without juries, or political issues such as taxation without representation, from the outset there were men who asserted that even where law was upheld, it was invalid if it violated natural law and the natural rights of man. This ideal of social equality was never realized in practice, but the absence of classes and estates and the relative prosperity of the people resulted in a society that was much more homogeneous than those found in Europe. The economic conditions in the colonies were generally favorable. Few people starved, and while property ownership yielded "substantial differences of personal wealth, [it] gave a livelihood to all who worked on [the land]" (Pole 1978, 27). Hartz calls Americans "the national embodiment of the concept of the bourgeoisie," even as they lacked the "passionate middle-class consciousness which saturated the liberal thought of Europe" (1955, 51). In nineteenth-century America there was little to be passionate about: without the drain of "economic parasites" and the constraints of "guilds," and with ample opportunities available, the conditions for conflict and passion did not exist (Hartz 1955, 53).

The abundance of economic opportunity that characterized the North American continent was an important contributor to ideas of equality, but the conscious rejection of European corporate society was also a factor. Classes existed in the United States, but they "were not built on laws of privilege. No one claimed that colonial society was composed . . . upon a legally implanted hierarchy of rights" (Pole 1978, 36). And while it was accepted that "inferior classes existed, they were not denied all possibility of self-respect" (30). However far reality may have diverged from principle, the principle held that differences in rank and style were earned, not inherited.

This ideal of equality in no way presupposed that all men were equal in natural abilities. To the contrary, inequalities in wealth and status were widely accepted because in a society where initiative and hard work were to be rewarded with social and economic advancement, they offered proof that the "American way of life" was succeeding. Equality, at first a vague and ambiguous concept, had come to stand for equality of opportunity by the Jacksonian era (Pole 1978, 143–47). Regardless of a man's position at birth, the social ideology affirmed that he stood an equal chance to achieve greatness in a society governed by the Jeffersonian ideal of a natural aristocracy.

The joining together of the cultural concepts of individualism and equality was accomplished in a fundamentally American myth, the myth of Horatio Alger. Alger himself was not particularly successful in achieving financial greatness, but the stories he and his successors wrote celebrated how poor, orphaned boys who were adopted by benevolent men rose through ambition and hard work to positions of greatness. Although the stories written by Alger were much more modest in their depictions of rags-to-riches success than the myth suggests (Cawelti 1965, 108–10), Alger came to serve as a symbol of individual initiative in a free-enterprise system.

> the Alger hero represents a triumphant combination—and reduction to the lowest common denominator—of the most widely accepted concepts in nineteenth-century American society. The belief in the potential greatness of the common man, the glorification of individual effort and accomplishment, the equation of the pursuit of money with the pursuit of happiness and of business success with spiritual grace; simply to mention these concepts is to comprehend the brilliance of Alger's synthesis. (Lynn 1955, 7)

The notion of upward mobility was hardly new to American culture; Benjamin Franklin had exemplified the ideal American in the eighteenth century, with his *Autobiography* standing as "the archetypal story of a young man who, though poor, attains success by dint of hard work and careful calculation" (Bellah et al. 1985, 32). The Alger myth encompassed the Franklin success story and its Poor Richard aphorisms and extended them to the late-nineteenth- and early-twentieth-century world of economic capitalism. In addition to offering an exemplar of the path to worldly success, it delineated what the boundaries of state activities should be in order for an individual to make the most of opportunities to achieve the American way of life (Hartz 1955, 203–55).

The reality of racial inequality was clearly at odds with these principles of individual rights and equality of opportunity, for to exclude individuals solely on ascriptive characteristics flew in the face of the professed American commitment to allow each individual to realize his or her own potential based on his or her talent. In the first few decades of the republic this contradiction was less glaring because politics was still essentially a gentleman's arena, and many white men of humble origins and economic position were excluded as well. But after the Jacksonian democratic revolution, and as immigration expanded the boundaries of who was to be accorded the rights and privileges of citizenship, the continued banishment of blacks became harder to justify.

Race

The most critical social, political, and economic institution that provided encouragement for the emergence of affirmative action as a policy choice was that of race relations, first as defined by slavery and later by de facto and de jure racial discrimination. But the conditions for affirmative action did not appear until well into the twentieth century. Even as Americans based their arguments for independence from Britain on the philosophical precepts of equality and liberty, the potential contradiction between these claims and the widespread use of slave labor in the colonies did not receive much attention. After all, many European countries including Britain were active in the slave trade, and blacks were considered to be in a different and considerably inferior position to whites. Slavery was not an issue that divided Americans from the British; rather, it produced cleavages within each population. The debate over slavery in the colonies, however, was qualitatively different than those occurring in Europe.

As David Brion Davis notes,

> Clearly there was nothing novel about the freedom and independence of some men depending on the coerced labor of others. What distinguished American colonists was their magnificent effrontery. They rejoiced to find their ideals of freedom and equality reflected in the actual social order, but resolutely denied that the social order rested on a "mudsill" of slavery, as Southerners would later acknowledge. (1975, 263)

In the South the debt white society owed to slavery was straightforward: the presence of slave labor made it possible for whites to avoid developing a lower class of the type found in England and on the Continent. In the North the connection was less apparent but still strong, as many states had profited from their direct or ancillary participation in the slave trade.

Abolitionists were able to make headway in the northern colonies because slave labor was not economically critical for them. They had smaller populations of blacks, and as a result most of these colonies had abolished slavery by the time of the Revolution. But for the southern states slavery was an economic necessity, and they insisted on continuing to define slaves as property. In order to keep slaves but still affirm their commitment to an equal society in the face of this subjugation, southern whites "formally [read] blacks out of the polity, thereby separating black slavery from white freedom" (McLeod 1983, 231). No northern representatives felt as strongly about the abolition of slavery as southerners did about its continuation, and after prolonged debates among the founders during the Constitutional Convention, the Constitution did not in the end contain direct reference to slaves or slavery. And later, when the new Congress discussed the institution in any form, "the debate was acrimonious and laden with threats to the Union" (McLeod 1983, 231).

Despite the southern interest in keeping blacks from being recognized as human beings, and therefore entitled to rights and benefits, in the nineteenth century abolitionists continued to advocate the extension of this equal opportunity to blacks (Fredrickson 1971; Pole 1978). The abolition of slavery in England strengthened the dissenters' positions, and in the first half of the nineteenth century antislavery sentiment increased sharply (Pole 1978). The Missouri Compromise was designed to avoid continual debates over the extension of slavery, but the Dred Scott case demonstrated that complications were almost impossible to legislate away.

Abraham Lincoln's Emancipation Proclamation in 1863, the victory of the North in the Civil War, and the passage of the Fourteenth and Fifteenth Amendments and the Civil Rights Acts of 1865 and 1875 all contributed to the guarantee of equal protection under the law for blacks, while Reconstruction policies encouraged blacks to vote, to become educated, and to participate in government (Foner 1988). But these legal and military victories failed to sustain African-Americans' hard-won equality of opportunity. The North proved unwilling to occupy the South indefinitely, and the withdrawal of northern troops was succeeded at first by southern laws that segregated black and white society and later by Supreme Court decisions that upheld the states' rights to pass such laws. By the beginning of the twentieth century, the formal equality blacks had attained had been almost entirely undermined by the establishment of these legal restrictions on African-Americans, known as Jim Crow laws, throughout the South (Woodward 1974). Slavery had been abolished and blacks guaranteed equal treatment under the Constitution, but in the South they soon returned to a second-class status despite being free rather than enslaved.

The intimate identification of the Civil War with the abolition of slavery has sometimes led people (and school history textbooks) to cite the conflict over slavery as the cause for the war. Most scholars agree, however, and evidence from the period confirms, that each side was fighting primarily to assert its own view of the legitimate sphere of state influence and to impose its own political vision on established and new states in the Union. Anne Norton has pointed out that while many northerners opposed the institution of slavery, few were supportive of real equality for blacks. Moreover, blacks frequently encountered substantial racism in the North, albeit of a different type. New Jersey "had abolished slavery by reclassifying its slaves as 'apprentices for life.' . . . Massachusetts prescribed flogging for nonresident blacks who stayed longer than two months. . . . Ohio passed a law expelling its entire black population (Norton 1986, 227–28).

The emancipation of slaves during the Civil War, the strides southern blacks made during Reconstruction, and the passage of the Thirteenth, Fourteenth, and Fifteenth Amendments to the Constitution reinforced the northern view of itself as more egalitarian and advanced than the South, and of the South as the repository of racial inequality. The introduction of Jim Crow laws at the turn of the century made it even easier for the non-southern United States to read race out of its consciousness except as a peculiarly southern problem. This blindness allowed many northerners to ignore that the Supreme Court almost immediately began to uphold very narrow interpretations of the Fourteenth Amendment and then validate southern Jim Crow laws in the late nineteenth and early twentieth century (Woodward 1974; Tushnet 1987).

The first decision handed down by the Court that had an important effect on blacks was not even directed explicitly toward them. The *Slaughterhouse Cases* (83 U.S. 36 [1873]), marked the Court's first interpretation of the Fourteenth Amendment. In this decision the Court established and formalized the concept of states' rights. It essentially invalidated the "privileges and immunities" clause, taking the position that there was a distinction between privileges and immunities of persons as citizens of the United States and as citizens of the states. The Court held that Fourteenth Amendment protected rights held by U.S. citizens but did not mention state citizens, and since most civil rights were derived from state citizenship, they were not protected against state action by the Fourteenth Amendment.

Ten years later the Court further limited the ability of the Reconstruction amendments and laws to protect blacks from discrimination. In the *Civil Rights Cases* of 1883 (109 U.S. 3), it held that in the case of public accommodations, the Fourteenth Amendment outlawed discriminatory practices only when taken by the states themselves and not by private persons. In its opinion, the Court stated that the excluded blacks had suffered private wrongs to their "social rights," not to their political or civil rights by the state or under state authority.

Finally, in 1896, the Court issued one of its most famous decisions, one that was to legitimate discrimination against blacks for over fifty years. *Plessy v. Ferguson* addressed the constitutionality of a Louisiana law that provided separate railway carriages for whites and blacks. The Court found that the concept of "separate but equal" facilities was consistent with the Fourteenth Amendment. In its opinion it stated that

> the object of the amendment was undoubtedly to enforce the absolute equality of the two races before the law, but in the nature of things it could not have been intended to abolish distinctions based on color, or to enforce social, as distinguished from political, equality, or a commingling of the two races upon terms unsatisfactory to either. (163 U.S. 537)

The court went on to address the "separate but equal" issue directly:

> We consider the underlying fallacy of the plaintiff's argument to consist in the assumption that the enforced separation of the two races stamps the colored race with a badge of inferiority. If this be so, it is not by reasons of anything found in the act, but solely because the colored race chooses to put that construction upon it. (163 U.S. 537)

The *Plessy* decision was immensely important because it legitimized the segregationist trends that were spreading throughout the South by the mid-1890s. Furthermore, the Court specifically referred to education in its statement, and its phrases implied the rightness of segregation in education.

> Laws permitting, and even requiring, their separation . . . have been generally, if not universally, recognized as within the competency of the state legislature. . . . The most common instance of this is connected with the establishment of separate schools for white and colored children, which has held to be a valid exercise of legislative power even by the courts of States where the political rights of the colored race have been longest and most earnestly enforced.
>
> One of the earliest of these cases is that of *Roberts v. City of Boston*, 5 Cush. 198, in which the Supreme Judicial Court of Massachusetts held that the general school committee of Boston had power to make

provision for the instruction of colored children in separate schools established exclusively for them, and to prohibit their attendance upon the other schools. (163 U.S. 544)

By focusing on education and drawing attention to an 1849 decision supporting segregation in the North,[1] the Court granted legitimacy to the dual systems of primary, secondary, and higher education that were being developed, even though they were contrary to the intentions of Congress when it passed the civil-rights and land-grant-in-education acts. The *Plessy* decision became the standard by which the segregation of blacks and discrimination against them were judged, and it served as a strong precedent for the Supreme Court in the twentieth century.

Although the position of blacks in American society was marked by oppression and discrimination throughout the eighteenth and nineteenth centuries, there was considerable conflict within the majority white community over how blacks were to be treated. To the extent that their mistreatment could be seen as a peculiarly southern problem, white discomfort was limited primarily to abolitionists and other racial liberals, who were a minority of the northern population. But when racial inequality appeared to taint the North as well, as it did in the Missouri Compromise, the Dred Scott case, and in the post–Civil War Supreme Court cases, it became harder to rationalize away. Myrdal's American dilemma is captured in the Supreme Court's record on civil-rights cases in the first half of the twentieth century. Within twenty years of the *Plessy* decision the Supreme Court was finding it difficult to sustain the argument that separate facilities for blacks were in reality equal to those provided for whites. But it took nearly sixty years for it to overturn the principle, and even then some justices feared the court was moving too quickly (Kluger 1975). When the Warren Court pronounced that separate was not equal in its 1954 Brown decision, there was rejoicing from civil-rights supporters, but the question remained in the background as to whether justice delayed had been justice denied. At least part of the basis for this tension was the ideological primacy of the ideal of individual equality of opportunity. This tension was mirrored in ambivalence over how injustice might be rectified: through the voluntary actions of individual, or through the intervention of the state.

The Role of the State

The tension between the ideals of American society and the reality of race relations finds an analogy in American attitudes toward the state. At the same time that American political thinkers affirmed the legal equality of the individual and the primacy of natural rights, they were also constructing a limited view of the power of the state. The Lockean view of the state emphasized that "government came into existence only by the consent of those who voluntarily entered into it, and who lived under it, for the protection of rights already recognised by natural law" (Pole 1978, 8). The state of nature could not guarantee adequate protection of natural rights, and therefore civil society and the state were necessary, but these institutions could never take precedence over individual rights. This construction of the state gave primary importance to the rule of law because of the need for laws to establish forms and procedures, but it created a society that "[did] not understand the meaning of sovereign power (Hartz 1955, 7).

It seems less accurate to say that Americans did not understand sovereign power than to say that they were more concerned about its excesses than its advantages. Having fought a revolution to rid themselves of a "corrupt" English state (Pocock 1975), American political leaders were determined to limit the power of the central government. At the Constitutional Convention there were sufficient supporters of strong states' rights that Federalists and republicans were forced to compromise. In the new constitution, the federal government was primarily given residual powers that consisted of responsibilities that were clearly in the national rather than individual states' interests, such as foreign policy, and duties that were beyond the states' powers to carry out efficiently, such as the regulation of interstate commerce, postal services, and the like. Fearing tyranny of the majority as much as tyranny of the minority, as well as the ability of factions to accumulate power, Madison and his colleagues further divided power within the federal government between three branches and provided that the legislative branch have a bicameral legislature.

The Federalists' fear of factions and majorities was not unfounded, because of the relationship of citizen to state that the establishment of democracy created. Political elites had expected the new, virtuous American state to serve a "distinct public interest to which people would willingly surrender some their private pecuniary interests" (Wood 1991, 252). But most Americans expected their new state to be responsive to their demands, and they pressed these demands in local and national assemblies. Thus, the ideal of virtuous politics in which the state was "a 'disinterested and dispassionate umpire in disputes between different passions and interests'" competed with the emergence of "popular legislative practices that we today have come to take for granted—parochialism, horse-trading, and pork-barreling that benefited special interest groups" (Wood 1991, 251, 253).

This tension suggests that despite the widespread, enduring, and articulate view of the state as perpetually corruptible, there has existed since the founding a strain of thought that supports the legitimate intervention of the state, as embodied in the federal government, in economic and social matters. Beginning with debates over the formation of a national bank and conflicts over the state's support of commercial over agricultural interests (and vice versa), citizens have expected benefits from the state even as they have expressed concerns about the scope of its power. The republican call for limited government in the early nineteenth century was characterized by its political rivals as a cover for state bias toward the aristocracy, and Jackson's calls for limited government attempted to roll back these favors. But Jackson focused on these abuses at the same time that the federal government pursued a policy that can best be described as expansionist and interventionist, albeit in a different sphere (Hanson 1985). In more recent times this challenge has been embodied in the debate over states' rights and the framing of the twentieth-century civil-rights debate in terms of that ideology. It might be argued, then, that Americans have a real concern about the potential abuse of power by the state, but they are also well aware that state power can provide them with benefits.

The nineteenth-century U.S. state has frequently been characterized by scholars as weak, underdeveloped, and without a coherent economic policy (Keohane 1983; Skowronek 1982; Higgs 1987; North 1981). Nonetheless, this weak state was still responsive to interests, particularly the interests of commerce and agriculture. In the first half of the nineteenth century tariffs on textile and iron were set high in response to northern businessmen who wanted southern textiles for their industries; this policy was "a means of redistributing income in favor of the cotton textile producers" (Keohane 1983, 79).

Government intervention was also important in another major arena: transportation. Keohane notes that in the 1830s state and local governments were very active in financing public-works projects: "70 percent of the canals built in the United States during this period were constructed with public funds borrowed from private investors" (1983, 65). These enterprises were not very successful, as the 1840s witnessed widespread defaulting on state debts, but they provide evidence of government interest in facilitating commerce and trade. The federal government was more fortunate with its support of railroad expansion, as it appropriated thousands of acres of land and then sold it cheaply to railroad companies to enable track expansion (Higgs 1987).

None of these actions could be used to characterize the American state as strong, but they all point to the ability of even a weak state to channel support and incentives to certain groups rather than others. The conflict over the tariff is particularly illustrative. Northern and Southern interests were diametrically opposed on this issue, and the tariff went up and down according to which group was in control of the federal government. Just as important, both sides saw control of the state as critical in this contest (Keohane 1983).

In the twentieth century the tension between an interventionist and a laissez-faire state has at once become less relevant and more stylized, as the growth of the state has perforce resulted in greater power and intervention, but specific instances of these expansions are deplored in the traditional language of limited-state theory. For example, the New Deal and the Great Society have been criticized by some as dangerously enlarging the power of the state and taking away private autonomy, even though millions of Americans have benefited from their social-policy programs. And liberals use the same kind of language when protesting state incursions into what they perceive to be civil liberties and privacy issues, such as abortion; they argue that the state has no right to interfere in the private lives of its citizens. If the strength of a political creed can be judged by its use by both sides of a debate, then the legitimacy of the limited state, however much it is violated in practice, is clearly supported in principle and in rhetoric.

Pocock ascribes these contradictory impulses to the historical peculiarities of the American experience. He argues that the United States represents the last stage of the "civic ideal of the personality" in which the "civic and patriotic ideal . . . [is] perfected in citizenship but perpetually threatened by corruption; [with] government figuring paradoxically as the principal source of corruption" (Pocock 1975, 505, 507). Thus, the American state is an expression of one of the greatest aspects of American democratic politics, the reality that every individual is a member of the polis through citizenship, but as an institution it is constantly threatened by its potential for adulteration and decline.

India

Caste and Hierarchy

If the exclusion of blacks from American conceptions of equality has been termed the American dilemma, the reconciliation of traditional hierarchical concepts of society with constitutional provisions for equality might be considered the Indian dilemma. Andre Beteille has termed this conflict "between the legal order with its commitment to complete equality and the social order with its all-pervasive stratification . . . the most manifest contradiction in everyday life in contemporary India" (1983, 81, 84). Throughout history groups comprised the primary unit of hierarchical organization, but since independence, individual rights have come to coexist legitimately with the rights of groups. The environment for reservation policies in India, therefore, is one in which dichotomous views compete for social and political legitimacy. This situation is exemplified in the Indian constitution, where individual rights are considered fundamental, but the state is directed to take steps to improve the conditions of social and educationally backward *classes*. To make matters even more confusing, the divisions do not occur neatly between "traditional" and "modern" values. Rather, preference policies are supported by some old and new values and undercut by others.

Hierarchical social organization and corporate identities have been fundamental organizing principles in Indian society for thousands of years, and the caste system has been viewed by lay and scholarly observers as one of the most salient aspects of Indian life. Since the nineteenth century, however, traditional emphases on hierarchy and group identity have been directly challenged by a new commitment to individualism and equality, embodied in a constitution that shares many characteristics with its U.S. counterpart.

Just as Louis Hartz is the most articulate exponent of the theory of the centrality of Lockean liberalism in American culture, Louis Dumont is the preeminent spokesman for the position that the hierarchy and corporate identity specified in Hindu law and ritual observance are central concepts in India. According to Dumont, hierarchy exists in different forms and across different social categories in all societies, but scholars of the West tend to see it as aberrant because of the dominant egalitarian ideology (1980). In India, however the concept of hierarchy is fully and explicitly realized as a basic unit of social organization through two systems: class, or *varna,* and caste, or *jati.*

The varnas date from the Vedic period and divide society into four great classes. The highest class consists of the *Brahmins,* or priests; the second class is the warrior, or *Kshatriya* class; the third class comprises the farmer/artisan groups, or *Vaisyas;* and the fourth class is constituted of the *Sudras,* who serve the three higher classes. Untouchables are completely outside this overarching class system, ranking beneath Sudras. Because the varnas provide such sweeping classifications, it is difficult to specify precisely their "functions in the modern age" (Dumont 1980, 67), but they certainly have strong symbolic value; the division between twice-born castes (those allowed to participate in a Hindu thread ceremony), which comprise the elite, "pure" group, and the rest of the society, is critical in the determination of status.

The second determinant of hierarchy is caste ranking. Castes, or *jatis,* are roughly derived from occupations and provide a much more precise status hierarchy than does the varna system. Unlike varna status, which provides "a common social language which holds good, or is thought to hold good, for India as a whole" (Srinivas 1962, 69), castes are regionally specific; not all castes are found in all regions, and their hierarchial position can vary from one part of India to another. Interaction between castes is determined by a complex and highly articulated series of exchanges based on the opposition of purity and pollution (Dumont 1980). Crudely speaking, high castes are pure and low castes are impure, and the kinds of exchanges that can be undertaken without violating the purity of high castes are minutely specified in the sacred texts and in practice. And while the material inequalities and indignities that frequently correspond to caste affiliation have been deplored, as recently as twenty-five years ago "the vast majority of people [did] not consider caste an evil" (Srinivas 1962, 71).

Traditionally, occupations were allocated among different social groups according to Hindu law and custom in "that classic expression of inequality, viz., caste" (Srinivas 1962, 88). While the division of labor among varna and caste groups was ideally supposed to grant all groups a certain dignity irrespective of their positions, this precept was contradicted in theory as well as in practice. Philosophically, "Shudras and women are marked out in the *Dharmashastras* for indignities of every conceivable kind . . . and they are debarred from most of the ordinary graces of life" (Beteille 1983, 82). In practice, the discriminatory treatment of Sudras by Brahmins was severe and encompassed every aspect of social life. Over time, Sudras became differentiated into different castes, with the lowest-ranking castes becoming "the classical forbears of the Scheduled Castes of today" (Beteille 1983, 82).

However, just as equality has never been as effective in practice as in principle in the United States, hierarchy has never been observed in society to the degree that it is specified in Hinduism. The strict hierarchical relations specified in Hindu law have frequently been violated, and since at least the nineteenth century there exist numerous examples of castes that improved their ranks in the hierarchy; low castes have come to wield considerable economic and political power, particularly in south India (Srinivas 1962; Rudolph and Rudolph 1967). In democratic independent India the Hindu idealization of hierarchy has become even more contested as low castes have mobilized to obtain political and economic benefits. Nonetheless, ritual ranking still carries considerable social weight, and perhaps for this reason egalitarian beliefs have not completely supplanted hierarchy in India.

Several scholars have noted that systems of hierarchy and corporate organization are not unique to India; for example, the feudal societies of

Europe were also distinguished by a hierarchical ordering of social groups. But corporate society is often considered to have found its most sophisticated and complete realization in the Indian context (Dumont 1980; Beteille 1983). And while the European feudal system of passions and virtue was eventually supplanted by an individualistic system of interests and rights (Pocock 1975; Hirschmann 1977), the Indian caste system has endured even though the individual has now become a legally and politically legitimate social unit.

The enduring yet flexible nature of caste as an institution provides both support for and opposition to reservation policies. Since caste doctrine privileges groups over individuals, the allocation of preferences according to group identity is not ideologically problematic and is even given legitimacy. But the concept of caste hierarchy, which distinguishes minutely among groups and privileges some over others, undercuts support for preferences that target low- over high-caste groups. The latter might oppose such policies because they violate high-caste groups' own interests, but the religious precepts of purity and pollution complicate the situation further.

The Emergence of Equality and Individualism

Throughout history there were attempts to challenge the supremacy of the social hierarchy, but these efforts did not result in any substantial weakening of the caste system because of its ability to absorb new groups and ideas; dissenters were usually accorded new positions within the overarching Hindu structure. Beginning in the nineteenth century, however, acceptance of corporate, unequal society was challenged by a Western emphasis on the primacy of the individual. This challenge arose largely because the Indian elite

> found itself in a peculiar historical predicament in the nineteenth century. It was essentially an upper caste intelligentsia which had within its traditional cultural context taken its own social superiority for granted. It now found itself despised, and its traditional culture denigrated by alien rulers acutely conscious of their own racial superiority. The situation itself called for an assertion of equality as a general value, not merely equality among races or among nations, but also equality among castes and among human beings in general. (Beteille 1983, 48–49)

Throughout the late nineteenth century Indians began to incorporate aspects of Western society, culture, and philosophy into their intellectual agendas. In art this included the development of the Indian novel; in fashion, the adoption of English dress. And in the political realm, Indian elites became increasingly attracted to Western philosophy's emphasis on the importance of the individual as the primary unit, standing above corporate religious and caste groups.

The shift from the group to the individual as the primary political unit was by no means universal among upper-class Indians. Muslims, in particular, felt threatened almost from the beginning by a system in which the majority would dominate unless sufficient safeguards were introduced to protect minority interests. Hardy's analysis (1971) details superbly the fears of Muslim elites that their defeat at the hands of the British would be compounded by Hindu predominance in a Raj with greater indigenous political representation. Because of these fears Muslim leaders were less eager to depart from the use of corporate categories in politics. And given the severity and the extent of the discrimination that separated untouchables from the rest of Indian society, it can hardly be surprising that early-twentieth-century attempts to improve their conditions were also met with considerable resistance by elite Hindus. In 1911 the question of whether the census was to record untouchables as Hindus or in a separate category arose. Even though it was clearly advantageous from a political point of view to count untouchables within the Hindu fold, Galanter quotes a contemporary observer as noting, "Ten years ago the answer would have been emphatically in the negative. Even now the conservative feeling of the country is for their exclusion" (Holderness 1911, quoted in Galanter 1984, 26n.).

From a different angle, Hindu nationalists saw increased political participation and the rise of the independence movement as an opportunity to recapture the lost glory of the pre-Mughal period of Hindu dominance (Chandra 1979). They advocated majority rule, but for different reasons than the Indian National Congress: Hindu nationalists saw in majority rule an opportunity to restore Hindu political supremacy. Indian political leaders were committed to granting the concept of equality a privileged status during the independence movement and in the new state. Led by Gandhi, who argued that "equality was a fundamental value in the Indian tradition" (Beteille 1983, 51), as well as by Nehru, and continually challenged by Ambedkar, the Indian National Congress emphasized the importance of equality as a guiding principle in independent India.

Although these differing approaches to political representation offered challenges to the secular nationalist trends, they did not succeed in supplanting the increasing desire for a politics that granted integrity to the individual. The greatest challenge to this new emphasis on the individual came not from within Indian society, but instead from the very representatives of Western political thought that governed India. Rather than perceiving India as comparable to contemporary European societies, the English left their Enlightenment concepts at home and treated India as a premodern society that was essentially feudal in nature.[2] To the English, India was made up of discrete groups, similar to guilds, whose interests were fundamentally separate from each other. The British perception that Hindus and Muslims were irreconcilably in conflict has been well documented (Hardy 1971). But the British construction of India went beyond the Muslim-Hindu division and saw many other groups as conflictually opposed: landowners, academic communities, industrialists, and other religious groups were all seen as discrete segments of society rather than interrelated parts of a whole.[3]

This British view of a corporate India had important political ramifications. From nearly the beginning of India's inclusion as a crown colony, the Raj formulated policy that treated different economic, religious, and social interests separately. Copeland quotes an 1892 dispatch from the Government of India that states that Indian society "was 'essentially a congeries of widely separated classes, races, and communities with divergences of interest and hereditary sentiment,' which could be properly represented only by those who knew and shared their sectional opinions" (Copeland 1945, 24). Not surprisingly, the introduction of political representation, beginning in the late nineteenth century, reflected this official position and offered separate representation by class, religion, and economic interest.[4]

This disjuncture between a British construction of India as essentially corporate and the growing conviction of the Indian elite that national unity and individual rights had to supersede "traditional" social groupings gave rise to the major paradox of the national independence movement. While Indian elites argued that India should be treated as a single entity with an undifferentiated electorate, their Western rulers maintained that the corporate nature of society was paramount and that political representation should be on a group rather than an individual basis. Thus, the British became the champions of the "traditional" hierarchical corporate conception of India, while secular, liberal Indian elites supported the "Western" emphasis on equality and the political importance of the individual. This conflict proved to have important ramifications for the nature of politics, first during the nationalist movement and later in independent India, and it shaped the process of state building that was being undertaken in the first half of the twentieth century.

Since 1947, the legitimacy of equality as a fundamental precept has increased. It has not displaced the traditional belief in hierarchy, particularly in the private sphere, but it has made headway in public, "secular" arenas of interaction. The twentieth-century Indian conception of equality is similar in many ways to the American concept of equal opportunity, but there is also a critical difference. Perhaps because of the pervasiveness of social inequality, Indians who are interested in ameliorating unequal conditions are well aware of the limitations of prospect-regarding equal opportunity as a path to equality. But they also value the emphasis on individual advancement and the concept of initiative being rewarded that accompanies equal opportunity. Almost from the beginning of the debate over reducing inequalities between groups, politicians and scholars have expressed concern on two counts: first, that the formal abolition of discrimination cannot by itself provide sufficient impetus to improve the conditions of the low castes and untouchables; and second, that strong preference policies will move society away from ever achieving equality of any kind. The framers of the Indian constitution placed great importance on reconciling these potentially contradictory concerns. They sought to provide ways to reduce inequality, but they did not want to abandon the focus on the individual in favor of a new corporate structure. It should be remembered that Ambedkar, the leader of the untouchable community who was in large measure responsible for the acceptance of reservations, was opposed to making them permanent because he feared that they would eventually lead to a division of society and prevent the assimilation of untouchables within caste Hindu society (Zelliot 1969).

However, unlike the situation in the United States, in India "it is thus not a question of choosing between the meritarian and the compensatory principles, but of achieving a proper balance between the two" (Beteille 1983, 98). Many Indians freely admit that there is substantial inequality in society and that it is important that these differences be lessened, and reservation policies are seen by backward classes and scheduled castes as a vital tool in the process. But at the same time, civil servants, scholars, and social groups opposed to extensive reservation policies fear that merit and talent will be discarded in the effort to improve the economic, social, and political circumstances of the disadvantaged.

While the legitimacy of individual rights has come to be more widely accepted among what Srinivas once labeled "enlightened Indians," Indian society is still organized primarily in terms of castes and communities, and the ideology of caste hierarchy continues to conflict with emerging ideologies of individualism and equal rights. Caste groups have proven to be resilient and innovative in taking advantage of new political, economic, and social opportunities (Rudolph and Rudolph 1967), and it is unlikely that they will wither away in the foreseeable future. Moreover, the Supreme Court has lent support to the concept of group rights in the modern context by devoting considerable energy to the development of constitutionally acceptable methods for classifying groups as backward (Galanter 1984). These efforts have been complicated, contradictory, and at times incomprehensible, but they have given new life to a traditional form of social organization.

The tension between individual and group rights is particularly evident in the development of preference policies. The Supreme Court has stipulated that caste cannot be the sole measure of backwardness, and opponents of reservation have argued that it is manifestly unfair for the children of privileged untouchables to take advantaged of reserved seats. This objection has been raised with increasing frequency in recent years, as reservation policies have entered their fourth decade and are being utilized by a second and even a third generation. Untouchables have their own response to this challenge. The late Jagjivan Ram, the first scheduled caste member to reach the highest circles of the national political elite in independent India, was asked why his son should benefit from reservations. He is said to have retorted that since there were still many tables at which his son could not dine, perhaps untouchability was not a dead issue and reservations were important for scheduled caste advancement.

The Role of the State

Conceptually and institutionally, the state has existed in India since ancient times. Moreover, analogies to the tension between state restraint and state intervention that have characterized American politics can be found in Indian state theory as well, from classical times to the twentieth century. The Indian state has been given strong powers to intervene in society and to command obedience, but it has also been restrained by its obligations to social groups and to its role in upholding the social order. This tension can be observed in periods of external rule as well as in the philosophy and practice of Hindu sovereignty.

The social need for the institution of the state, in the person of the king, dates back to classical times and is specified in Indian sacred texts. The king is "somehow necessary for the protection of the people through the maintenance of the moral order or *dharma*," and the texts "are unanimous in assigning the protection of the people and the maintenance of the order of the world or even of the whole universe to the king" (Heesterman 1985, 108, 109). However, the king's authority is not without constraints. On the one hand the king, in order to protect society, is allowed the use of *danda*, or legitimate force, and *artha*, the use of rational action to acquire and guard land (Dumont 1980, 302–5). But on the other hand he is not the ultimate repository of power and legitimacy, because the priest, who precedes him in the ranking of the varnas, has "transcendent" authority

(Heesterman 1985). In addition, the king has obligations and duties to groups within society, because society precedes and limits the state: "the state upheld and protected society and its values rather than itself constituting the highest form of community and the means for realizing value" (Rudolph and Rudolph 1987, 67). There is no "divine right of kingship" as there was in Europe; indeed, it may even be that "the king is just someone who is put in charge of the maintenance of public order, in exchange for which service his subjects leave to him a part of the crops they harvest" (Dumont 1980, 297).

Although the Mughal and British empires developed strong states in their conquest and rule of India, they did not depart entirely from this Janus-faced conception of the state. Habib notes that even though the Mughal empire was characterized by an "uncomplicated desire of a small ruling class for more and more material resources—an almost primitive urge to consume and acquire" (Raychaudhuri and Habib 1982, 172), it depended on alliances with regional kingdoms and on the loyalty of intermediaries who collected the taxes and levies that made possible the Mughal's rulers' lavish standard of living and continuous efforts to expand. Even at the peak of Mughal hegemony, "the emperor's power and wealth could be great, but only if he was skilled in extracting money, soldiers and devotion from other kings. He was a marshal of kings, an entrepreneur in power . . . Even under strong emperors, the hierarchy was always shifting and realigning" (Bayly 1988, 13–14). Bayly points to the incorporation of Hindus as well as Muslims into the administrative and ruling elite and argues that the decentralized nature of the Mughal empire made possible the flowering of regional kingdoms during the former's decline (1988). This interdependence between sovereign and society and the maintenance of the social order was important in spheres beyond the economic: Among the great Mughal emperor Akbar's many accomplishments, his tolerance toward Hindus is frequently cited, whereas Aurangzeb's preferential treatment of Muslims and persecution of Hindus is cited as one of his failures.[5]

The British Raj echoed this pattern of a strong state that was still constrained from intervention in issues considered to be primarily social in nature. In the eighteenth and early nineteenth the British state, as embodied by the East India Company, had the same coercive and extractive goals as the Mughal empire it gradually replaced. Like the Mughals, the British worked through regional rulers and took over direct administration of territories only when it resulted in superior revenue extraction (Bayly 1988). The Company was far less interested in social transformation than in economic conquest, and in the initial phases of English penetration into India it was satisfied to work behind the scenes politically.

By the eighteenth century this approach was being challenged by diverse Englishmen, who ranged from politicians to evangelical Christians to utilitarian economists, and who saw India as a laboratory for their ideas (Stokes 1959). They considered India to be a primitive, irrational, and immoral country that needed to be socially reeducated for its own good. While such direct interventionist approaches tended to be defeated by the hands-off policy of the British government, the requirements of an extractive economic system that was protected by a coercive political structure could not avoid bringing about major transformations in Indian society.

To cite only a few examples, the need for stable revenues led to the imposition of consistent land tenure systems across the Bengal and Madras provinces (Raychaudhuri and Habib 1982). The development of systematic political administration resulted in the codification of administrative law and the separation of Hindu and Muslim law from "secular" law for the first time and the movement of dispute resolution from localities to British courts. The census, which was initiated to codify and "make sense" of Indian groups for the British, imposed a rigidity and apparent permanence on a caste system that had historically been somewhat fluid and local in its scope (Bayly 1988). And finally, all these policies, regardless of their stated aims, had the effect of reshaping social relations as the demands of empire brought new groups to the forefront and pushed others to the back. Thus, despite British protestations that their policies were not designed to interfere with existing social relations except in special cases, Indian subjects and British representatives became accustomed to a strong state whose presence was felt not only in the economic and political arenas, but also in the social realm.

In bringing Western law and administration to India, the British introduced and legitimized the importance of the individual in politics and law, even as the Raj itself emphasized the fundamentally corporate nature of Indian society. This attention to individual rights, which became a key element of the nationalist struggle, provided one of the two major issues of contention in the development of the independent Indian state. The first was the balance between individual and group rights, and the second was the balance between a strong and a weak state, as embodied in the central government.

The debate over the scope of the state echoed the American founders' fears of the unbridled power of the state; like the American colonists, Indians knew only too well the disadvantages of such a system. But at the same time nationalist leaders were convinced that a strong state was necessary to propel the social and economic "revolution" that India needed to experience if it were to participate fully in the modern world (Austin 1966). Moreover, the "fissiparous tendencies" engendered by India's linguistically, religiously, and ethnically plural groups could best be countered by a strong central structure that could rise above provincial demands and quell separatist movements.

These apprehensions, which could easily have led to a state that was so strong as to verge on authoritarian (Rudolph and Rudolph 1967), were countered by the tension over the balance between individual and group rights. The protection of individual rights was perceived, on the model of the U.S. and Irish constitutions, to be a central government responsibility. But an authoritarian structure could not be considered a reliable guardian of individual rights and liberties. And the competing demands of groups and their corporate rights, which were vehemently supported by some constituent assembly members and which British policies had made impossible to ignore, gave support to a balance between central and regional interests (Austin 1966).

The resulting constitution has continued and institutionalized the contested position of the Indian state, and this ambivalence creates a complex set of expectations in independent India's democratic political system. On the one hand, the state has been given the power to lead the social and economic revolution and to formulate policy that is in the best interests of all India. But on the other hand the state is keenly sensitive to the demands of different groups within the electorate, groups that often have competing or contradictory demands. Reservation policies bring out this tension clearly, as the state can be seen promulgating strong policies at certain points in time and backing off from taking the policy initiative at others.

Conclusion

The political cultures of the United States and India have provided both support for and arguments against affirmative-action policies. In the United States the reality of racial discrimination and the history of selective state intervention in policymaking created a receptive environment for the development of government programs aimed at ending racial inequality. Since before the founding of the American republic, the cleavage of race has served as a rebuke to the idea that the United States provides equality of opportunity and equal treatment under the law for all its citizens. The most destructive war in American history, the Civil War, was fought in large part because of the political ramifications of the slavery issue. While citizens may hold diverse attitudes about race relations, there are few who would dispute that it is a critical U.S. concern. This importance helps explain why state intervention in civil rights has been accepted despite a political culture that tends to favor a weak state.

At the same time, however, Americans' philosophical and ideological commitments to the supremacy of individual identity over group membership, a restrained central state, and equality of opportunity created disincentives for these same programs. Affirmative-action targets by group, and the policies do not distinguish between members of the group; ascriptive identity is the only criterion for eligibility. This aspect challenges a central tenet of American political culture: the belief that the individual, not the group, is the proper target of policymaking, and therefore programs to achieve equality of opportunity should be oriented toward individuals. And finally, while Americans agree that the state should guarantee equal rights and equal access, they are much more skeptical about state intervention to develop programs that go beyond formal legal equality (Schuman, Steeh, and Bobo 1985).

In India, an increased commitment to equal opportunity and growing desires for upward mobility by a variety of actors, together with a historically strong state, created similar incentives for preferential policies. The colonial experience and the divide-and-rule tactics of the British exposed for Indians the problems attached to giving primacy to corporate identities. Concomitantly, expanding political and economic opportunities for those beyond the highest castes made policies that favored groups that were dominant in those arenas but had little religious ritual standing. And the unquestioned legitimacy of the Indian National Congress among Hindus joined with the historically strong position of the state to allow political parties to develop preferential policies.

Nevertheless, the enduring strength of caste hierarchies, suspicions about state motives, and a weak but growing support for individual rights provided important disincentives as well. Caste has been declared illegal in the Indian constitution, but it flourishes at all levels of politics as a proxy for interest-group mobilization. The successful adoption of electoral politics has led to suspicion about state policies, as excluded voters equate policies with electoral payoffs. And the introduction of market-based economics, albeit within a socialist framework, with its emphasis on individual reward, has made group rewards more suspect.

Although even a relatively brief discussion about the context underlying affirmative-action policy development yields too many factors to provide a clear connection between policies and their causes, it provides important substantive insights. In both countries the political cultures create ambivalent circumstances about the very issues that affirmative-action programs address. The simultaneous presence of opportunities and constraints suggests that it is not surprising that affirmative action became so controversial. Indeed, the surprise should be that there was a time when they failed to evoke controversy. In the next chapter I turn to the political conditions that preceded the initiation of policy development to suggest why this was so.

CHAPTER 3

The Precursors of Affirmative-Action Policy

In this chapter I explore the conditions under which African-Americans and untouchables were finally able to succeed in gaining benefits from the majorities that had historically oppressed and excluded them. The introduction, adoption, and expansion of affirmative-action policies was part of a longer process that included related but quite distinct programs to increase equality for these groups. I begin from the assumption that minority preferences over outcomes remained constant, that is, they were always aiming to achieve equal treatment from the rest of society. But until certain circumstances changed, these outcomes could not be achieved. These changes included the groups' political strategies, the receptivity of political elites to their demands, changing attitudes on the part of the majority groups, and what might be termed exogenous shocks to the political system that affected majority-minority relations.

In order for blacks and untouchables to gain equal treatment under the law, much less prescriptive policies like affirmative action, political elites had to be receptive to their demands. Until the twentieth century, politicians had few reasons to pay attention to the interests of blacks and untouchables. But then the changing political power of these groups, accompanied by more positive attitudes on the part of whites and caste Hindus, created a new structure of incentives. In the United States, changing social, economic, and demographic factors within the black community and society in general led to increased political power for African-Americans. At the same time, factors unrelated to race relations, especially U.S. participation in World War II, led to changes in the attitudes of whites toward blacks and toward policies that guaranteed equal opportunity. And in turn, minorities used new and more effective strategies to push elites to develop such policies, especially in employment and education.

In India, the changing conditions that accompanied the gradual extension of limited political opportunities to indigenous groups under colonial rule put untouchables in an advantageous political position vis-à-vis caste Hindu groups, while negotiating over equal rights helped to transform elite Hindus' attitudes toward caste and equality, not least in relation to untouchables. In these negotiations untouchables employed strategies that would gain them benefits in specific policy areas, including political representation, employment, and higher education.

In both countries, changing social, economic, and political conditions led to increased political power for blacks and untouchables. At the same time, changes exogenous to majority-minority relations led to changing attitudes on the part of the majority groups. These two factors, increased minority political power and changing majority attitudes, combined to make political elites more receptive to minority demands, a result that the groups exploited through strategic behavior. I discuss these transformations for the United States and India in the remainder of this chapter.

United States

In the twentieth century, changing political and social relations brought U.S. society to recognize and acknowledge the hypocrisy inherent in celebrating principles of equality and liberty while denying their practice to blacks and to take steps to reconcile ideals with reality. This transformation was facilitated by a number of factors. The end of southern dominance in agriculture and black migration from the South to the North made their votes increasingly important to politicians seeking votes. At the same time, black participation in World War II, the emergence of the United States as a world power after the war, and its rivalry with the Soviet Union helped to transform majority attitudes toward blacks. As African-Americans pressed their demands for equality, they encountered a more receptive political environment.

Demographic and Economic Transformations

Before World War I, the racial status quo was maintained because of the terms of the North-South economic compact. As long as northern mill owners were dependent on a steady supply of southern cotton, southerners were able to impose their view of race relations on the rest of the country, but by World War I the economic interests of North and South began to diverge. During the decades of the late nineteenth and early twentieth centuries, the increasing labor demands of northern industry had been met by an influx of immigrants. But the war caused immigration to decline sharply, and northern manufacturers began to come into conflict with southern plantation owners as they attempted to recruit southern black laborers. Despite fierce opposition from southern economic elites, northerners were successful in their efforts: whereas less than two hundred thousand blacks migrated from the South in the first decade of the twentieth century, the number increased to more than half a million in the second ten years (Lee et al. 1957). Thus, "for the first time since Reconstruction, the material interests of various segments of the nation's economic elite diverged on the 'Negro problem'" (McAdam 1982, 74).

The shift in demand for black labor did not end with World War I for several reasons. First, increasing feelings of nativism and isolationism in American society during the 1920s helped to bring about restrictive immigration laws, which left northern industry heavily dependent on black labor from the South. Second, the decline of cotton's preeminence in the southern economy made southern elites less inclined to combat northern attempts to draw blacks into their industrial economy (McAdam 1982, chap. 5). And the final blow to the hegemony of "King Cotton" was struck during the Great Depression, when plummeting cotton prices drove blacks off the plantation to look for jobs that could provide them a living, as the farm policies of the New Deal reduced acreage significantly in order to stimulate demand (Sitkoff 1978).

The demographic changes that accompanied the diminution of the role of southern agriculture had two important political consequences. First, the Jim Crow laws that had prevented blacks from voting in the South did not exist in the North, and there they were able to exercise their electoral rights. Second, the vast majority leaving the South came from states where they had been most severely constrained from voting, and they settled in those large northern and western industrial states that were key to electoral success in presidential races (Woodward 1974; McAdam 1982). Thus, the transformation of black electoral quiescence into electoral power was potentially very strong, and during the New Deal and war years this constituency began to take shape and become important (Lawson 1976).

During the 1932 election, African-Americans were skeptical of Franklin Roosevelt because he was a Democrat and because his vice presidential candidate was a southerner. Indeed, in Chicago, less than 25 percent of the black electorate cast its ballots for Roosevelt (Myrdal 1944). But African-Americans soon became some of Roosevelt's strongest supporters. Despite discrimination in the implementation of many New Deal programs, no other president had done as much for blacks since Lincoln, and "the debit side of the New Deal's efforts to assist Negroes fell far short of its material and psychological credits. Never before had Negro leaders participated in government affairs as freely and as frequently" (Fishel 1969, 12). Moreover, while Roosevelt did not develop programs aimed specifically at the African-American community, he did not exclude it either. And his refusal to countenance traditional methods of subordination were extremely important to blacks; as Du Bois remarked, Roosevelt "declared frankly that lynching is murder. We all knew it, but it is unusual to have a President of the United States admit it. These things give us hope" (quoted in McAdam 1982, 109). By 1936, Roosevelt's approval rating among blacks was nearly 85 percent (Myrdal 1944).

From the beginning of Roosevelt's term of office, African-Americans had a staunch supporter within the White House. Eleanor Roosevelt made no secret of her opposition to race segregation and discrimination. As First Lady, she "included Negro and mixed organizations on her itineraries, welcomed mixed groups of adults and children to the White House, and spoke up for the race at critical times" despite the heavy criticism she received from whites (Fishel 1969, 13). Emboldened by her example and by Roosevelt's enormous popularity, Harold Ickes, Harry Hopkins, and other New Deal administrators took steps to control discrimination in housing, labor, and agricultural policies (Sitkoff 1978).

After the 1940 elections, when Roosevelt lost his huge margin in the Congress, African-American support became pivotal, and with this new political strength, they were able to gain benefits that were more than symbolic. During World War I, blacks had subordinated race issues in order to support the war effort fully, but the postwar period had brought few changes. When World War II commenced, black leaders changed their strategy and determined to protest even as they encouraged all citizens to contribute to the war effort. This changed approach was motivated partly by the economic circumstances in which the United States found itself as it entered the war. World War I had coincided with a boom in industrial employment and a favorable labor market for blacks due to decreased immigration from abroad. But in 1941 "the nation was well stocked with unemployed whites. . . . Discrimination [was] the rule practically everywhere" (Myrdal 1944, 1005). It is noteworthy that the March on Washington in 1941 was organized by A. Philip Randolph to protest discrimination in defense industry and government employment.

Attitudinal Transformations

The changes that demographic and economic transformation produced were complemented by developments in society at large in the 1940s and 1950s. In particular, World War II catalyzed American assessment of the black position in society. The United States had played a limited role in World War I because it entered the conflict near the end and did not need to mobilize many troops. World War II, on the other hand, required the mobilization of large numbers of men to serve in the military, and blacks were heavily recruited. They had also been recruited into the army in

World War I, but primarily in service and domestic positions rather than as combat troops. In World War II, by contrast, they served in important combat units, but they were always segregated from white soldiers.

This separation of African-Americans from the rest of American society impressed itself on the white majority in two ways. First, it made clear that although they were fulfilling the greatest sacrifice demanded of citizens, that of giving their lives to protect their country, they were not accorded the full rights citizenship entailed. African-American servicemen on home leave were barred from many whites-only establishments, and blacks abroad were often prohibited from patronizing facilities for white soldiers. Second, the ideological character of World War II highlighted the race problem in the United States. As Myrdal noted, "This War [was] an ideological war fought in defense of democracy. . . . Moreover, in this War the principle of democracy had to be applied more explicitly to race" (Myrdal 1944, 1004), since Nazism promulgated the theory of a master race and the Japanese appealed to antiwhite feelings in Asia. Within the United States, the rhetoric used by leaders to justify participation in the war pointed up the discrepancy with reality: "The hypocrisy and paradox involved in fighting a world war for the four freedoms and against aggression by an enemy preaching a master-race ideology, while at the same time upholding racial segregation and white supremacy, were too obvious" (Dalfiume 1969, 247). Blacks were being asked to give their lives so that citizens of other countries could gain the freedom that they themselves were denied at home.

The contradiction between ideology and practice did not end with the war but continued to be an issue in the postwar years. The United States fought in World War II as a defender of democracy, freedom, and equality, and it emerged from the war as a world power. Almost immediately, it found itself in competition with the Soviet Union for influence with new nations. Against this backdrop, the issue of segregation was no longer strictly an internal matter, but one that had international repercussions. The establishment of the United Nations in New York "suddenly threw open to the outside world a large window on American race practices. . . . To many of these people the Jim Crow code came as a complete shock" (Woodward 1974, 132). The international importance of U.S. court decisions on desegregation can be inferred from the fact that the Supreme Court's 1954 *Brown* decision was broadcast within a few hours by the Voice of America in thirty-five different languages. Similarly, throughout the 1950s members of Congress and cabinet members pointed to the international benefits of pressing forward civil-rights legislation, and the State Department was assiduous in recruiting blacks to posts, sometimes of high rank, in the Foreign Service (Woodward 1974).

The Effectiveness of African-American Political Strategies

From the 1930s, black elites developed political strategies that were more effective than those they had used previously. These strategies ranged from activism directed at elected officials to legal strategies. Changes in approach were exemplified by the different ways black activists treated participation in the first and second world wars. In the interwar years African-Americans became more educated, more organized, and better able to communicate with each other as the black press grew in sophistication and breadth. Furthermore, the leadership had become increasingly outspoken and unwilling to postpone demands to a more convenient time: "The elderly DuBois renounced with bitterness the credulous advice he once gave his people in the First World War to 'close ranks'" (Myrdal 1944, 1005). Despite charges from whites that blacks, and especially the black press, were constituting themselves as a fifth column, they continued to press their demands and challenge unequal treatment whenever possible.

The March on Washington never materialized because the threat was sufficient to cause Roosevelt to issue Executive Order 8802, which introduced the principle of nondiscrimination in federal-government contracts. Of greater symbolic than substantive value, it prohibited discrimination in the employment of workers in defense industries or government on the basis of race, creed, color, or national origin, and it stated that "it is the duty of employees and of labor organizations . . . to provide for the full and equitable participation of all workers in defense industries" (Benokraitis and Feagin 1978). In addition, Executive Order 8802 established the Fair Employment Practices Commission (FEPC), located in the Office of Production Management, to administer the order. The FEPC had almost no real power because no sanctions for noncompliance had been specified; rather, its distinction lay in the fact that it was the first administrative unit created to investigate discriminatory practices. In 1943 Roosevelt issued a second executive order, EO 9346, which extended nondiscrimination to federal agencies and all government contracts and strengthened the FEPC. However, the FEPC's vigorous exercise of its authority to solicit testimony on discrimination soon caused it to run afoul of business and conservative politicians. In 1944 it was transferred to the authority of the Committee on War Manpower, which was hostile to the FEPC's mission and quickly curtailed its activities (Sovern 1966; Ruchames 1953).

These high-profile mobilizing strategies were accompanied by a less well known, but equally effective, attack on the legal underpinnings of Jim Crow, particularly in the area of education. The struggle to achieve formal legal equality for blacks has ranged across a number of arenas, including political representation, public accommodations, and employment, but perhaps its most well known and enduring focus has been public education. *Brown v. Board of Education* addressed access to primary education, and even in *Plessy,* which was essentially an accommodations case, the Supreme Court cited an education case in Massachusetts to support its argument. This centrality for education is due to the importance that education plays in American society and political culture; the right to equal opportunity in the use of one's individual abilities contains within it the assumption of a level playing field, and access to quality education is considered to be a basic means to achieve genuine equal opportunity.

Among developed countries, the United States has been a leader in providing education to large numbers of citizens. In contrast to other social-policy areas such as health care or old-age support, the United States consistently acted prior to European countries in expanding all levels of education (Heidenheimer, Heclo, and Adams 1983; Rubinson 1986). Education is considered to be a governmental responsibility; not necessarily a federal responsibility, but nonetheless an arena in which at least local and state governments are expected to play a part (Tyack, James, and Benavot 1987). Throughout the United States, the number of colleges and universities increased dramatically during the nineteenth century. This general expansion of higher education, however, was largely closed to African-Americans, who were excluded from many public and private colleges and universities. In order to benefit from postsecondary learning they were forced to establish their own institutions.

Beginning in 1854 and continuing throughout the latter half of the nineteenth century, African-Americans founded dozens of colleges and universities that trained lawyers, doctors, businessmen, and skilled artisans. Over time, these graduates comprised a small but critically important black middle class. They were never able to compete effectively with whites, to break into white society, or to achieve a status comparable to college-educated whites, but they provided important resources for their own community, and they established a vanguard of an educated elite that could lead the fight for equal rights in the 1950s and 1960s.

Black colleges were generally considered to be inferior in resources to predominantly white institutions, and the major reason for this inferior status lay in their lack of money. Three acts of Congress that provided for the enormous expansion of higher education to the mass of Americans, and therefore could have supported the growth of black higher education, were written and administered in such a way that the African-American community was virtually excluded from sharing in the benefits. The Morrill Act of 1862, which enabled states to provide scientific and practical training at land-grant colleges, preceded the abolition of slavery and made no special provision for the education of blacks. The Hatch Act, passed in 1887, specified that funds were to be equally divided between white and black colleges, but the state legislature was given the prerogative to direct otherwise; with this latter qualification, Congress "proffer[red] equality with one hand, [and] quietly withdrew it with the other" (Preer 1982, 7).

In the second Morrill Act, passed in 1890, congressmen sympathetic to blacks' educational concerns specifically mandated an equitable distribution of funds, but left a gaping loophole: "the maintenance of colored schools as branches or departments of white universities did not violate the prohibitions of distinctions based on color" (Preer 1982, 9), even if these branches or departments were located in entirely different cities. The practical consequence of this loophole was to allow state governments to allocate the majority of federal resources to predominantly white campuses while leaving black campuses woefully underfunded and understaffed.

Deprived of financial assistance by state and federal governments, African-Americans were forced to find alternative means of support. Much of the funding they received was provided by white northern philanthropists. This funding, as Myrdal has remarked, had "strategic importance: first, to give [education] a start during Reconstruction, later to hinder its complete destruction during Restoration, and to advance it in recent decades" (1944, 890). The General Education Board, founded by John D. Rockefeller, provided money for fellowships, colleges, and libraries. The Phelps-Stokes Fund assisted black and white college students studying black problems. The Carnegie Corporation supported African-American colleges and libraries, as well as research projects on black conditions. When Myrdal was conducting his research, three of the four best black colleges and universities, those Myrdal considered equal to white institutions, were privately supported; only Howard University was supported by the federal government.

There was a negative aspect to this philanthropic aid. Black colleges and universities tended to be controlled by the philanthropists who supported them, so that even though African-Americans had produced their own educational institutions, these institutions were subject to white, even if it was well-meaning white, domination. This domination manifested itself not only in white control of the university administrations, but in white control over the type of education these institutions would provide. Benefactors were divided between favoring training that would give African-Americans practical skills and a more liberal education similar to that received by elite whites.

Perhaps more important for long-term black strategies in higher education, this opposition was reflected in the African-American community as well, and it hindered its ability to present a sustained and unified alternative to white exclusionary policies in higher education. It was best exemplified by the debate between W. E. B. Du Bois and Booker T. Washington in the late nineteenth and early twentieth centuries. Washington advocated a "vocational" form of education that would emphasize skills, trades, and self-sufficiency for the black community, and he played down political activism and integration in favor of practical training and job skills. In his view, blacks would be able to compete with whites only after they had attained a certain level of self-reliance and educational competence. In contrast, Du Bois and his supporters argued for a "classical" education similar to that which college-going whites received. They stressed the importance of providing comparable education so that blacks could compete with whites from the outset, and they advocated political action to improve the position of blacks (Myrdal 1944; Franklin 1980).

This conflict over the best type of education was part of a more extensive debate within the African-American community over whether members were best off improving their own segregated schools or obtaining access to white colleges and universities. Some argued that African-Americans were best served through a separate educational system and would not be able to compete successfully with whites until they had improved all of their levels of schooling; until this was done, they should continue to educate themselves separately (Franklin 1980). Opponents of this position asserted that the only way to become fully integrated into the larger society was to receive the same education as whites (Preer 1982).

Beginning in the 1920s the dissension subsided as lawyers targeted the Supreme Court in an attempt to achieve the reversal of *Plessy v. Ferguson.* For nearly two decades the Court frustrated this ambition, managing to address numerous cases that invalidated discriminatory acts without directly confronting *Plessy.* In the education arena, several cases from the 1930s to the 1950s established the right of black students to have access to equal educational facilities. The first case considered by the Court was *Missouri ex rel. Gaines v. Canada* in 1938 (305 U.S. 337). The state of Missouri refused to allow black students to attend the state university law school. In its place, the state provided payment of tuition for blacks to study at the university of "any adjacent state." In ruling on this case the Court held that Gaines had been denied equal protection of the laws and stated "that is a denial of the equality of legal right to the enjoyment of the privilege which the State has set up, and the provision for the payment of tuition fees in another State does not remove the discrimination" (349–50). The Court went on to stipulate that a state must either provide separate educational facilities for blacks and whites or must admit blacks to whites-only institutions.

In 1950, the Court specified further the conditions under which blacks and whites could be segregated in higher education in the *Sweatt v. Painter* decision (339 U.S. 629). Following upon the *Gaines* ruling, the state of Texas had quickly established a separate law school for African-Americans so that it would not be forced to admit them to the prestigious, whites-only University of Texas Law School. But this new school was vastly inferior and clearly a makeshift solution to maintain segregation. Alternatively, blacks could attend the law school at the Texas State University for Negroes, which was established after the case went to trial. The court held that both these schools failed to provide the plaintiff with an education that "is substantially equal to that which he would receive if admitted to the University of Texas Law School" (634). It cited as factors contributing to inequality the "number of faculty, variety of courses . . . scope of the library. . . . What is more important, the University of Texas Law School possesses to a far greater degree those qualities *which are incapable of objective measurement* but which make for greatness in a law school" (633–34; emphasis added). Thus, in this decision the Court went farther than it had in *Gaines* by stipulating that the educational facilities must not only exist, but that they must, in tangible and intangible ways, be equal.

On the same day as the *Sweatt* decision, the Court ruled on another case involving segregation within a university. *McLaurin v. Oklahoma State Regents* (339 U.S. 637 [1950]) concerned an African-American student who was admitted to the state law school but was then internally segregated, being forced to sit at special "colored" seats and tables in classes, the library, and the cafeteria. The Court held that segregation within the university would "impair and inhibit his ability to study, to engage in discussion, and exchange views with other students, and, in general, to learn his profession" (641).

With these decisions the Supreme Court had been tiptoeing around the issue of separate but equal without confronting it directly. In each of the higher education cases the Court had found that separate was unequal, but it shied away from addressing the question raised by *Plessy* of whether separation could ever be accompanied by equality. Finally in 1954 the Court stated that it was not. In the unanimous *Brown v. Board of Education of Topeka* decision (347 U.S. 483), invariably (and justifiably) referred to as "the landmark *Brown* decision," the Court overturned *Plessy* and outlawed de jure, state-supported segregation in primary and secondary schools. The Court directly stated that "Separate educational facilities are inherently unequal" (495). The Court, feeling that the decision had been enough of a bombshell, did not address the question of how unitary educational facilities might be achieved but invited concerned parties to submit suggestions on desegregation might best be accomplished. It heard arguments in its next session and in 1955 issued a second *Brown* decision (349 U.S. 294), often referred to as *Brown II,* in which it assigned the implementation of 1954 decision to the federal district courts, to be undertaken "with all deliberate speed" (301).

Soon after the second *Brown* decision, the Court made clear that its desegregation order encompassed public higher education as well. In *Florida ex rel. Hawkins v. Board of Control* (350 U.S. 413 [1956]), the Court held that Hawkins's petition for admittance to the all-white University of Florida Law School was merited. Moreover, the opinion stated firmly that "there is no reason for delay. He is entitled to prompt and immediate admission under the rules and regulations applicable to other qualified candidates" (413–44).

The Receptivity of Political Elites

Roosevelt had embraced the black vote during his terms as president, but its importance of African-American political support was confirmed in the 1944 and 1948 elections, when they were pivotal in securing Democratic control of the presidency. Soon after assuming the presidency upon Roosevelt's death, Harry Truman signed Executive Order 9664, which continued the FEPC, and in December 1946, he issued Executive Order 9808, which established the President's Committee on Civil Rights. This committee investigated the status of civil rights and submitted a comprehensive report, but its remedies were ignored by Congress (Benokraitis and Feagin 1978). Nevertheless, Truman continued the provision on nondiscrimination in government contracts, and in 1951 he issued Executive Order 10308, creating the Committee on Governmental Contract Compliance, which was able to request limited compliance. In 1948 Truman ran on a pro-civil-rights platform and became the first Democrat to fail to carry the former Confederacy in decades. During that election year he issued an executive order calling for the gradual desegregation of the armed forces (McAdam 1982, 84).

It is well known that Truman was aggressive in his attempts to place civil rights high on the governmental agenda during his elected term. But even Dwight D. Eisenhower, who courted the southern vote during his first election campaign, extended desegregation in explicitly federal spheres. Compared to the Truman administration, Eisenhower's accession to the presidency marked a decrease in executive efforts in the area of civil rights, because while Eisenhower was not personally opposed to the extension of civil rights to blacks, he was strongly motivated by his belief in the limited federal role in social-policy development. Early in his term Eisenhower revoked Truman's Executive Order 10308 and transferred the compliance activities of the Committee on Governmental Contract Compliance to the President's Committee on Government Contracts (Benokraitis and Feagin 1978).

Despite these retrenchments, Eisenhower took steps to advance desegregation in those areas that were explicitly the province of the federal government. Under the combined pressure of northern Republicans fearful of losing black support and Eisenhower's own cabinet members and advisors, the armed forces were completely desegregated, discriminatory practices were outlawed in military base schools and veterans' hospitals, and formal discrimination was abolished in theaters, hotels, restaurants, public housing, and federally sponsored employment in Washington, D.C. (Sundquist 1968; Burk 1984). And despite Eisenhower's belief that legislation could not change "the hearts and minds of men," the aggressive strategies of pro-civil-rights legislators and Eisenhower's attorney general, Herbert Brownell, produced successful legislative efforts to provide blacks with electoral and civil rights (Anderson 1964; Sundquist 1968).

Senators and representatives had been regularly introducing civil-rights bills since the early 1940s, but none of these efforts had made any progress, with few bills even making it out of committee (Burstein 1985). Supporters of Truman's civil-rights measures attempted to introduce them in the House of Representatives and the Senate, and two bills were passed in the House, but the Senate's filibuster rule created an overwhelming obstacle.[1] By the mid-1950s, however, civil-rights proponents were finally able to make some headway, and in 1957, the first civil-rights legislation since the post–Civil War era was enacted (Sundquist 1968). Fierce debate weakened the original bill, which contained both organizational measures and extensions of federal power, and the bill that was ultimately passed represented a compromise between civil-rights proponents and southern Democrats. It had been stripped of the original Part III, which had authorized the federal government and the attorney general to seek injunctive remedies where civil rights were violated and provoked intense and sustained debate within and outside the Senate.

The final form of the Civil Rights Act of 1957 created the Civil Rights Commission, elevated the civil-rights section of the Justice Department to divisional status under an assistant attorney general, and strengthened voting rights by extending the election provisions of the criminal code to cover primary and secondary elections and by authorizing aggrieved individuals or the attorney general to sue for injunctive relief in voting-rights cases (Sundquist 1968, 226).

In the remaining years of Eisenhower's terms, civil-rights activists sought to pass a bill containing Part III, as well as to introduce stronger civil-rights measures to enforce the *Brown* decision and voting rights. But the Senate's procedural rules continued to defeat these attempts. In 1960, a slightly stronger but still moderate voting-rights bill passed both the House and Senate; it provided court-appointed "referees" to oversee elections once a "pattern or practice" of discrimination was revealed (Sundquist 1968, 246). These bills represented the first successful congressional efforts to achieve enforceable civil rights for blacks since Reconstruction.

India

In the early part of the twentieth century, changing political, social, and economic conditions under colonial rule brought minority interests on to the political agenda and gave disadvantaged groups a new influence. These groups, which included untouchables, were quick to take advantage of the opportunities available to press for special policies. At the same time, the experience of elite Hindus with the British Raj and their need to negotiate with the Raj for power made them more sympathetic to untouchables' concerns and opened a policy space for egalitarian and preferential policies that targeted them.

British Rule and the Origins of Reservation Policy, 1862–1930

In the late nineteenth and early twentieth century, the British government introduced incremental changes in the political governance of India that were to have profound ramifications for the eventual development of reservation policies. The earliest harbingers can be found in the early days of India's establishment as a British crown colony, when Indian independence was unthinkable, democratic institutions were limited in Britain and nonexistent in India, and preferences were granted to one's allies, not to the disadvantaged. To the British, individualism was a modern concept that evolved in societies from an earlier, less advanced emphasis on the tribe, clan, or other corporate entity as the social unit. India might eventually, with proper guidance, learn to value the individual as the British did, but until that time individuals were defined (and presumably defined themselves) by their ethnic or religious identity.

After the 1857 mutiny and the annexation of India as a crown colony, the British government, especially the Government of India, began to think it would be advisable to allow prominent Indians to serve on limited advisory councils. The first of these efforts was embodied in the Indian Councils Act of 1861, which reduced the concentration of government power in Calcutta and established provincial councils in the Bombay and Madras presidencies as well. In 1892 the act was amended to allow very limited population-based representation, and it introduced the notion of political participation for Indians. This participation was still highly circumscribed; indeed, the secretary of state reminded the viceroy, "There must be no mention of anything like 'election' in them; recommendations, if you like, but the ultimate responsibility of 'nomination,' must rest with the Governor General and the Governor absolutely."[2]

Given the British view of Indian society, it is understandable that this new Indian representation was based on "communities of interests," not individuals.[3] The British were careful to ensure that their allies were certain to be members of the council, and places were reserved for commercial interests, large landowners, university faculties, Anglo-Indians, and Muslims among others. More than fifteen years later the British government took another hesitant move in the direction of increased indigenous participation. The Morley-Minto reforms were similar in principle and spirit to the 1892 act, but they increased the scope of indigenous representation. In doing so, however, they also codified and reinforced the policy of using group membership as the appropriate basis of representation.[4]

These policies were carefully thought out and extensively deliberated at the highest levels of British government before being adopted. The British had several motives in introducing limited indigenous participation. Their assumptions about Indian attitudes toward colonialism, especially the attitudes of Muslims, had been shaken by the scope and intensity of the 1857 mutiny, and liberal and moderate officials argued that the best way of ensuring loyalty was to offer advisory roles to elite Indians (Hardy 1971). The most sympathetic among British elites also considered the political socialization and education of their subjects to be an important goal. And finally, by the end of the nineteenth and the beginning of the twentieth centuries, indigenous political groups had begun to organize and demand access to power, and intelligent British actors were aware that the selective apportionment of political benefits would allow Britain to retain influence as Indian political organization and participation expanded.

While all these interests shaped British strategies, however, their choices of action were dominated by the desire to maintain existing hierarchies of power. Each time that political reforms were introduced or expanded, officials were concerned about maintaining the three major pro-British interest groups: commercial, landed, and Muslim.[5] These interests cannot be classified quite as they would be in a democratic political system, because the important actors were neither elected officials nor the classic career civil servants found in bureaucracy-centered explanations. Rather, they were high-level appointed officials who were members of the ruling economic and political elite.[6] They saw their government positions as embodying their service to their country and Crown, and they had very definite ideas about what the interests of these institutions were. Among British elites of all political persuasions it was conventional wisdom that Muslims were more loyal than Hindus, and that they, along with British economic interests, formed the bulwark of support against indigenous political challengers, who were increasingly recruited into the Indian National Congress (Hardy 1971; Seal 1971; McLane 1977).

The range and extent of interest that policy developments in Indian occasioned can be gauged by the actors involved in the process. When the amendments of 1892 were being debated, the viceroy of India received a personal communication from Queen Victoria reminding him of Britain's interests:

> The Queen-Empress has naturally watched with great interest—not unmixed with anxiety—the passing of the great measure of the Indian Councils' Bill. She wishes to impress the Viceroy with the great importance of securing an adequate representation of the great body of the Mahomedans. The Mahomedans are undoubtedly far the most loyal of the Indian people, and would be a great support in Council.[7]

The Indian Councils Act was formulated by the secretary of state for India and the viceroy in India, and it was then vehemently debated in Parliament. Lower-ranking civil servants no doubt assisted in the details of the bill, but the process was far from the relatively bloodless, expert decision making set forth in bureaucracy-centered models. The central actors may not have been elected officials, but they were clearly motivated by political (as well as more altruistic) interests, and they were not without expert knowledge of their own.

A cynical view of the council reforms might suggest that British officials were primarily interested in elevating their indigenous allies and saw the councils as a way to achieve this. This is a bit ungenerous, but to the extent that councils were supposed to help retain status quo power relations, the policies that they put in motion raised problems for the British. By 1906, when the debate over the Morley-Minto reforms began, there were new indigenous interests who were not British allies, but who had become adept at incorporating themselves into the new political arrangements. That the British were aware of this development and unhappy about it is evident from their concerns over the form the 1909 reforms would take: a Home Department dispatch noted that the result of the 1892 act was to place "a monopoly of voting power in the hands of the professional class."[8] The term *professional class* usually meant lawyers, who were predominantly Hindu and often sympathetic to the Indian National Congress. At the same time, the groups the British wanted to encourage were faring poorly, and the introduction even of carefully limited electorates would not necessarily help them. Muslims were too dispersed in some regions to make territorial electorates favorable for them, while commercial and landed interests were not always sufficiently organized to elect their own representatives through peak associations, the method favored by the British.

In 1908, the Morley-Minto reforms expanded political opportunities for Indians beyond the 1892 act. Indians were to be given representation in the provincial legislatures and in the Viceroy's Legislative Council, and they were to be elected, either directly or indirectly by associations. This representation was not general but was to be allocated in proportion to major groups' percentage of the population. In 1906, one month after the announcement that reforms would be considered, the earl of Minto, then viceroy of India, received a deputation of Muslims from all the regions of India, who asked that they be granted separate political electorates (Hardy 1971). The conservative Muslim elite feared that they would be dominated by liberal Muslims of the new generation and by Hindus in joint electoral bodies. This request was favorably received by the British, who wanted to maintain the power of landowning, traditionalist representatives of the Muslim population (Robinson 1974).

Although, as Peter Hardy has stated, the British did not unilaterally invent the Muslim League as a counterpoint to the less cooperative Indian National Congress, they "amplified the weakest call for help from conservative Muslims into an alarm siren shrieking in the ears of the Secretary of State in London" (Hardy 1971, 159). The Morley-Minto reforms were more an extension of the 1892 act than a departure from it, but they went beyond the act in two crucial areas: first, they introduced a limited system of elections to select representatives, and second, they extended the group-based selection process previously used in appointments to the new electoral system by establishing separate electorates for Muslims (Government of India 1909).

Untouchables were not granted separate electorates at this time, but the opportunity for them, as well as for Anglo-Indians, Christians, and others to receive them, was presented as an option. The British had determined that "Where there are no representative Associations, and electorates cannot be formed the only possible alternative is to have recourse to nomination" until methods that produced the desired outcome were developed.[9] Not surprisingly, the Indian National Congress and other nontargeted groups objected to this policy, leading to a peculiar situation in which the supposedly corporate Indians preferred territorial, individual-based representation, while the individualist British insisted on representation based on groups. Since the British were the rulers, however, the policy outcome was inevitable.

The introduction of these reforms and the potential for political benefits marked a turning point for the untouchable community. Until this point they had been politically quiescent, but as governance relations between the British and the Indian elites began to change, untouchables realized they would have to mobilize to demand advantages for themselves. Their initial demands were humble.

> We do not aspire to high political privileges and position, since we are not educationally qualified for them, but humbly seek employment in the lowest grades of the Public Service, in the ranks of Police Sepoys and of Soldiers in the India Army. (Zelliot 1969, 141)

The Morley-Minto reforms reinforced the existing status quo on representation, which had been established by the Indian Councils Act, but they also brought the policy of separate electorates into the public arena. The Indian Councils Act was an elite, selective policy that was unnoticed by most Indians and dismissed as ineffective by many of those who were aware of it or participated in it. By 1909, however, when the reforms were instituted, informal and formal political participation was more widespread, and Indians were increasing their levels of political socialization. As this process continued, separate electorates became one of the issues about which people were politically aware.

The importance of the status quo on separate electorates and its ramifications became critical in the next policy reform watershed, the Montagu-Chelmsford reforms that led to the Government of India Act of 1919. At the end of World War I, the British government took up the question of additional political reforms for India. The climate and the circumstances were strikingly different from those surrounding the previous two reform periods. Indian participation in the allied cause during the war had been high, and there was an implicit understanding that this loyalty would be rewarded by a greater role in their own governance. As the 1918 report noted,

> the war has come to be regarded more and more clearly as a struggle between liberty and despotism, a struggle for the right of small nations and for the right of all people to rule their own destinies. Attention is repeatedly called to the fact that in Europe Britain is fighting on the side of liberty, and it is urged that Britain cannot deny to the people of India that for which she is herself fighting in Europe,

and in the fight for which she has been helped by India's blood and treasure. (Government of Britain 1918, 21)

The Montagu-Chelmsford reforms delivered on this understanding by introducing the concept of dyarchy, in which power was decentralized to the provincial government, the military and civil services were opened to greater and more influential Indian participation, and the franchise was expanded.

In contrast to the Morley-Minto reforms, which merely included Indian minority representation within the governance structure, the Montagu-Chelmsford ("Montford") policy, as enunciated in their report of 1918, had a much more ambitious aim: "It will be apparent that we have now gone as far as is possible upon the old lines. No further development is possible unless we are going to give the people of India some responsibility for their own government" (Government of Britain 1918, 147). Concretely, this was specified to mean the gradual Indianization of the civil and military services, an expansion of the franchise, and some decentralization of power to the provincial governments. The Montford policies advocated the continuation of separate electorates for Muslims and extended them to Sikhs. They did not provide separate electorates for untouchables, non-Brahmins, low-caste Hindus, or any other groups that asked for them, but the door was left open for their later extension to these communities.

Changes in the world environment, the decreasing economic importance of India to Britain, and the expansion of democratic political institutions within Britain all contributed to a political environment that seemed hospitable to the introduction of limited self-rule. However, while this policy was noble and worthy in principle, there were numerous difficulties in its implementation. India's economic importance may have diminished in the twentieth century, but it was still the jewel in the crown of the British empire, and its psychological, political, and strategic importance was high. The introduction of the power-sharing concept of dyarchy did not mean independence or even dominion status for India, but it did assume greater and more extensive participation by more Indians.

The British government's decision to incorporate indigenous interests into the political process need not have given political influence to untouchables, and certainly there does not appear to have been any deliberate intent to do so. But the Raj's interest in diluting the claims of the Indian National Congress to represent all Indians led them to encourage all demands for separate minority representation, which created an opening for groups other than the already organized Muslims. And, as I will discuss more fully below, it forced the Congress to take them seriously.

Changes in Caste Hindu Attitudes

The British decision to include Indians in the governance process was in part an acknowledgment of elite Indians' challenges to the British constructions of Indians and an Indian response to imperial perceptions of the colony. The British tended to view India as feudal, premodern, and irrevocably divided into corporate groups with no importance accorded to individuals (Copeland 1945). This response occurred primarily at two levels, the cultural and political. At the cultural level, Indians examined their own culture to understand whether British supremacy was due to the superiority of Western culture. Faced by a colonizing power that was transforming India at every level, elite Indians turned inward to comprehend why they could be subjugated, while Hindu reform movements seized the opportunity to attack caste restrictions, using Western concepts to support their charges (Tucker 1972). At the political level, British conceptions of how Indian society was organized led to a new, Western-influenced emphasis on the preeminence of corporate groups. At the same time, barriers to high-caste advancement in the colonial administrative system and Indian National Congress leaders' desire to appeal to Indians across religious and caste lines led to a reexamination of aspects of caste doctrine (McLane 1977). And finally, non-Brahmin movements in south India offered a concrete challenge to the historical allocation of power in favor of Brahmins.

During the British Raj, castes that had traditionally held high religious, economic, and political status were not only conquered by and subordinate to the British, they were also considered genetically and culturally inferior by their colonizers. This attitude came as a particular shock to high-caste Indians, who were used to looking down on their low-caste brethren for many of the same flaws the British were now attributing to them (e.g., dark skin, heathen religious practices). Reactions to this treatment by the British took a number of forms. At the extreme end, some younger high-caste Indians began wholeheartedly to reject Indian culture and to embrace British literature, language, art, and fashion in the movement known as the Bengal Renaissance. A more moderate response to the advent of Western norms and beliefs was exhibited by those elite Hindus and Muslims who went to Europe to study and became enamored of certain Western attitudes. These men returned to India to encourage the acceptance of some aspects of Western life and to challenge certain deeply rooted caste dogmas that were disdained by the British, such as the prohibition of widow remarriage (McLane 1977; Brown 1985).

The difficulties in reconciling Hindu doctrine with participation in the British political system gave new life to Hindu reform movements. Hinduism's emphasis on ritualism and hierarchy had been challenged by reform efforts throughout the centuries. During British rule, however, the activities of Christian missionaries presented a new threat and spurred Indian self-examination of religious doctrine and social customs. Among the main targets of reform Hindu movements such as the Brahmo Samaj, the Prarthna Samaj, Arya Samaj, and the Ramakrishna Mission were Brahmin social, economic, and political dominance and the inequalities generated by caste (Gupta 1985). These movements gained added legitimacy because they were often supported or led by important social, political, and religious figures such as Ranade, Dayanand, and Vivekananda, and they lay the foundation for the more encompassing reform efforts during the independence movement (Tucker 1972).

From a different perspective, exposure to Western political theories led some Indian nationalist leaders to believe that the rigid doctrines and social hierarchies stipulated in caste dogma were as more of a hindrance than a help to development in the modern world environment. Nehru, in particular, was deeply influenced by Fabian socialism and the writings of Marx. While he rarely attacked caste by name, he was concerned about the number of "restrictions" in Indian society and the barriers these placed on development and change. Nehru praised "the old Aryans, [who] were a very positive people. . . . They looked forward in the realms of thought, as well as towards the countries of the earth, for fresh advances and conquests" (Gopal 1983, 469). And he distinguished these innovators from those prominent in the present.

> Today the keepers of our consciences are men, narrow and bigoted and with no knowledge of anything except empty forms and ceremonials. . . . We must get rid of this inertia and woodenness and recover elasticity of thought. . . . Everything that removes the barriers that keep apart one man from another and make a common humanity possible; everything that raises large numbers of human beings and makes life more endurable for them; everything that substitutes reason for ignorant and blind bigotry is ever welcome. (Gopal 1983, 470)

By stressing the philosophical and tolerant aspects of Hinduism over the ritual and confining, and by advocating a more scientific and rational approach to social change, Indian leaders helped to make untouchability and caste hierarchy seem not only unjust, but also backward and premodern.

At the same time that religious reformers and intellectuals were questioning fundamental tenets of Hindu doctrine, the conditions for individual advancement in colonial India had begun to change, providing yet another challenge to caste (Hardy 1971; Seal 1971). In order to participate in the new bureaucracy of the British Raj, high-caste Indians sometimes had to make choices between caste rules and political advancement. For example, Hindu law forbade travel over the sea; any such action resulted in the loss of caste. In nineteenth century India, however, Indians who wanted to join the colonial civil service found their prospects greatly enhanced by the acquisition of an English education, which required an overseas journey (McLane 1977). The first high-caste Indians who traveled to Britain endangered their marriage arrangements and their standing in their native communities, and some were ostracized from their caste groups. In spite of these hardships, however, elites determined to advance in the British hierarchy persisted in their goals, and some aspects of caste doctrine slowly began to change to conform to the evolving social and political environment.

In the early years of its existence, Congress leaders were more concerned with access to administrative and political positions than with issues of equality and social reform; their attempts to introduce Western ideas and behavior stemmed in large part from their desire to take advantage of colonial opportunities without renouncing their traditional positions. But the growing influence of Hindu nationalists and the success of the Hindu revival movement forced Congress to become more reform-oriented (Gupta 1985). In this changing environment, Congress members such as Gandhi, who considered caste reform and the social incorporation of untouchables a high priority, gained a greater voice. The legitimacy of Congress as representative of Indian interests against the British depended on its ability to represent most, if not all, of the Indian people. If the Congress were to appeal across caste lines, it could not discount the importance of low-caste and untouchable groups. In practice, high-caste groups' control of lower and untouchable castes, especially in the rural areas, assisted mobilization during the struggle for independence. But the rhetoric of the period was one of equality and dignity for all Indians.

This new egalitarian orientation was influenced in part by the political conflict that had arisen in south India. The historical dominance of Brahmins in the south had long been resented by the other far more numerous castes, and expanding opportunities for indigenous political representation led to fears by the latter groups that Brahmins would come to control these arenas as well. Consequently, the early twentieth century witnessed the rise of social movements in British Madras as well as in the princely state of Mysore, as non-Brahmin groups challenged the age-old political, economic, and social monopoly of the tiny Brahmin minority.

Political Mobilization in South India

Untouchables did not mobilize as quickly as elite Hindus and Muslims, in part because they were excluded from educational institutions in India. But the British award of separate electorates "brought the idea of communal electorates for minorities to the forefront in the minds of all communities which feared for their submersion in a government run by the dominant caste Hindu community" (Zelliot 1969, 141). Apart from a desire to share in the developing political reforms, untouchables had no clear program, and it was not until 1917 that they even met as a group. That year marked the convening of the first Depressed Classes Conference, which was attended by more than twenty-five hundred representatives from western and southern India. In south India they were able, however, to piggyback on to the policy demands of more politically active groups in southern princely states and provinces.

At the same time that Muslims and later untouchables were successful in gaining separate electoral privileges from the British, low-caste Hindus were demanding and receiving preferences at the provincial level. Since the 1910s, a variety of policy approaches had been attempted, with the two most comprehensive and notable cases being the princely state of Mysore, which emphasized preferences and programs, and the British provincial state of Madras, which emphasized political access.

Returned to native rule by the British in 1881, princely Mysore gained a reputation as a model state during the late nineteenth and early twentieth centuries. Under the maharajah of Mysore, social services were expanded, and the state was noted for its efficient and enlightened administration (Gustafson 1968). In the early twentieth century, as opportunities for political participation by indigenous elites increased, dominant castes began to seek ways to break the Brahmin monopoly on professional and governmental employment. The maharajah, who was not Brahmin, was receptive to the demands for greater representation by these numerically strong middle and lower castes and he perceived that his own political fortunes would be enhanced by improving their access to political and economic power (Manor 1977). When these groups protested the dominance of Brahmins in government, the professions, and higher education, the maharajah appointed a commission, headed by Leslie Miller, to study backward-class representation in these areas (Dushkin 1974).[10]

In its 1922 report, the commission noted that while Brahmins comprised less than 4 percent of the population, they held nearly 80 percent of government positions (Chandrasekhar 1985). The report contained over two dozen recommendations for changes in the public services and education. Using the enumerations of caste and religious community units that had been developed by the British government in the census, it defined backwardness through the sole criterion of literacy in English: any group with less than 5 percent literacy was considered backward (Dushkin 1974). This meant that every community was eligible for the special benefits, with the exception of Brahmins and those for whom English was the mother tongue.[11] Among the recommendations for increasing backward-class percentages in public service were the abolition of competitive examinations for jobs, reservations in every grade, and the preferential hiring of non-Brahmins until the proportion was fifty-fifty, with a time limit of seven years (Dushkin 1974). These recommendations were weakened by the government, and the final policy was one in which non-Brahmins were to be given preference but no quotas or time limits were to be imposed.

In the area of education, the recommendations set forth by the commission received greater support. The number of educational institutions, from primary to university level, was greatly increased. In higher education, scholarships were provided both on general merit and for backward classes, and they were allocated proportionate to each group's percentage of the population. Scheduled castes, which were called depressed classes, were counted twice: they were included in the backward-class category, but they also had benefits through the depressed-classes programs. These included special schools, hostels, and scholarships (Chandrasekhar 1985). While scheduled caste representation in schools and universities remained low until independence (less than 5 percent), it did represent an increase from zero percent before the Miller Commission report (Sivakumar 1982).

Mysore's policies represented an early step toward increasing backward-class and untouchable access to employment and education. Dominant castes had been successful in convincing the maharajah of Mysore to counter the Brahmin monopoly and provide for greater non-Brahmin representation. Beginning in the early 1920s non-Brahmins took advantage of reservation and preference policies to increase their representation in the court, in employment, and in education. While the political and social animosity toward Brahmins never reached the heights that it did in other areas of south India like Madras, it was still apparent in the less conflictual environment of Mysore that fears of Brahmin dominance would have to be assuaged by any political party hoping to win the electoral support of the large non-Brahmin population.

As the possibility of increased political participation in British India became evident, the British Presidency state of Madras was notable for its upsurge of social and political activity. The majority of citizens of Madras did not view the expansion of political rights as necessarily advantageous, and they did not wholeheartedly support the Indian National Congress's efforts in this direction. The reasons were straightforward. In Madras, as in much of south India, the population was unevenly divided between a tiny minority of Brahmins and low- and out-caste groups. Although some of these low-caste groups had achieved fairly high political and economic status in their localities and had become what Srinivas terms "dominant castes" (1962), there were no ritual middle castes to speak of, and education was confined to Brahmins. As a result, Brahmins overwhelmingly comprised the economic, social, and political elite. In the late nineteenth century, when very limited political participation was introduced by the British, dominant castes had pressed their demands, but they had been largely unsuccessful in breaking the Brahmin monopoly. By the twentieth century they were determined that if political opportunities were indeed going to increase, this increase was not simply going to augment existing Brahmin spoils (Irschick 1969).

Non-Brahmins viewed the Indian National Congress almost as suspiciously as they did Brahmins, seeing the organization as a vehicle primarily designed to further Brahmin interests. Annie Besant's Home Rule movement of the 1910s and her appointment as president of the Indian National Congress in 1917 confirmed non-Brahmin suspicions about the organization and intensified their desire to ensure that additional political benefits would be distributed across all groups. In order to counter Brahmin influence and to articulate their own cause, non-Brahmins formed the Justice party specifically to press for special preferences for non-Brahmins (which originally included untouchables) in the Montagu-Chelmsford reforms. Since the Justice party competed against the Congress party in the new political system, the Congress party was forced to broaden its appeal and allay non-Brahmin fears that it represented only the Brahmin elite.

Montagu's 1917 announcement that Britain was committed to including Indians in the governing process raised fears among non-Brahmins that Brahmin social dominance would soon be extended to the political realm. In response, politically active non-Brahmins began to formulate policies that would avert this occurrence in order to present them to Montagu on his impending visit to India. While the non-Brahmin political groups were divided on a number of issues, such as Home Rule, they quickly reached unanimous agreement that "the only way to prevent Brahmans from assuming power under the new constitutional regime was to assure non-Brahmans a special position in the franchise arrangement" (Irschick 1969, 67–68). This special position was formalized in requests to Montagu that separate electorates be established for non-Brahmins in Madras.

When the Montagu-Chelmsford report was issued, non-Brahmins were dismayed to learn that their hopes for special political representation had been dashed. Although the report retained communal representation for Muslims and extended it to Sikhs, the authors rejected all the other demands for minority representation. In referring to the non-Brahmins of Madras, they parenthetically noted that "in that presidency these actually constitute a majority" and recommended that nomination be the preferred means for assuring adequate minority representation (Government of Britain 1918, 188–89).

However, Montagu left non-Brahmins a narrow window of opportunity when he "admitted that the Reforms would presume the granting of some provincial autonomy" (Irschick 1969, 94). In addition, the report was only the beginning of the reform process; the 1919 Government of India Bill to implement the changes was to be refined and elaborated after further investigation by the Joint Select Committee, which would hear from Indian representatives. The Select Committee's report was more supportive of non-Brahmin demands; it recommended that they

> must be provided with separate representation by means of reservation of seats. The Brahmins and non-Brahmins should be invited to settle the matter among themselves; and it would only be, if agreement cannot be reached in that way, that the decision should be referred to an arbitrator appointed for the purpose by the Government of India. (Quoted in Irschick 1969, 158)

After Brahmins and non-Brahmins were unable to reach a compromise, the Government of Madras appointed an arbitrator, Lord Meston. Meston's Award, announced in March 1920, reserved twenty-eight seats, far less than the non-Brahmins had expected. But even though the number was lower than they had hoped, the principle of reservations had been formalized in practice in time for the government to complete its franchise arrangements for the 1920 elections.

The Receptivity of Political Elites

When I discussed the United States previously, political elites were implicitly defined as elected and appointed officials within the three branches of the federal government. This assumption was made because it was perceived to be the key arena of civil-rights change. In India, however, the political elites with the ability to formulate and implement affirmative action cannot plausibly be simplified in the same way. The primary political power was clearly the British government, which had the ability to implement almost anything it chose. But while the Raj exercised considerable influence over the princely states that were not part of British India, the rulers of these states also had the capacity to implement policies within their borders. And finally, the third group of political actors were the governors of the British provinces, who could, with the acquiescence of the Government of India, implement a wide range of policies within their own borders.

Untouchables benefited from the receptivity of all three of these actors. The Government of India encouraged untouchables to ask for electoral protection after the practice of elections had been introduced in the Morley-Minto reforms,[12] because it helped counter the challenges posed by the Indian National Congress. By the time that the Montagu-Chelmsford report was issued at the end of the World War I, untouchables had begun to organize and had received protected electorates as indigenous political representation was expanded. By the 1920s, when British commissions were touring India, untouchables were articulating their own desires for electoral protections to consistently sympathetic British political elites.

The Reforms Enquiry Committee of 1924, also known as the Muddiman Committee, was constituted to examine how the implementation of dyarchy was proceeding; it also examined the position of untouchables and called attention to their lack of adequate political representation. Partly as a result of the committee's findings, untouchables were given greater representation in all the provinces, and one nominated member was granted for the central Legislative Council (Zelliot 1969, 156–58). And in 1928, the controversial Simon Commission, which was boycotted by the Indian National Congress because of the absence of Indian members, provided a receptive forum for the concerns of religious and other minorities, including untouchables (Government of Britain 1930).

At the provincial level, untouchables found that they were able to benefit from the political power of more numerous and politically sophisticated low-caste Hindus. Since non-Brahmin castes far outnumbered other groups in south India, the introduction even of limited democratic institutions made their demands important to ruling elites. And the nature of their demands made untouchables a natural simultaneous target for policy responses. In both Mysore and Madras, non-Brahmins demanded representation that was more proportional to their numbers and preferential policies that would help them achieve this goal. But untouchables were even worse off than non-Brahmins. When policies were developed for non-Brahmins, untouchables were included. These decisions were not motivated by altruism or generosity alone. By extending preferential treatment to untouchables, both indigenous princely and colonial British rulers were hoping to gain their loyalty at the expense of the Indian National Congress, and the British at least were temporarily successful.

Conclusion

The political and social events that preceded the development of affirmative-action policies were transformative in their scope and intensity. In the United States, participation in World War II and the birth of the civil-rights movement led Americans to reconsider enduring ideologies and behaviors. For Indians, the increased political participation introduced by the British and the beginnings of the movement for independence were equally crucial. Moreover, these phenomena had critical implications for majority-minority relations and attitudes. Blacks and untouchables came to the forefront of majority consciousness in both countries, and they simultaneously became electorally important as well. In the United States, World War II and the civil-rights movement sped majority acceptance of efforts to promote true equality of opportunity, which culminated in the Civil Rights and Voting Rights Acts. In India, the British Raj treated all groups separately when it introduced indigenous political participation, which both mobilized untouchables and forced the Indian National Congress to take them seriously in the new political environment. These conditions enabled blacks in the United States to gain formal legal equality at last and untouchables in India to be recognized as important political actors in the independence movement. And in these contexts, policies that went beyond formal legal equality in the United States and British-imposed preferences in India made sense.

This chapter and the one that preceded it have established the immediate and the historical political contexts in which affirmative-action policies were introduced and expanded. In the next four chapters I turn to a detailed analysis of the process by which affirmative action was conceived, developed, and adopted by Indian and U.S. political actors. Using a framework that joins rational-choice methods with comparative historical analysis, I show why affirmative action was initially adopted without opposition and why it has endured even in the face of increasing controversy over its legitimacy and its effectiveness.

CHAPTER 4

Affirmative Action under Kennedy, Johnson, and Nixon

In the preceding two chapters I discussed the historical and cultural context in which affirmative action could emerge as a policy choice in the United States and India and the conditions that facilitated positive political responses to African-American and untouchable demands for such policies. In this chapter and the three that follow, I explore why affirmative action in particular was adopted as a policy choice and explain its subsequent trajectory. To do so I use the theoretical approach presented in chapter 1, which draws on rational-choice and comparative historical methods to develop an explanation that is both theoretically rigorous and sensitive to substantive issues.

Following the assumptions laid out in chapter 1, I hypothesize that policies are developed to make individual politicians and political parties more appealing to specific vote blocs. The specific contours that these policies take are dependent on the particular constituency being targeted, the number of actors involved in the policy process and their respective preferences, and the institutions in which they interact. Chapters 2 and 3 provided the context of the policy process, while chapters 4 through 7 take the long view of policy histories. Recalling the assumptions presented in chapter 1, I argue that policy processes are punctuated equilibria. Large-scale changes can only be fully explained by reference to their contexts, but within periods of equilibrium institutions and preferences are stable and can be modeled formally. Combining comparative historical analysis and rational-choice methods, I structure the discussion of affirmative-action policy development by providing a narrative history of the overall process and modeling crucial policy shifts using the preferences of relevant actors and the sequences of their moves.

Following the traditions of positive political theories of American politics, I use simple spatial models that have been developed to explain voting and policy outcomes. Roemer and Rosenthal initially introduced the "setter" model to formalize Niskanen's explanation of how bureaucrats achieve their budgetary preferences. Shepsle and Weingast (1981), Denzau and MacKay (1983), and Gilligan and Krehbiel (1986) then extended that approach to congressional voting decisions under different conditions.[1] Ferejohn and Shipan (1990) have adapted the model to incorporate multiple institutional actors within the U.S. government. I build directly on the Ferejohn and Shipan model because it most closely approximates the case examined here. It arrays the preferences of bureaucrats, legislators, the president, and the courts in a specific policy situation, stipulates the order in which the actors move, and then predicts the policy outcome based on these sequences and preferences. The model is very simple by the standards of formal theory, but it captures the important preferences, moves, and institutional configurations that affect the policy process.

In rational-choice uses of these models the preferences of the actors are usually assumed and the circumstances are hypothetical or abstracted from actual cases. In this analysis, however, the models are expected to capture the salient aspects of real-world actors as they develop and bargain over a specific policy. For those answers we need to turn to some of the methods of qualitative comparative analysis. In addition to providing evidence that allows identification of actors' incentive structures and preferences, it directs us to examine policy formulation from the earliest period and to consider not only those choices that were adopted, but also those that failed to take hold. And it emphasizes that many players can have effects on the policy process, not just the most obvious ones.

Therefore, this analysis begins with a framework derived from rational choice and formal theory. The emphasis is on those actors responsible for the institutionalization and enforcement of policies, that is, elected officials and appointed bureaucrats, and the behavior in which they engage when making decisions about policies. But it also embeds these actions within the particular historical and political context in which they occurred, in order to determine what the structure of incentives, preferences, and institutional configurations were. And by doing so, it depicts how wider social interests and contexts are channeled into the governmental process of developing, bargaining over, and passing legislation to implement policies.

In this chapter I look at the initiation and expansion of affirmative action in the United States, beginning in the early 1960s and concluding with the second Nixon administration. Affirmative action originated as a way for President Kennedy to show the civil-rights community that had supported his election that he was moving forward without forcing him to confront Congress in a battle he was unlikely to win. The rationale that guided the development of this policy emerged from the civil-rights movement. As a political issue affirmative action had been incorporated in various forms within the movement debate, but it was not part of the legislative agenda that culminated in the Civil Rights Act of 1964. As the growing support for the civil-rights movement made the redress of existing inequalities in American society compelling to more and more citizens, the concept of affirmative action in its early formulations seemed an appropriate means of achieving these goals in a timely manner. The early approach was too innocuous to provide cause for alarm, and there was nothing to suggest the forms that the policy would later take and that would give rise to controversy. *Affirmative action* was a phrase used to signal a strong commitment to the enforcement of nondiscrimination, but while it conveyed good intentions, it carried little intimation of how this might be accomplished.

Affirmative action as a policy directive can be found at least as far back as the 1935 National Labor Relations Act. There the phrase was used to describe Congress's command in the act that the National Labor Relations Board "redress an unfair labor practice by ordering the offending party 'to cease and desist from such unfair labor practice, and to take such *affirmative action* . . . as will effectuate the policies of this Act'" (quoted in Graham 1990, 33; emphasis added). In this context, affirmative action combined with cease-and-desist powers to enforce the government's labor laws when confronted with unwilling employers. Labor did not gain an advantage beyond the original intent of Congress through this provision; instead, the provision ordered the government to enforce the spirit of legislation when employers were able to evade the letter of the law. In the 1960s, the phrase was used to signify active efforts to eradicate discrimination, as opposed to the more passive "nondiscrimination."

Once affirmative action was introduced, some elected officials and bureaucrats had incentives to expand these policies, while other elected officials had incentives to stop them. In the early stages of affirmative-action policy development, the relative obscurity and ineffectiveness of the programs gave their supporters stronger incentives to expand them than their opponents had to push for their elimination, and the institutional structure of the Congress aided affirmative-action supporters as well. Once the policies became more effective and more public, however, they were subject to concerted challenges by opponents.

In the preceding paragraphs I described policymaking as a sequential process in which different actors were involved at different times. In the case of affirmative action, the initial efforts were made within the executive branch. But most policies cannot become very strong or effective without legislation and funding, which fall within the purview of the legislative branch. Once the policy was developed as far as possible within the framework in which it had begun, and when civil rights came on to the congressional agenda, affirmative-action policy was negotiated between Congress and the president. Once negotiations were resolved and legislation passed, the policy reverted back to the bureaucracy and executive branch for implementation. If the executive and the bureaucracy wished, they could expand the policy using executive and administrative orders. But the policy development that could be achieved through this authority was limited. If additional funds were required, then Congress had to appropriate and authorize the expenditure, and any major administrative changes were subject to congressional review as stipulated in the Administrative Procedures Act (APA) (Page and Shapiro 1992; McCubbins, Noll, and Weingast 1987). This process repeated itself throughout the development of affirmative action. In the remainder of this chapter I focus on how affirmative action was increased and expanded by the government, using qualitative historical data to describe the substantive process and simple formal models to capture the periods of negotiations among governmental actors.

1961–64: Initial Efforts to Enforce Nondiscrimination

When John F. Kennedy assumed the presidency in 1961, he did so after an extremely close election and a campaign in which debates over civil rights played a major role. Richard Nixon was not a favorite of the liberal wing generally because of his involvement in the McCarthy hearings and the Alger Hiss case, but his civil-rights record was strong. He had won praise from King and other leaders for his positions, and he had consistently opposed Jim Crow legislation (Lawson 1976). Kennedy, by contrast, had little obvious record or interest in civil rights before the campaign, but the Democratic party platform was the strongest in history, and he had reached out to the civil-rights community, endorsing the sit-ins and characterizing the movement as a moral crusade.

Once in office, however, these public pronouncement ceased. Although he had won the presidential campaign, Kennedy's coattails had had a negative effect, and the Democrats had lost seats in both the House and the Senate. This meant that the actual programmatic coalition was even thinner than the Democratic majority, especially on the policy issue that most alienated the southern wing of the party. So Kennedy remained silent on civil rights, asking advocates to be patient and understanding, and above all to give him time.

The President's Committee on Equal Employment
Opportunity and the Roots of Affirmative Action

In the meantime, Kennedy took actions in the executive branch that were possible without the agreement of Congress. In one of his early moves as president, he reorganized the two committees that were assigned responsibility for ensuring nondiscrimination in government contracts and employment during the Eisenhower administration into the President's Committee on Equal Employment Opportunity (PCEEO). The PCEEO was extolled by the administration as having a greater commitment to nondiscrimination enforcement and a much higher profile within government. This latter claim was probably true, given the public-relations effort accompanying its creation and its stellar membership. Vice President Johnson was its chairman and Secretary of Labor Arthur Goldberg its vice chairman, and the remainder of the committee included cabinet members, labor leaders, and distinguished public servants.

Critics of the PCEEO assailed its effectiveness and the administration's commitment to civil rights, and in part they were correct. As an interagency committee, the PCEEO had neither statutory authorization nor a budget (Graham 1990, 40). Johnson seemed an inauspicious choice to lead it, given his steady and effective opposition to congressional civil-rights bills in the 1950s. And while its establishment was accompanied by great fanfare, its specific agenda remained murky. However, given the stringent limits set about the committee, it was relatively effective, and the policies it was able to formulate and implement provided the foundation for later, more vigorous policy action.

Johnson's actions as chairman refuted his critics' expectations. Certainly he had no desire initially to serve on the PCEEO, and he and the civil-rights community viewed each other with mutual suspicion. Johnson chafed at the restrictive nature of the vice presidency, but his efforts to increase his power were unsuccessful. The PCEEO was one of his few opportunities, and once he had accepted the position, he took a very active role, apparently deciding that if he was to be exiled onto a weak committee he would make it as effective as he could (Graham 1990, 31–33). This goal was accomplished through four strategies: publicity for the committee and its efforts, the establishment of voluntary nondiscrimination programs with employers, the development of compliance-reporting procedures for government contractors, and the collection of statistics on African-American representation in government employment.

Publicity for the PCEEO and voluntarism in nondiscrimination was initiated through a high-profile program called Plans for Progress. This program sought to convince employers to adopt voluntarily measures to increase minority representation. These measures included a promise to observe nondiscrimination in hiring and promotion, to increase recruitment of blacks, to visit traditionally black colleges, and to allow the PCEEO to evaluate the outcomes of these actions (Graham 1990, 50–59). To some observers, Plans for Progress epitomized both the PCEEO and the Kennedy administration's initial approach to civil-rights policy: it was voluntary, it was ambiguous, it tried not to antagonize conservative and business interests, and the civil-rights constituency hated it.

They hated it because the public and committee focus on Plans for Progress diverted attention from the development of PCEEO's third strategy, the development of compliance-reporting procedures for contractors. By providing a way for employers to circumvent the compliance authority of the PCEEO (they could sign up with a program with less demanding requirements than the contract compliance approach), and by mounting a high-profile publicity campaign that diverted attention from the other activities undertaken by the PCEEO, Plans for Progress emphasized "persuasion" to the exclusion of "enforcement," rather than uniting them.[2] Supporters of the program, on the other hand, argued that the voluntary approach was the best option available, and that Plans for Progress would at least provide some jobs and help fuel the rise of the black middle class.

Several of the members of the House Committee on Education and Labor were among those who were dissatisfied with the administration's willingness to rely on voluntary programs. In 1961 the committee reported out a bill that would replace the PCEEO with a new five-member Fair Employment Practices Commission (Graham 1990, 54). This legislation was unlikely to succeed, because Education and Labor was more liberal than the House as a whole, and far more liberal than the chairman of the powerful House Rules Committee, which was responsible for reporting the bill to the floor for consideration. But like many of Education and Labor's bills, it was important in terms of signaling, or position taking: it sent the message that the committee would be watching the PCEEO and applying pressure to keep enforcement of nondiscrimination a high priority (Fenno 1978; Mayhew 1974).

By 1963 Johnson and other members of the administration had begun to see the program as a liability. The approach relied so much on business cooperation that it appeared to be captive to business interests. But given the publicity it had received, it could not be scrapped without considerable embarrassment to the PCEEO and the administration. Therefore, a compromise was reached: the head of Plans for Progress and its most vocal critic within the PCEEO departed simultaneously. The program was not abandoned, but the development of compliance-reporting procedures for contractors became the primary enforcement mechanism to ensure nondiscrimination. The Kheel report's recommendation to join persuasion and enforcement shaped the PCEEO's strategy for effecting nondiscrimination in employment.

The less publicized policy initiative of the PCEEO was the establishment of reporting requirements for government agencies. At the committee's first meeting, Johnson called attention to the executive order's directive to gather statistics on government employment patterns. Agency response was slow and uneven, and many pro-civil-rights officials were concerned about making racial headcounts, since these had historically been used against minorities rather than for them. Nonetheless, according to Graham, by 1963 "the federal agencies formally understood not only that they could once again identify employee records by race, but that they *must* do so" (1990, 62).

These racial headcounts were potentially quite controversial, but they aroused little attention, especially in Congress. This legislative neglect can be attributed to the nature of the institutional relationship between the executive-bureaucratic and legislative branches. Responsibility for the oversight of bureaucratic activity is divided among congressional committees. The committees have the ability to schedule hearings, call witnesses from within and outside the bureaucracies, and threaten to withhold funding if they disapprove of the actions being taken (McCubbins and Sullivan 1987). If there are conflicts in preferences or interests between the committee and the implementing agencies, the latter's life can be made quite difficult. But for the PCEEO, congressional supervision was at times a nuisance but rarely threatening. This was because the oversight responsibility for the PCEEO lay with the Committee on Education and Labor, which was traditionally one of Congress's most liberal committees. Its members might want the president or his agencies to move more strongly on civil rights, but it was unlikely to call their behavior to the attention of the full Congress, since that body was unlikely to be sympathetic. As a result, the committee often wound up shielding agencies from congressional scrutiny rather than the reverse.

The limited achievements of the PCEEO were inadequate by the standards of civil-rights advocates, and in the face of mounting social protest and pressure for change in the early 1960s they seemed timid and weak. But they were much stronger than those undertaken during the Eisenhower administration.

> As a result of the PCEEO's greater visibility and commitment, after only on year the staff had received and processed almost as many complaints (1,850) as had its *two* predecessor committees under Eisenhower in *seven* years (2,095). (Graham 1990, 60)

In addition, the policies that emerged from the early period helped to lay the foundation and shape the debate that arose in the watershed changes of 1964. The successes and failures of the PCEEO, and the experience gained by the implementation process, helped point the way to more effective and vigorous civil-rights policies.

The Civil Rights Act and the Creation of the Equal
Employment Opportunity Commission

In the years just prior to the debate over the 1963 and 1964 civil-rights bills, Congress had not been deeply involved in civil-rights legislation. Kennedy did not submit a bill until 1963, and the PCEEO was a purely executive creation. The House Committee on Education and Labor pressured the PCEEO to take stronger action, which may have had some effect, but without statutory authority there was little the latter could do. After Kennedy's assassination, however, the interaction between the executive and legislative branches over civil-rights legislation became intense.

In 1963, after American public opinion had been galvanized by the attack of Bull Connor's police force on nonviolent protesters in Birmingham, Kennedy had submitted his first civil-rights bill to Congress. It was more cautious than advocates had wanted, but in the hands of a sympathetic Judiciary Committee it proceeded through the initial phases of subcommittee hearings and markup (Sundquist 1968; Whalen and Whalen 1985). After Kennedy's assassination, however, the prospects for civil-rights legislation changed considerably. Civil rights became part of the unfinished Kennedy legacy, and Johnson singled out the civil-rights and tax bills currently being considered in Congress as his first legislative priorities. With the heightened attention of the American public and the new symbolism attached to the bills, civil-rights advocates within and outside Congress and the executive branch realized that they had the opportunity to put a stronger package together than Kennedy had initiated.

The civil-rights bill that had cleared the House Judiciary Committee before Kennedy left for Dallas was much weaker than civil-rights advocates and their congressional allies proposed, although it was stronger than the original June bill (Sundquist 1968). It scaled back the attorney general's authorization to sue to protect individual rights, it reduced the scope of the public-accommodations title, and it limited voting-rights protection to federal elections. On the question of most immediate interest to supporters of affirmative action, that is, what would succeed the PCEEO, the bill was stronger than the original Kennedy bill but still fairly restrained.

Since Roosevelt's original FEPC, its supporters had been attempting to create a strong enforcement agency on the lines of the NLRB, whose most effective power had proved to be cease-and-desist authority. Just as the NLRB could force recalcitrant capitalists to bargain with unions, civil-rights advocates hoped that a powerful FEPC could compel nondiscrimination. But conservative Republicans and southern Democrats viewed an activist FEPC with alarm, the former on the grounds that government was intrusive enough already and the latter on the additional grounds that a strong FEPC would focus on southern employment relations first. These two blocs had joined together since the demise of the original FEPC and been able to block such authority for any new employment commissions.

The House Education and Labor Committee had voted out a bill that provided for an NLRB-type agency, a quasi-judicial body with cease-and-desist authority. But the Judiciary Committee, which was almost as liberal ideologically but whose chairman, Emmanuel Celler, was considerably more pragmatic, chose a more moderate strategy. The agency proposed in its 1963 bill was called the Equal Employment Opportunity Commission (EEOC), and it was designed as a prosecutorial body rather than a quasi-judicial one. As such it had less scope than the NLRB, the Federal Trade Commission, or the state FEPCs. But it was able to file civil suits and seek injunctive relief for plaintiffs (*CQ Almanac* 1969, 364).

In the Senate, the opposition, led by Everett Dirksen of Illinois, was able to extract further compromises from the House bill concerning the powers of the new EEOC. The EEOC could not file suits on its own, but instead it had to refer cases to the attorney general. Moreover, these suits could only be initiated when a "pattern or practice" of discrimination had been documented. A second amendment stated that only the direct victims of discrimination had standing to file complaints; no third parties, such as civil-rights groups like the National Association for the Advancement of Colored People, had standing. Third, the EEOC was ordered to defer to state FEPCs wherever they existed; the state and local agencies were given sixty days to respond to complaints before the EEOC was allowed to take action. And finally, as Hubert Humphrey put it, the "respondent must have intended to discriminate." Accidental or inadvertent discrimination would not violate what was to become Title VII (Graham 1990, 150). The House leadership accepted these amendments, and the provisions were written into the Civil Rights Act.

Proponents of a strong EEOC patterned after the old FEPC or the NLRB were disappointed by the outcome, because they saw the debate over the Civil Rights Act of 1964 as their best chance for success. But if we model these events, it becomes clear that given the actors involved in the process, their preferences, and the institutional context, this outcome could have been expected.

Modeling the Debate over the EEOC

A single-dimensional model is able to capture the salient aspects of the negotiation over the EEOC, including the relevant actors, their preferences, the relative locations of these preferences on a spectrum representing the liberal to conservative range of possibilities for the EEOC, and the institutional configurations that affect the policy outcome. In this debate or game, there are several actors that can affect the policy process. Two committees in the House, the Education and Labor Committee (EL) and the Judiciary Committee (J), reported bills with their favored EEOC provisions. EL is slightly more liberal than J, as reflected in their policy provisions for the new agency and by the ratings given them by Americans for Democratic Action.[3] The House is more conservative than either committee. The president (P), who indirectly affects the process by signaling to Congress his preferred legislation and directly affects it through his veto capacity, is characterized as preferring the Judiciary Committee bill. The final actor is the Senate (S). The model is presented in figure 4.1, with each position representing the actor's preferred outcome, or ideal point.

The winning policy outcome, Q, falls at Sc, the Senate's cloture point. This result is somewhat surprising, since it is the most conservative of the actors' preferences. Moreover, Sc is not the Senate median, which is the preference of the member whose vote is necessary for passage of the bill. This median is at 50 percent plus one member. The cloture point is critical because the rules of the Senate allow for unlimited debate, or a filibuster, on a bill as long as any member wishes to take the floor. In 1964, in order for debate to be terminated, two-thirds of the senators needed to vote to end debate, which is called invoking cloture. For bills on which members held strong opinions, such as southern Democrats on civil rights, a filibuster was certain to occur and cloture would have to be invoked. This effectively turned the normal majority needed to pass a bill into a two-thirds "supermajority." The House and the president are forced to accept this outcome because anything to the left of Sc will be subject to filibuster and the leadership will be unable to gain enough votes to invoke cloture. This is a simple model, and it is unable to capture many aspects of this complex and sophisticated negotiation. It is all the more impressive, therefore, that it is able to capture the essential features of the policy outcome, mostly importantly the position, Q, of the EEOC that was written into the Civil Rights Act. Surprisingly, it also provides a more balanced view of the relative importance of the actors involved in the process. Historical accounts make much of the roles of President Johnson and Senate minority leader Everett Dirksen in the passage of the act, and there is no question that they played critical parts (Sundquist 1968, chap. 6; Graham 1990, chap. 5; Whalen and Whalen 1985, chap. 6). But these accounts tend to remove the actors from their institutional positions.

The model suggests that Dirksen was able to wring concessions from the House because the position of the Senate's cloture point meant that without concessions there would be no bill. Had the cloture point been dif-

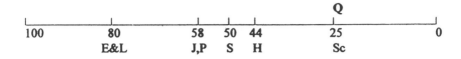

Fig. 4.1

ferent, Dirksen's bargaining position no doubt would have been different as well; Dirksen was undoubtedly a superb negotiator, but his parameters were set by the preferences of his colleagues. Similarly, President Johnson signaled his commitment to a strong civil-rights bill by stating that he would suspend all other government business if necessary. But the type of bill he could get was constrained by what the House and Senate were willing to pass. And since Johnson was to the left of the House, he could never get his ideal bill. The passage of the Civil Rights Act was a great and historic achievement. But the model shows why it was, above all, a product of compromise in which one-third of the Senate was able to force weakening amendments on a liberal president and the rest of the legislature.

The End of the PCEEO and the Fate of Compliance Reporting

Had proponents been able to establish a strong EEOC that was analogous to the NLRB, then the PCEEO might well have become redundant. But the compromise EEOC had neither the statutory authorization nor the institutional makeup to take over the PCEEO's most important responsibility, that of overseeing government contracts to ensure that Executive Orders 10925 and 11246 were being followed. The design of the EEOC was such that remedial action could only be taken *after* a discriminatory incident had occurred and been reported to the commission. The approval of nondiscrimination provisions in government contracts, on the other hand, had to take place *before* the contract could be awarded. Thus, while the goals of the new and old agencies may have been the same, their methods diverged, and the EEOC could not easily take over all the duties of the PCEEO.

These questions were not taken up within the legislative arena. Having spent months hotly debating the passage of the Civil Rights Act, Congress then left details and implementation to the agencies, which gave the initiative for further refinements back to the executive branch. Officials at the PCEEO were well aware both of the potential for overlap between the two agencies and the inability of the EEOC to carry out the former's responsibilities. A Department of Labor memo circulated after the passage of the Civil Rights Act discussed in detail the problems that might arise.[4] With the establishment of the EEOC, the memo noted that there might be "possible criticism from Congress, industry and labor that the government contract program is unnecessary and burdensome."[5] In addition, funding could become a problem. The PCEEO's activities had been funded by the contracting agencies, thus minimizing congressional involvement. But now, unsympathetic agencies could ally with like-minded members of Congress and interest groups to reduce agency support.

The memo's recommendations were directed at alleviating these obstacles. First, it argued that the president or vice president

> should make a clear statement that the government contract program will continue and that agencies are to carry it out fully and to contribute funds needed to the Committee. Unless unavoidable, an appropriation request should not be submitted to the Congress for the PCEEO.[6]

In the context of 1964, this action would ensure the program's support by a hugely popular president, and it would make congressional intervention more difficult. The memo went on to recommend that wherever possible, the PCEEO and the EEOC coordinate their activities and information, with the former yielding authority to the latter where appropriate.[7] The PCEEO staff appeared to view the new EEOC as a potential ally rather than a rival, and therefore they sought to find ways to coordinate responsibilities without scaling back existing programs or diminishing their own authority.

The EEOC did not come into being immediately after the Civil Rights Act was passed. The act had authorized it to begin in 1965, and in the meantime its commissioners had to be appointed and staff hired, and there was initially some confusion over how to coordinate nondiscrimination activities within the executive branch. The most public manifestation of this uncertainty was history of the short-lived President's Council on Equal Opportunity, chaired by Vice President Hubert Humphrey. Humphrey's council was charged with coordinating the civil-rights activities of the executive branch, admittedly a difficult mandate. His main recommendation was the abolishment of the PCEEO, with its federal-employment nondiscrimination duties to be transferred to the Civil Service Commission, and its lesser duties (education, community relations, surveys, and the like) to the new EEOC. The PCEEO's main job, contract compliance enforcement, would be transferred to Humphrey's council (Graham 1990, 182). Although there was some discussion about moving this last area to the EEOC as well,[8] this option was rejected because the EEOC was not equipped with the power to fulfill it.

Johnson, however, did not approve of this solution. It was not noticeably more streamlined than the existing arrangements, and the establishment of a Council that needed congressional funding, with its attendant oversight, would invite hostile intervention. In addition, Humphrey's leadership of the council would give executive civil-rights jurisdiction to "a chairman whose loyalty was above reproach, but whose unrestrained loquacity was legendary, whose prudence was increasingly suspect in the White House environment, and whose star was clearly plummeting in the presidential firmament" (Graham 1990, 183). So Johnson, with a loyal Humphrey valiantly backing him up, issued a new executive order, 11246, that terminated the Council and the PCEEO and transferred its compliance review responsibilities to the Department of Labor. Such a location was appropriate since the focus of the program was minority employment, and since both secretaries of labor, including Arthur Goldberg but especially Willard Wirtz, had been major forces on the PCEEO. Wirtz then created a new agency to administer compliance review, the Office of Federal Contract Compliance.[9]

Both Johnson and Wirtz had a variety of incentives to use their executive and bureaucratic authority to overcome legislative constraints. From a substantive point of view, Johnson saw civil-rights enforcement and the expansion of antipoverty policies as the cornerstone of his domestic agenda, and electorally he was even more reliant on the black vote after alienating the South through his championship of the Civil Rights Act. Wirtz shared his substantive policy goals, and from a strategic perspective the location of compliance review in the Department of Labor increased the prestige and power of a relatively weak and low-status agency. The creation of the OFCC circumvented important constraints Dirksen and the other conservatives had attempted to place on active civil-rights enforcement, especially in the growing arena of affirmative action. Dirksen won the battle during the Civil Rights Act debates when he succeeded in weakening the EEOC. But ironically, his success caused him to lose the war, because his weak EEOC was unable to absorb the PCEEO, and the latter's successor agency was able to develop a set of programs that surpassed what all but the strongest possible EEOC could have envisioned.

1965–68: The OFCC and the Beginning of Affirmative Action

The delegation of authority by Johnson to Wirtz to create the OFCC did not attract a great deal of attention; it was overshadowed by other aspects of Executive Order 11246. Indeed, it is difficult to find reference to its establishment in the Department of Labor archives. But the OFCC soon became a powerful agent in the development of affirmative-action policy. The PCEEO had been a high-profile interagency committee; it is arguable that it had been established as much to signal Kennedy's commitment to civil rights as to transform nondiscrimination policy. The OFCC was different. It was quintessentially a bureaucrat's agency, and its main directive was to make certain that affirmative action was being taken to ensure stipulated levels of minority employment in government contracts. Its success would not be determined by levels of public support or by media attention to the agency itself, but by tangible increases in minority representation that could be presented to civil-rights advocates. It was still important to avoid attracting negative publicity or raising congressional hackles, but it was imperative to develop programs and policies that could achieve this new and quite specific goal.

The OFCC and the Early Expansion of Affirmative Action

In 1965, the Civil Rights Act and its battles were part of the past. Public and congressional attention now turned to the passage of the Voting Rights Act and Johnson's new War on Poverty programs. In this environment, the combination of a low public profile and a clear administrative mandate made the OFCC an ideal institution for the development of strong contract compliance. Programs could be developed quietly, without the pressures that had attended the high-profile approach of the PCEEO. And since the OFCC was going to be judged in terms of tangible results in contract compliance, it had a strong incentive to develop clear and precise programs to achieve these results.

In the period following its establishment, the OFCC moved steadily to develop policies that would increase minority employment in government contracts, and these policies led inexorably toward more precise requirements. While the EEOC concentrated on processing individual complaints of discrimination and increasing public awareness of Title VII requirements, the OFCC focused on compliance review programs. The EEOC, in a move that was to increase greatly its power and influence, had taken responsibility for gathering and coordinating compliance reports. But the final authority to review and approve was vested in the Department of Labor and implemented by the OFCC.

Although the PCEEO had become somewhat demoralized during its last months, it had continued to fulfill its obligations. In addition, the impending changes in civil-rights enforcement and administration had provided the staff with an opportunity to evaluate the effectiveness of its programs. Staff assessments tended to support the charges by critics that the PCEEO was ineffective in carrying out its mandate. Internal memoranda were candid in laying out the shortcomings of the compliance review program and the reasons for them. A May 1965 memo laid out what the staff considered to be the "fundamental problems" in the program: insufficient cooperation by contracting federal agencies; insufficient full-time, trained manpower to carry out compliance reviews; inadequate preaward procedures that failed to take advantage of the greatest strength of the program; and the routine exemption of many major government contractors.[10]

As a member of the PCEEO since 1962, Wirtz was well aware of these problems. When the compliance review program was transferred to his Department of Labor, Wirtz shared with many others in the administration the desire to enforce vigorously the civil-rights protections and promises implicit in the Civil Rights Act. A letter from Attorney General Nicholas Katzenbach articulated this position clearly.

> One further point should be made clear at this initial stage. I believe that the compliance and implementation programs should not rely merely upon complaints. Each department or agency with financial assistance programs governed by Title VI should have in operation a regular, periodic system of inspection to insure that nondiscrimination assurances are in fact being carried out.[11]

In addition, written administration statements continually distinguished between nondiscrimination as a goal and the actions required to enforce civil-rights policy and thus achieve this goal. An internal PCEEO memo circulated days before its abolition stated the difference clearly and left no doubt about which it favored.

> The Committee will continue to place primary emphasis on the affirmative action obligation as opposed to the nondiscrimination obligation. In implementing the nondiscrimination requirement the burden of the proof rests with the contracting agency to prove the existence of discriminatory policies and practices. On the other hand under the affirmative action obligation the burden is upon the contractor to prove that he has established and is implementing an effective program of affirmative action to insure that minorities are reached during recruitment and are hired, placed, promoted, and upgraded.[12]

On the issue of how compliance could be ascertained, the memo went on to declare that

> the best indicators of whether such a program is established and effectively implemented are statistics . . . and statistical comparisons between numbers and types of hires, placements, promotions, etc. involving Negroes and those involving whites.[13]

It is clear, then, that as early as September 1965, the prohibitions against racial balance and numerical requirements that had been promised in the congressional debates over the Civil Rights Act were being challenged by the realities of enforcing and documenting nondiscrimination in employment. The EEOC and OFCC did not set out to violate these congressional assurances. Indeed, most liberal staffers were uncomfortable with "record-keeping by race" (Graham 1990, 200), because they were acutely conscious that the practice had been used to exclude blacks, not to increase their numbers. In 1962, the Department of Labor had barred using race as a category in personnel records for this reason. But the informal visual headcounts used in place of statistics to determine minority representation were inadequate, and contractors participating in Plans for Progress had been asked to provide information on employees' and applicants' race. However uncomfortable liberals were made by racial statistics, there was no other practical way to determine minority representation. Serious attempts at enforcing the spirit of Congress's intent to eliminate discrimination led the bureaucracy to violate the promises made in the debates.

With these tensions before them, the OFCC began to address the shortcomings that PCEEO staffers had documented. The lack of adequate trained manpower to conduct compliance reviews had been ameliorated in part when contracting agencies increased their allocations of full-time personnel to a total of 130 from a previous high of 100,[14] though still short of the goal of 180 suggested by the PCEEO. The second major response had much greater eventual consequences however: the OFCC began seriously to institute comprehensive preaward review programs, a policy that led ultimately to the highly controversial Philadelphia Plan.

Strengthening Compliance Review

At the outset the OFCC was able to develop its programs without attracting much attention. But as it became more effective, it inevitably began to invite scrutiny. The origins of the Philadelphia Plan, which came to the public's and Congress's attention in 1968, can be traced back to 1965. A memo from Humphrey circulated just before the announcement of Executive Order 11246 referred to city-level development of comprehensive and centralized affirmative-action plans, with five cities to be selected for the initial program implementation. Humphrey noted that eventually the anticipated new Department of Urban Affairs might be the appropriate agency to direct the program, but until such authorization was made the Department of Labor could undertake its employment components.[15]

In 1966 the OFCC, in conjunction with Justice and other agencies, took on its first large government contractor, the shipyards at Newport News, Virginia. The government was able to achieve a favorable settlement, and the terms of the settlement, as well as attacks by critics, sound remarkably similar to charges leveled at affirmative action today. A long front-page *New York Times* article on the agreement, whose tone could be described as neutral-to-favorable toward the settlement, noted in the third paragraph that

> the concept of at least partially compensating Negroes for past injustices has long by advocated by civil rights groups, but it is not known to have been put into force to any significant degree. Usually when discrimination is brought to an end employees are free to compete on an equal basis.[16]

Critics charged that the agreement violated the nondiscrimination provisions of the Civil Rights Act, the Peninsula Shipbuilders' Union denounced it as a violation of union bargaining protection, and members of Congress transmitted their constituents' concerns.[17] Nevertheless, the government stood fast behind the agreement as negotiated.

Unfortunately for the OFCC, the Newport News settlement represented the high point of its compliance review activities in its first year and a half of operation. By designing its operations to avoid congressional oversight, the OFCC had also given up any positive power it might be able to draw on from sympathetic committees, and the agency simply did not have sufficient direct control in most instances to enforce compliance regulations. Instead of being able to appeal to Congress, it had to depend on the contracting agencies that funded the OFCC's work, and their behavior was uneven; they ranged from supportive to frankly obstructive. At its inception the OFCC sent letters to agency heads stressing the importance of preaward reviews in ensuring compliance with 11246. In response, Department of Health, Education, and Welfare (HEW) secretary John Gardner wrote a blunt letter to Wirtz in which he stated that the burden of implementing Title VI regulations left no time or manpower for contract compliance reviews.[18] Paul Nitze at the Department of Defense, on the other hand, simply refused to undertake such actions on the grounds that with over fifteen million contract actions it would be impossible to carry out compliance reviews expeditiously (Graham 1990, 283). The lack of support by these two departments prevented affirmative action from being extended to two major areas of federal funding: defense contracts and education aid.

The one area where Labor and the OFCC did have a potential advantage, however, was in construction contracts, because of the transitory nature of contractor-agency ties and the concentration of contracts within the sympathetic (and new) Department of Housing and Urban Development (HUD). The OFCC began with a three-city program reminiscent of Humphrey's memo recommendations, in St. Louis, Cleveland, and the San Francisco Bay Area. None of these attempts was ultimately successful; the St. Louis plan was challenged in the courts, San Francisco contractors managed to look like they were complying without actually doing anything, and Cleveland produced strong resistance by unions. But lessons learned in these failed attempts were applied to a fourth city, Philadelphia, where the plan was put into effect more comprehensively.

The Cleveland experience had yielded one programmatic point that had profound ramifications for affirmative-action policy. It offered a concrete implementation procedure for affirmative action, it aroused the ire of some of the institutional actors who would have to comply with it, and it finally drew the attention of Congress. This procedure was the "manning table," a document in which concrete numerical projections of minority hiring were stated. Unions in Cleveland had objected strongly to the manning table, which ironically had been proposed by a hopeful contractor, as well as other aspects of the policies, arguing that they required

> employment of a percentage of Negroes as a condition of "Affirmative Action" which violates the preferential hiring and quota prohibitions of the Federal Civil Rights Act of 1964, the Ohio Civil Rights Act, and the Fifth Amendment to the United States Constitution.[19]

Responding to this letter and to inquiries from several members of Congress, Wirtz, OFCC director Edward Sylvester, and their staff denied that these programs were new, that they infringed on union rights, or that they introduced quotas into the hiring process. Assistant Director for Construction Vincent Macaluso responded that preaward procedures had been in operation "for over a year and a half" and maintained that "there is no suggestion of a quota requirement, nor is one intended" in Cleveland or elsewhere.[20] For his part, Wirtz rejected all requests by union officials and members of Congress to hold public hearings on the preaward process on the grounds that it had been policy "for several years."[21] Far from backing down, in fact, Wirtz attempted to extend the preaward compliance and the manning table requirement to the new compliance program in Philadelphia. The Philadelphia Plan, as it was termed, extended compliance review with strong enforcement and controversial components such as the manning table to all contractors in the city, and it required that no contracts could be awarded until minority hiring had been guaranteed by the builders and unions.

Builders, unions, and their allies in Congress immediately challenged the plan. The congressional response was given additional support by the entry of the Comptroller General Elmer Staats into the debate. Staats asserted that the General Accounting Office had the authority to review all agency contracts, and he claimed that this authority gave him the capacity to rule the Philadelphia Plan illegal on the grounds that it violated existing bidding procedures and failed to define the standards by which its requirements could be met (Graham 1990, 293–95). Wirtz and the administration challenged Staats's interpretations of his authority and the plan, but Staats nevertheless ruled the plan illegal.

The Johnson administration's failure to implement the Philadelphia Plan may seem surprising given the vigor with which the president and his Department of Labor bureaucracy had expanded the role of the OFCC and developed more effective compliance programs. But the majority of affirmative-action expansion during the Johnson administration had been carried out without public scrutiny and when the president's popularity was high. In the waning days of Johnson's presidency, with his attention focused on the Vietnam War and the party's attention focused on a difficult presidential campaign, there was little enthusiasm from a lame-duck president and an outgoing cabinet secretary for pressing the plan on a combative Congress. Johnson's successor, having finally achieved his goal to be president and finding himself confronted with a Democrat-dominated Congress, showed no such hesitation.

Graham has comprehensively addressed what he rightly calls "the irony of the Philadelphia Plan" (1990, chap. 11). The irony lies in the circumstances of its initiation, termination, and reintroduction. The Philadelphia Plan was initiated in 1967 by a strongly pro-civil-rights president and bureaucracy, but it was then rescinded. Given that Johnson was followed as president by Richard Nixon, who was accused of winning his first election with a "southern strategy," it was reasonable to assume that the plan, and affirmative action in general, would be at least scaled down and perhaps eliminated. Instead, the reverse occurred. The plan was successfully revived, and affirmative action was strengthened and expanded in scope.

1969–74: The Philadelphia Plan, Order No. 4, and the
Triumph of Affirmative Action

Retrospectively, it is difficult to accept that during the two Nixon administrations, affirmative action was not only not rolled back, during the first
few years it was greatly expanded. But this surprise stems more from a
tendency to recall the entire Nixon presidency as much more conservative
than it was. Two factors need to be kept in mind. First, Nixon was considerably more active in domestic issues from 1968 to 1972 than he was after
1972, and this activity was much more along moderate lines than that of
the Republican presidents who followed him. Second, with reference to
affirmative action specifically, there was no clear public or partisan consensus on the policy until the early 1970s.[22] In 1969, when Nixon assumed
office, affirmative action had only recently entered the popular lexicon,
and it was still limited to government employment in the area of contracts.
Public opinion polls do not even begin to ask questions about affirmative
action until 1972, by which time most government policies were firmly in
place.

The usual reason for assuming that Nixon had no interest in promoting affirmative action is the fact that Nixon's 1968 platform was more conservative on the issue of civil rights than his 1960 platform. But again, it is
important to remember that while there was a civil-rights backlash in
1969, it was primarily responding to the riots of the 1960s. Busing, which
became such a lightning rod in succeeding years, had not yet moved north.
Fears about excessive civil-rights legislation was beginning to become
apparent, but it had not yet crystallized. Nixon ran for the presidency on
an antibusing platform, but neither he nor his appointees were opposed to
civil rights generally. And many incoming administration officials were
moderate Republicans like Secretary of Labor George Shultz, the kind
whose support had been crucial for the passage of civil-rights legislation.

Moreover, many early Nixon appointees shared a goal for government that distinguished them from Johnson administration officials but
gave them similar interests in some policy areas: they placed a high pre-
mium on rationalizing policymaking and government activities in general.
Therefore, even when civil-rights or affirmative-action policies were not of
primary importance to the administration, they seized opportunities to
improve, from a bureaucratic viewpoint, policymaking in these areas. And
there was certainly plenty of room for improvement. The decentralized
nature of civil-rights policymaking made enforcement difficult from the
start, and the division of responsibilities for compliance reporting between
OFCC and the contracting agencies exacerbated the problem.

Wirtz's OFCC was well aware of these shortcomings and had continued to try and find solutions for them, although these efforts had been overshadowed by their unsuccessful attempts to begin implementing the Philadelphia Plan. When Wirtz and OFCC head Edward Sylvester told critics that preaward reviews had been in operation for years, they were essentially correct. Since early 1966 the OFCC had been ordering contracting agencies to "emphasize pre-award reviews that require a compliance program and review before the contract is awarded."[23] A few months later, perhaps in response to Comptroller General Elmer Staats's attack on the Philadelphia Plan, the Department of Labor issued new regulations stating that "all contractors doing government work will be required to have written affirmative action programs verified by a senior company officials, establish timetables, and set target dates to correct deficiencies in minority employment."[24] While the public announcement did not refer to numerical targets, an internal memo noted that the regulations would require an affirmative-action compliance program to "be based on a study of utilization of minority group employees and must contain specific goals and timetables if deficiencies are found."[25] The OFCC was unable to enforce these regulations because, except in the case of construction contracts, they were the responsibility of the contracting agencies, but the parameters of enforcement had been defined.

The Revival of the Philadelphia Plan

The incoming Nixon administration made changes in the organization of the Department of Labor, including the OFCC, and it reviewed policy priorities, just as most new executive appointees do. But these changes were in the direction of strengthening nondiscrimination and affirmative-action policy, not weakening it. Shultz created an Assistant Secretary for Wage and Labor Standards, headed by veteran bureaucrat Arthur Fletcher, and placed the OFCC within its jurisdiction. In addition, he raised the level of the OFCC director to GS-18 from GS-17, which Wirtz had sought unsuccessfully from the time of the OFCC's creation. Initially Shultz had been receptive to the suggestion that the OFCC be moved to the EEOC (Graham 1990). but by August 1969 he was arguing against such a move and urging that the OFCC remain within the Department of Labor. Testifying before the Senate Subcommittee on Labor, he asserted that the department "is the focal point of the manpower programs of the Government . . . the effective marriage of equal opportunity and job development will be facilitated by retention of the present organizational arrangement."[26]

Simultaneously with these organizational efforts to strengthen the OFCC, Labor moved to improve the enforcement of existing programs.

Shultz immediately initiated correspondence with the least compliant contracting agency, the Department of Defense, and obtained assurances from Secretary David Packard that he would personally demand and monitor affirmative-action reports from their contractors.[27] While the OFCC continued to be dissatisfied with Defense contractors' efforts, the publicity accorded the issue and the efforts of the agency improved the situation somewhat.

Finally, the Nixon administration also moved quickly to revive the Philadelphia Plan in a slightly revised form; by June, Arthur Fletcher had circulated a memo to all agency heads outlining its main provisions.[28] In the comptroller general's attack on the plan in 1968, his main objection had been to the requirement that contractors submit affirmative-action programs without any specific instructions as to their content. Moreover, once a contractor won an award, there was still a negotiation period over the affirmative-action aspects. The revisions to the plan attempted to overcome these obstacles.

Existing OFCC regulations required written affirmative-action programs but were not otherwise specific, and contractors and unions had been complaining about the vagueness for years.[29] Fletcher's revised guidelines attempted to respond to this criticism by setting "definite standards" of affirmative action. These standards included a "range" of minority group employment expected, based on current representation and local availability. The bidder would then submit a goal of minority employees to be utilized within this range.[30] In a statement designed to preempt any further intervention by the comptroller general, Solicitor of Labor Laurence Silberman affirmed that this revised plan was legal and also addressed the questions raised previously.

Responding to a request for review from Republican congressman Paul Fannin of Arizona, Staats reentered the debate. In a seventeen-page letter to Shultz, he pointed out that "the original Philadelphia Plan was suspended because it contravened the principles of competitive bidding" but acknowledged that "The present statement of a specific numerical range into which a bidder's affirmative-action goals must fall is apparently designed to meet, and reasonably satisfies, the requirement for specificity."[31] But Staats then went on to raise another, more fundamental objection.

> we have serious doubts covering the main objective of the Plan, which is to require bidders to commit themselves to make every good faith effort to employ specified numbers of minority group tradesmen in the performance of Federal and federally assisted contracts and subcontracts.[32]

Staats justified his opposition on the grounds that Titles VI and VII prohibited discrimination in hiring and in federal programs, and that this prohibition covered the OFCC's affirmative-action program as clearly as it did discrimination against minorities. He went on to note that section 703(j) of the Civil Rights Act states,

> Nothing contained in this subchapter shall be interpreted to require any employer . . . to grant preferential treatment to any individual . . . on account of an imbalance which may exist with respect to the total number or percentage of persons of any race, color.[33]

Staats then argued that the establishment of ranges of minority employment by the OFCC and its requirement that contractors set goals of minority hiring directly contravened this provision and therefore was in violation of federal statutes.

The administration refused to accept this reading of the Civil Rights Act. Furthermore, they argued that the comptroller general, as an agent of Congress, was acting outside of his scope of authority as well as beyond his area of expertise. But Staats's position was taken up by conservative senators, who used the conflict to introduce an amendment that would give the comptroller general the authority to determine whether a wide range of executive statutes and bureaucratic regulations were legal. The rider, which was attached to an appropriations bill for victims of Hurricane Camille, held that no congressional appropriation "shall be available to finance, either directly or indirectly or through any Federal aid or grant, any contract or agreement which the Comptroller General of the U.S. holds to be in contravention of any Federal statute" (*CQ Almanac* 1969).

The Nixon administration was taken by surprise at this action. Shultz and Sylvester appeared at a press conference and denounced the proposed legislation. They pointed out that the language of the rider was not limited to civil rights, but rather would apply "to all appropriations and it goes across the board to the whole affirmative action concept," not just quotas.[34] Moreover, they claimed that the comptroller general was setting himself up as a quasi-judicial agent. Staats, however, had two potential sources of support in the House: those fearful of encroaching executive and bureaucratic power, and those opposed to civil-rights legislation in general.

Faced with the possibility of losing a major employment and nondiscrimination initiative, the White House swung into action on both the lobbying and public-relations fronts. Nixon issued public statements in support of the Philadelphia Plan, Sylvester publicly appealed to the civil-rights community, which he claimed had been too quiet on the issue,[35] and Shultz lobbied key House members.[36] The process was not an easy one, because the debate cut across usual coalitions and created some strange new alliances. For example, labor found itself on the same side as anti-civil-rights southern Democrats, while civil-rights leaders and other liberals stood with the administration of the antibusing Southern Strategist. In the end, however, the administration coalition prevailed and the rider was defeated.

Modeling the Debate over the Philadelphia Plan

In this debate the relevant actors are the Senate Appropriations Committee (Sa), the full Senate (S), and the President (P). The Philadelphia Plan is considered the status quo point, or Q. The Appropriations Committee adds the anti-Plan amendment to the Hurricane Camille bill. The president then threatens to veto the bill because it invalidates the plan. A continuing resolution is passed to keep the previous appropriations bill in effect. The House (H) vetoes the amendment in an analogous House bill. The president again threatens to veto the bill if it contains the amendment. The Senate then reverses itself and defeats the amendment, and the plan is upheld.

We array the House, Senate, and Senate Appropriations Committee in a single-dimensional model, with the dimension reflecting attitudes toward the plan. We categorize the president as falling to the left (liberal) side of the Senate, because he supports the plan, while the full Senate and the committee are both opposed at points in the process. The model is shown in figure 4.2.

We place the status quo point at P. The House prefers the committee amendment, Q*, to the status quo, Q, but the Senate does not. If the presidential veto threat is considered credible, then both chambers will need supermajorities (two-thirds plus one for a veto override), and the Senate's preferences suggest it will not override. Therefore the president gets his ideal policy.

One question raised by the model is, why did the Senate bother to invalidate the Philadelphia Plan? Perhaps conservative senators thought, after the election campaign and Nixon's widespread use of the "southern strategy," that having staved off the plan during Johnson's tenure, they would do at least as well with Nixon. But they underestimated his administration's support for affirmative action. And, as will become evident shortly, Nixon's position as a moderate-to-liberal Republican president on affirmative action gave him a strong bargaining position.

Viewed intuitively and retrospectively, Nixon's support of affirmative action is indeed difficult to reconcile with his emphasis on curbing urban violence during the election campaign and his firm antibusing stance. But

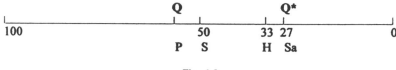

Fig. 4.2

there are alternative explanations quite separate from civil rights that may account for his position on the Philadelphia Plan: protecting executive and bureaucratic power against congressional encroachment and taking the opportunity offered to split the Democratic coalition (unions opposed the plan, while civil-rights groups supported it). But these reasons, although consistent with Nixon's interests in expanding presidential power and his Machiavellian delight in fomenting dissension within the Democratic party, cannot fully explain his administration's commitment to expanding affirmative action in quiet, bureaucratic ways. This latter strategy is exemplified by the development and implementation of Revised Order No. 4.

Administrative Initiative and Revised Order No. 4

Opponents of affirmative action had barely recovered from their defeat over the Philadelphia Plan when they made another unwelcome discovery. While public and congressional attention had been focused on the debate over the Philadelphia Plan, OFCC officials had quietly been specifying and extending the scope of affirmative-action compliance programs. In October 1969 the OFCC circulated Order No. 1, which specified each contracting agency's responsibility for contractor monitoring.[37] The order also set the minimum percentage of preaward reviews each agency was required to carry out at 50 percent, estimated the average man-hours needed for the reviews, and ordered each agency to submit their appropriations estimates to the Bureau of the Budget within ten days.[38]

Less than a month after issuing Order No. 1, the OFCC issued a set of regulations that are considered to be the most important and durable guidelines on affirmative action that the government has ever issued. These directives, which were promulgated in Order No. 4, comprehensively invalidated critics' charges that the affirmative-action requirements had been too vague to follow.[39] Order No. 4 stated precisely the obligations that contractors had with regard to affirmative action in employment and what steps they could take to fulfill those obligations. They even offered helpful sample illustrations. For example, "New York office plans to hire 20 sales representatives by March 1, 1970. Ten of the twenty will be minorities. Six of the ten will be Negro."[40]

Order No. 4 clarified as no other regulation, speech, or executive order had done just what were the guiding principles behind affirmative-action policy. First, neither intentional nor inadvertent prior discrimination needed to be proven. Instead, remedial action had to be taken if "the rate of minority applicants recruited [did not] approximate or equal the ratio of minorities to the applicant population in each location."[41] Second, affirmative action was not designed to compensate specific individuals who had been excluded from employment, because there was no connection required between previous victims and current beneficiaries. Instead the relevant issue was societal underrepresentation; affirmative action was based on an assumption that proportional representation in employment was the goal. Third, goals and timetables had to be specified numerically and were not negotiable. It was unclear whether these targets had to be met or if a good faith (failed) effort would be sufficient. But numbers had to be stated and at least attempted in hiring procedures.

In many ways, Order No. 4 represented everything that opponents of affirmative action disliked and feared. With its specific numerical targets, it seemed to confirm the worst fears of those who equated affirmative action with the imposition of quotas, and its justification was based on a contested and expansive reading of Title VI of the Civil Rights Act. And perhaps most intolerable to critics, the order paid no attention to the administration's previous assurances that the regulations would apply only to the construction industry. Instead, it extended coverage to *all* federal contractors with fifty or more employees and with contracts of at least fifty thousand dollars; this latter requirement was a significant increase from the Philadelphia Plan, which covered contracts of five hundred thousand dollars or more.

Opponents of affirmative action were quick to respond, challenging the administration on two fronts. First, they seized on the extension beyond the Philadelphia Plan and the proportional-representation aspects of Order No. 4. The OFCC, caught in the act of initiating a major policy shift that had neither been published nor considered in hearings, revised the wording slightly to mute the proportional-representation issue: in the Revised Order No. 4 issued in February 1970, underutilization was defined as "having fewer minorities in a particular job class than would reasonably be expected by their availability" (Graham 1990, 343), but the expansion of coverage remained intact.

Second, opponents tried once again to have the OFCC shifted from Labor to the EEOC through congressional legislation. This move was described by Shirley Chisholm as "a building trades amendment which was generated by their outrage over the Philadelphia Plan,"[42] although the charge was denied by its sponsors. To strengthen the EEOC, a bill was once again introduced that would give it cease-and-desist authority. But neither bill was successful; among liberal and civil-rights groups, organized labor could only get the Leadership Conference on Civil Rights to support the OFCC transfer. The coalition supporting affirmative action was strange but strong: with a Republican president and administration backing the policy, Republican members of Congress were induced by party discipline to support it, and with liberal Democrats already on board there were only the southern Democrats and staunchest labor supporters in opposition.

In the end, therefore, the administration was able to implement its sweeping new affirmative-action policy with only a few changes. And as a result, Revised Order No. 4 became and has remained the government's primary directive on affirmative action. Graham attributes this success to the social context of the policy, and he is no doubt correct; discrimination was still considered to be a real problem, riots in inner cities had been a summer occurrence for years, and there was no indication they would cease, so many people were still of the opinion that more needed to be done (Graham 1990).

In addition, three other factors probably played a role in muting opposition. First, the public's antipathy to affirmative action had not yet become fully apparent. Second, while business was opposed to more regulations and paperwork requirements, there were also some advantages. Businesses stood to gain public-relations benefits by implementing affirmative-action plans, and they also benefited from an increased labor supply. So while on balance they would have preferred to be left alone, they may not have fought as hard as they would if there had been no positive aspects to affirmative action. And finally, it was not clear how rigorously these new directives would be enforced. Civil-rights advocates perpetually berated OFCC for failing to use its cutoff and sanction authority, and the monitoring of compliance review programs remained inadequate.

The Role of the Supreme Court

Faced with the growing scope of affirmative action within government, opponents turned to the only other government institution that could put a brake on this policy development: the federal courts. But two critical cases left them worse off than when they began. The first defeat was a direct hit. In *Contractors Association of Philadelphia v. Secretary of Labor* (311 F. Supp. 1002 [E. D. Pa. 1970]), an appellate court rendered its verdict on the Philadelphia Plan. It ruled against the plaintiffs, who had argued that the plan was unconstitutional because it had not been approved by Congress and because it violated the Civil Rights Act. The court instead accepted the federal government's argument and agreed that since evidence had been introduced (and not challenged by the plaintiffs) that there had been inadequate minority representation in employment, and since the OFCC had determined this in hearings, then affirmative action was an appropriate remedy in the circumstances. In addition, the court held that Title VII's prohibition of quotas for racial balance only applied to Title VII circumstances, not to Title VI or to executive orders.

Had the OFCC not presented their "findings" of discrimination, and had they not presented affirmative action so explicitly as a *remedy* for past discrimination, the court might have ruled in favor of the plaintiffs. But given the evidence, the court appeared to believe that the obvious and documented lack of minorities in construction contracts made affirmative action a permissible policy despite the administration's adoption of clear numerical targets, which the court called "color-conscious" remedies. The decision was a double blow to opponents of affirmative action, first because it failed to invalidate the Philadelphia Plan, and second because it appeared to provide the means by which numerical targets could be used and considered constitutionally acceptable.

The next case was a private-party case, but it was one that had direct ramifications for affirmative action and for the acceptable range of bureaucratic interpretation of congressional preferences on the subject. *Griggs v. Duke Power Co.* (401 U.S. 424 [1971]) was a class action suit brought by thirteen black workers at a steam plant in North Carolina. After the passage of the Civil Right Act, Duke Power had stopped restricting blacks to the lowest-paying and least desirable jobs. But they imposed two new requirements for workers trying to move into the better jobs: they had to possess high-school diplomas, and they had to achieve satisfactory scores on two aptitude tests. While these requirements appeared to be racially neutral, they had the practical effect of limiting black advancement, because white workers were grandfathered out of the diploma requirement in a neutral-sounding clause.

The circuit court that had heard the case had ruled in favor of Duke Power on the grounds that there was no evidence of an intent to discriminate. But the Supreme Court, in a unanimous opinion written by Chief Justice Warren Burger, reversed the lower-court ruling. Burger supported this move with two main arguments. First, he argued that the language of section 703(h) of Title VII stated that tests could not be "used" to discriminate, with the meaning of that verb encompassing both intentional and unintentional discrimination. Second, he held that it was best to defer to the EEOC's reading of the statute, which was that intention was less important in determining whether an employment practice was unlawful than whether the practice had a clear and convincing business motive

(430–31). In the case of testing, this meant that unless there was a demonstrated "business necessity" for the test or requirement, it could be deemed unlawful if it resulted in an underrepresentation of minorities.

Burger based his decision on statutory grounds rather than constitutional ones, which meant that Congress could pass a law overruling the bureaucratic interpretation if it so desired (Eskridge and Frickey 1988). And given how far that interpretation ranged from the deliberations surrounding the Civil Rights Act in 1964, a remedy certainly seemed politically feasible. Title VII, both in the language and in the record of the debates surrounding its drafting, strictly stipulated that discrimination had to be intentional and that the discrimination had to have occurred after July 2, 1965, when Title VII went into effect. The EEOC guidelines, by contrast, stated that any tests with discriminatory effects were suspect and had to be justified for each racial group separately (differential validation). Intention was no longer the touchstone; effects were.

Modeling the Debate over Title VII

Congress did not take up the opportunity to clarify Title VII and restore the Dirksen compromise as the Civil Rights Act had intended it, and modeling these events makes clear why they failed to do so. The EEOC created by the Civil Rights Act was located, as shown in figure 4.1, at the 1964 Senate cloture point. This location was not at the 1964 House's ideal point, but the House had been forced to give ground in order to overcome the filibuster staged by southern Democrats and conservative Republicans. The EEOC (B) has now established a new policy that is further from the 1971 House median (H) but further away from the 1971 Senate median. The policy outcome is shown in figure 4.3.

For passage of a bill to restore the original status quo point, Q, both the House and Senate would have to pass it. But the bureaucracy's interpretation, Q*, which was upheld by the Supreme Court, is closer to S than Q was, so S has no incentive to pass new legislation. Thus, the bureaucracy, in its interpretation of Title VII, has actually come closer to the full Senate's median position, as opposed to its cloture point. The *Griggs* decision is deservedly criticized because of its suspect reasoning and interpretation of congressional intent. Nevertheless, the decision moved policy closer to the median positions of the Senate and removed the power of the conservative minority that was able to force the original compromise.

The model's predictions are borne out by the debates surrounding the passage of the amendments to the Equal Employment Opportunity Act in 1972. This bill ended years of unsuccessful attempts by House members to strengthen the EEOC bill beginning in the mid-1960s. The Senate had been

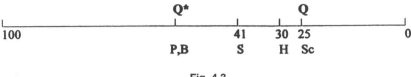

Fig. 4.3

less active, but in 1968 it introduced an EEOC bill that Everett Dirksen called "offensive" (*CQ Almanac* 1972) and threatened to filibuster. In 1970 the Senate approved a bill that gave the EEOC the liberals' coveted cease-and-desist powers. A similar bill had been reported out of the Education and Labor Committee in the House, which was chaired by Augustus Hawkins, but it died in the Rules Committee after a discharge petition effort failed.

The 1972 EEO Amendments

In 1971 Hawkins was more successful. His committee again reported out a bill that greatly strengthened the EEOC's powers. In addition to providing cease-and-desist powers, the EEOC's jurisdiction was expanded to cover state and local governments and educational institutions, and the Civil Rights Commission and the OFCC were brought under its control.[43] This bill was much stronger than what the Nixon administration wanted; the latter preferred a court-enforcement approach, in which the EEOC could bring suit against discriminatory employers, over cease-and-desist powers, and they kept the OFCC within the Department of Labor (Graham 1990). Republic John Erlenborn of Illinois, a member of the Education and Labor Committee, attempted to amend the Hawkins bill in committee so that it reflected the administration's interests, but he was voted down, and the Hawkins bill was sent to the full House (*CQ Almanac* 1972)

Here Erlenborn had more success. The House rejected the Hawkins bill and adopted the Erlenborn amendments, substituting the text of the administration's bill in its place. The amended bill featured the judicial approach rather than the NLRB-style prosecutorial one, and it left the Civil Rights Commission and the OFCC alone. This bill was sent on to the Senate in late 1971, where the Labor and Public Welfare Committee chose to report out a bill that was essentially identical to the Hawkins bill rather than the successful House bill pushed by Erlenborn and the administration (*CQ Almanac* 1972).

In early 1972 the Senate began debate on the bill. It became quickly apparent that the southern Democrat–led minority that wanted to roll back the *Griggs* decision by adopting strong anti-affirmative-action language would be unable to pass such legislation. It was equally apparent, however, that they would be able to obstruct passage of a strong cease-and-desist bill by filibustering. Therefore, the debate centered around compromises that could invoke cloture but still satisfy the proponents of strong EEOC powers. The result was one that gave the administration, which fell between these two poles, much of what it wanted.

The first significant amendment passed created a general counsel for the EEOC, in an attempt to reassure those who were afraid that with prosecutorial powers the agency "would operate as investigator, prosecutor, judge, and jury" (Graham 1990, 426) in discrimination cases. The Senate then agreed to an amendment that left the OFCC in the Department of Labor, but it defeated an attempt by Senator Dominick to substitute court enforcement for cease-and-desist authority. In the debate process, the forces that opposed *any* strengthening of the EEOC were outnumbered, but they were able to stave off votes by threatening filibusters. The Senate voted down court-enforcement substitutes for cease-and-desist powers three times. But they were unable to cut off debate and force a vote. After their second cloture motion failed to pass, the advocates of cease-and-desist admitted defeat and set about crafting a compromise. Dominick's modified amendment proved finally to be acceptable; it authorized the EEOC general counsel to bring suit and kept the expanded EEOC jurisdiction. After more than six weeks of debate, the Senate invoked cloture (with Robert Byrd of West Virginia signing his first cloture petition!) and sent the bill to a House-Senate conference committee (*CQ Almanac* 1972).

The final bill was an amalgam of House and Senate compromises. The House accepted the general counsel, stronger conditions under which the EEOC would bring suit against violators, and the transfer of the Judiciary's role in labor discrimination suits to the EEOC. The Senate accepted language reiterating that discrimination had to be intentional and restrictions on class action suits. And President Nixon was able to sign into law a bill that contained all of his preferred options.

Graham attributes the passage of the Equal Employment Opportunity Act of 1972 in part to the "bipartisan consensus that the equal employment principles of 1964 were sound but the enforcement mechanism was not. Congress was weary of seven years of debate over enforcement" (Graham 1990, 439). But another critical factor, one that Graham notes in his accounts of the debates, was the nature of the political alliances that were possible. Although Democrats controlled both houses of Congress, the strong presence of southern Democrats made it impossible for them to pass civil-rights legislation on their own. But if civil-rights bills could gain the support of the Nixon administration, then at least some Republicans could be counted on to vote in the affirmative for party reasons. If the administration was opposed to a bill, like the cease-and-desist provision for the EEOC, then the southern Democrats could defeat it. But if the administration wanted to protect the Philadelphia Plan, it could draw on Republican and liberal Democratic support. The key ingredient was the presence of what has proved to be the last Republican president who was relatively liberal on civil-rights issues.

Modeling the 1972 Debate

In 1971 opponents had been unable to impose their preferences, which was to return bureaucratic interpretation to the pre-*Griggs* era as stipulated in the 1964 debates by Dirksen. But their liberal counterparts, as represented by the House Education and Labor Committee and the Senate Labor and Public Welfare Committee, were also unable to pass their favored bills because they were too far from the medians of their full chambers. This time, however, the president's position was more conservative than before and therefore more in line with the House and Senate medians. The results are shown in figure 4.4.

The final bill, Q*, was located at the House's ideal point and to the right of the Senate median. And, intriguingly, if we assume that the administration's position was equivalent to the Erlenborn bill passed by the house, then the president once again achieved his ideal point, even though his relative position had shifted considerably.

The 1972 amendments expanded and strengthened affirmative action beyond what it had been in the Johnson administration, and they represented the last major initiative undertaken by the Nixon administration. Nixon was frustrated by what he saw as a lack of gratitude on the part of the civil-rights constituency for the gains he had made in that area; he grumbled that "the NAACP would say my rhetoric was poor if I gave the Sermon on the Mount" (quoted in Graham 1990, 345). And in 1972, responding to George Wallace's surprisingly strong challenge as well as increasingly vocal public opposition to busing, he stepped up his anti-affirmative-action rhetoric even as his administration was implementing policies. In public statements Nixon repudiated any association with the hated quotas, and in the runup to the election the OFCC was ordered to slow down enforcement of its regulations (Graham 1990, 447).

Richard Nixon was far less supportive toward affirmative action than Lyndon Johnson had been, and his policies were more conservative than could have been achieved had he desired to push the policy more strongly. Nonetheless, and contrary to many peoples' memories of the period, Nixon continued to advance the policies Johnson had begun, and he did not abandon civil-rights policies until his second term.

Fig. 4.4

Conclusion

The early development and subsequent expansion of affirmative-action policies in the United States were characterized by a sequential process in which executive action pushed policies forward for a time, then Congress became involved in considering legislation, then the policy responsibility reverted to the executive, and the sequence repeated itself. With supportive presidents in the White House between 1960 and 1974, the policy was expanded from a weak, voluntary one that only incorporated those businesses that were willing to develop their own programs to an agency-enforced program that covered almost all government employment and considerable portions of private, government-funded employment as well. Moreover, these policies were deemed constitutional by the Supreme Court.

While the executive branch was unfailingly supportive, albeit at varying levels of enthusiasm, Congress was considerably less enthusiastic. Liberal and nonsouthern moderate legislators of both parties, who considered African-Americans an important part of their electoral coalition, were favorably disposed toward affirmative action throughout this period, but their support was countered by the strong opposition mounted by southern Democrats and conservative Republicans. In the early and mid-1960s, before affirmative-action programs had become strong and expansive in their coverage, sympathetic members of the relevant oversight committee, the House Education and Labor Committee, had kept the responsible executive agencies from receiving much scrutiny; their task was made easier by the fact that few constituents were affected. But by the late 1960s, and especially after the Cleveland program, hostile members of Congress began to demand more accountability.

Both the theoretical and substantive evidence reveal how critical are the institutional structures within which policies develop. In the United States, with its separation-of-powers system, the structure either impels policy outcomes that are compromises among the first choices of the actors, or it results in outcomes that are the most conservative of the choices. Since each actor has potential veto power over the policy choice, no one player can impose a unilateral solution. In the early stages of compliance review during the Kennedy administration and during the first years of the OFCC it may have appeared that the executive branch was dominating Congress. However, it is more likely that not enough Congress members were opposed to the policy to take action. By the late 1960s, when their constituents were starting to become upset with the policies, they swung into action.

The evidence also suggests that the structure of incentives for many politicians led them to support the expansion of affirmative-action policies. All three presidents in office during this period considered the black vote part of their potential electoral coalition, and they did not believe that any other significant vote bloc would be alienated by their support of these policies. This belief was reasonable given that affirmative action was not really part of the public consciousness until the early 1970s. Even Richard Nixon, who was railing against quotas on the campaign trail even as his appointees enforced the strongest affirmative-action programs ever, was still courting African-Americans.

By the mid-1970s, however, it was no longer feasible to appeal to the traditional civil-rights constituencies by citing support of affirmative action without antagonizing other parts of a potential winning coalition. The strategy that had worked to serve politicians' interests for more than a decade became fraught with problems as the American public grew more knowledgeable about affirmative action and liked little of what they learned. In the next chapter I address policy changes in this transformed context.

CHAPTER 5

Affirmative Action under Carter, Reagan, and Bush

In this chapter I analyze the final expansion of affirmative-action policies during the Carter administration and their subsequent retrenchment during the Reagan and Bush presidencies. During the Kennedy, Johnson, and Nixon administrations, affirmative-action policy experienced a secular positive trend in which a voluntary, weak policy was transformed into a strong and compulsory one, and this trajectory seemed likely to continue after 1976. Jimmy Carter's election provided the first instance of unified government in eight years, and the elections following Watergate provided large Democratic margins in Congress, helping Carter to defeat Nixon's appointed successor, Gerald Ford. The Carter administration was not as supportive of affirmative action as his Democratic predecessors had been, and public opposition to affirmative action had increased since then, but African-Americans were key to the winning coalitions of most Democrats, so policy proponents were justifiably optimistic.

In the 1980s, however, this scenario abruptly shifted. Ronald Reagan was elected president on a platform that was pointedly hostile to affirmative action, and his coattails swept in enough Republicans to allow them to capture the Senate for the first time in decades. Within a few years, this Republican dominance made its impact felt on the Supreme Court as well. In contrast with the Nixon years, when Republican party loyalty helped to bring about a pro-affirmative-action coalition of liberal and moderate Republicans and liberal Democrats, Reagan and Bush drew on party loyalty and the votes of conservative Democrats to frustrate civil-rights and affirmative-action enforcement.

To explain the policy outcomes that resulted from this political transformation, I continue to apply the theoretical framework used in the previous chapter. Rational-choice methods are embedded in a qualitative historical context, with empirical evidence being used to determine the preferences of actors, the structure of incentives they face, and the institutional configurations in which they negotiate to develop policies. Substantively, the political landscape was transformed in the 1980s, but theoretically and formally many of the factors remained constant. Actors faced essentially the same structure of incentives: they needed to initiate, continue, or expand policies that would please their existing constituencies, and perhaps also appeal to new groups. And the institutional configurations remained constant as well: the arena of action continued to be the U.S. federal government, with its separation-of-powers system. The major changes came in the preferences of constituents, and therefore in the preferences of the actors involved in the policy process.

As I observed in the preceding chapter, until the early 1970s affirmative action was not a salient policy for the American public. But beginning in 1972, this circumstance changed. The debate over the Philadelphia Plan and the EEO amendments had brought attention to affirmative action as a new type of civil-rights policy. At the same time, actors outside the government had begun to implement policies of their own, which increased the policy's visibility. Public and private schools had begun voluntarily to adopt affirmative-action programs in admissions, while government regulations on affirmative action in hiring subjected university faculty-hiring policies to greater scrutiny. These two changes were challenged within the academy, which brought greater publicity to the concept of affirmative action as part of the civil-rights agenda (Glazer 1987; Bennett and Eastland 1979).

At the same time, civil-rights policies that had already been more visible were facing strong and increasingly organized opposition. Once court-ordered busing began to move north, beginning with the Supreme Court's *Keyes* decision, there was considerably less support for it, with public opinion eventually reaching a negative level of 90 percent in polls (Page and Shapiro 1992). Finally, in the enduring recessionary economy that characterized the economy, American began to be less generous in their attitudes toward policies targeted toward disadvantaged groups. Table 5.1 summarizes these attitudes.

TABLE 5.1.   Attitudes about Preferences versus Ability for Black Access to Employment and Higher Education

	Preferences	Ability	Don't Know
1977	11	81	8
1980	10	83	7
1984	10	84	6

Source: Gallup Poll data cited in Steeh and Krysan 1996.
Note: The Gallup Poll asked, "Some people say that to make up for past discrimination, women and members of minority groups should be given preferential treatment in getting jobs and places in college. Others say that ability, as determined by test scores, should be the main consideration. Which point comes closest to how you feel on this matter?" The possible responses were 1) preferential treatment, 2) ability, 3) don't know.

The juxtaposition of preferences with ability may have inflated the negative response to affirmative action, where responses are particularly sensitive to question wording. In 1977, a Roper Poll question that asked whether quotas should be retained or made illegal received a 59 percent response from whites that it be made illegal. However, the next year, when the Harris Poll asked whites if they supported affirmative-action programs provided there were no "rigid quotas," the positive response rate rose to 67 percent for employment and 68 percent for education, with only 17 percent and 15 percent opposing them, respectively (Steeh and Krysan 1996).

Clearly Americans, and white Americans specifically, were ambivalent about the policies, and in this environment, politicians became warier of supporting civil-rights policies in general, and lightning rod policies such as busing and affirmative action in particular. For many northern liberal Democrats, civil-rights support was a given, because African-Americans represented a core constituency. Other bedrock groups in their electoral coalition, notably Jews and unions, tended to oppose affirmative action, but they were unlikely to defect to the Republican camp. But the rest of the New Deal coalition, especially the working-class vote (which was increasingly nonunion) and southern male voters, were much less solid. Over the course of the 1970s, emerging Republican candidates abandoned the black vote in an attempt to woo these potential defectors from the Democratic party. And by the end of the decade, their success was exemplified by Ronald Reagan, who spoke out directly against affirmative action as quotas and was less than lukewarm toward the rest of the civil-rights agenda.

In the 1980s, then, the winning political coalition for parties and politicians at the national level appeared to include an appeal to opponents of affirmative action and other policy legacies of the civil-rights movement and the War on Poverty. Later in the chapter I discuss the effect this transformation had on the direction affirmative-action policies could take. Before these events occurred, however, affirmative action continued to be expanded and institutionalized in Congress and the Supreme Court.

1975–80: Policy Consolidation and Extension

While bureaucratic implementation of affirmative-action policy continued after Nixon's resignation through the Ford administrations, no further legislation was passed. Ford himself was moderate on civil rights generally and resistant to affirmative action specifically. The next opportunity for affirmative-action proponents was with the election of Jimmy Carter to the presidency, and they took full advantage of it.

Affirmative-action Expansion during the Carter Presidency

When Carter took office in 1977 the U.S. economy was in recession and plagued by high unemployment. One of the new administration's and Congress's first priorities was to amend the 1976 Public Works Employment Act in order to pump money and jobs into the economy as quickly as possible, and before it was accompanied by inflation. The act was essentially a pork barrel bill and had no explicit affirmative-action provisions.

When the amendments reached the House floor, however, Parren Mitchell of Maryland proposed a rider that would set aside a specific percentage of contracts for Minority Business Enterprises (MBEs). Mitchell noted that the Small Business Administration (SBA) had the authority, under section 8(a) of the Small Business Act, to provide special assistance to "socially or economically disadvantaged" persons, and he contended that a similar set-aside for minorities was both legitimate and necessary (Eskridge and Frickey 1988). An average of only 1 percent of government contracts went to minority contractors, and even under the SBA program the number was only increased to 3 percent. The amendment proposed that 10 percent of all federal contracts be set aside for MBEs. This rider was then amended to allow administrators to waive the 10 percent requirement in cases of demonstrated infeasibility, and it passed the House with no recorded opposition (*CQ Almanac* 1977).

A similar amendment was introduced in the Senate by Edward Brooke of Massachusetts and eight cosponsors. As in the House, the tiny number of contracts awarded to minorities was presented as the reason. And also as in the House, the amendment was adopted without debate. This action marked the first, and so far only, legislative use of a specific numerical measure to signify fulfillment of an affirmative-action target (Benokraitis and Feagin 1978).

Given this development, as well the growing public unease with affirmative-action policy, one of the remarkable aspects of this legislative debate was the absence of opposition. From the Democrats' point of view, it can probably be explained by their desire to support a new president early in his term. But the acquiescence of conservative Republicans is more difficult to understand. It may have been their interest in the larger bill to which the amendment was attached; in 1977, recession and inflation had created an environment in which Congress felt public pressure to "do something," and a public-works bill was a time-honored response that cut across party lines. But if we think in strategic terms, affirmative-action opponents simply may have known that they didn't have the votes to sustain a filibuster, much less defeat the amendment. The fact that the amendment passed the Senate by voice vote suggests that this may have been the case.

The PWA amendments of 1977 were the most publicly visible policy development during Carter's term. At the less visible bureaucratic level, the administration left the structure it inherited from the Nixon-Ford presidencies essentially intact while strengthening its enforcement powers. The OFCC and the EEOC were reorganized and given additional powers. The EEOC was given the responsibility to coordinate all employment discrimination activity. The OFCC became the OFCCP (the P stood for *Programs*), its funding and staffing were increased, and it was given the power to order back-pay awards in discrimination cases. In addition, the Office of Management and Budget, which had at times been a hurdle for enforcement officials because of its budgetary responsibilities, acquired a civil-rights unit to coordinate and oversee funding for enforcement (Benokraitis and Feagin 1978).

When opponents of affirmative action were unsuccessful at persuading the president and Congress to stop or roll back affirmative action, they continued to turn to the courts to try and overturn federal enforcement regulations, including the set-aside legislation passed in 1977. The Supreme Court was growing more conservative toward civil-rights issues,[1] but it continued to support policies drafted under certain conditions. Three cases in particular were critical in defining the parameters by which affirmative-action policy would be considered constitutionally permissible.

The Supreme Court

In 1976 the Court was asked to consider its first case on affirmative action in higher-education admissions. The plaintiff, Marco DeFunis, had been rejected by the University of Washington Law School even though his board scores were higher than other students who had been admitted. DeFunis argued that the school's affirmative-action policy constituted a case of "reverse discrimination" because as a white male he had been held to a higher standard than minority applicants. The Court rendered the case moot because by the time it reached them DeFunis had reapplied, been admitted, and was about to graduate (Schwartz 1988). But the following year, when it received another case very similar to this one, it granted certiorari.

Regents of the University of California v. Bakke (438 U.S. 265 [1978]) was brought by Allan Bakke, a white, male applicant who had been rejected twice by the University of California, Davis, Medical School. Upon learning that Davis had a minority-recruitment program in which 16 percent of the admissions places were set aside and considered in a separate process, Bakke sued the school on the grounds that his civil rights, as guaranteed by Title VI of the Civil Rights Act, had been violated. The

University of California defended its approach by arguing that the program would increase the numbers of minority physicians, some of whom might return to practice in those disadvantaged areas where they were sorely needed, and it provided a way to achieve diversity in the medical school. The facts in the case were not in dispute; the dispute was over whether Title VI permitted affirmative-action policy under these conditions (Sindler 1978; Schwartz 1988).

Bakke lost the case in superior court, although not on Title VI grounds. The judge ruled that Bakke would not have been admitted even if there were no minority program, and therefore the discrimination issue was irrelevant. However, the California Supreme Court reversed, holding that Davis had instituted a quota system and thus had discriminated against Bakke on the basis of race. In the words of one of the judges concurring in the opinion, "We saw quite clearly that this was a case of racial discrimination, and it was our feeling that discrimination against a person of any race is just bad" (quoted in Schwartz 1988, 24).

By the time the case reached the Supreme Court it had generated enormous public interest. The number of amicus briefs filed on behalf of the parties was fifty-seven, the largest number ever until the *Webster v. Missouri* abortion case in 1989. Groups that had traditionally ranged themselves on the same side in civil-rights cases were at odds, and there were also internal divisions within certain constituencies (O'Neill 1985). In one of its most unusual split decisions, the Court issued a two-part judgment. First, by a five-four margin it affirmed the California Supreme Court's verdict invalidating the Davis admissions system, but under constitutional rather than Title VI grounds. Second, also by a five-four margin, the Court reversed the California Supreme Court decision and held that "race may be considered as a factor in an admissions program."

In both the decisions the swing vote was cast by Justice Powell. Chief Justice Burger and Justices Rehnquist, Stewart, and Stevens all believed the Davis system was in violation of Title VI and as such there was no need to consider the constitutional question. Powell agreed that the system violated Bakke's rights, but he held that it did so on constitutional rather than Title VI grounds. Justices Brennan, Marshall, Blackmun, and White held both that the admissions system was valid "in every respect," and that race may be taken into account as a factor in the admissions process; on this latter point Powell concurred. This mixed ruling from a sharply divided court made it clear that numerical preferences without evidence of prior discrimination would not be allowed, but it also gave supporters of affirmative action and institutions looking for guidance encouragement by allowing the consideration of race among other criteria for admission.

In order to clarify the form that constitutionally permissible programs might take, Justice Powell cited at length the admissions process at Harvard College, which he acclaimed for its "flexible" use of race. The Harvard system considered race as a factor in some admissions decisions, but no target quotas were set and candidates were compared competitively (Sindler 1978, 310). The *Bakke* decision therefore gave colleges and universities the opening to develop race-conscious admissions policies if they so wished, but it provided no method to force reluctant institutions to do so. Since Powell's use of the Harvard program as a successful example of constitutionally permissible affirmative action provided a blueprint for how higher-education admissions could be structured to accommodate race-conscious selection, it is not surprising that *Bakke* remained the only higher-education affirmative-action case to be considered by the Supreme Court until 1996.

The second critical case occurred the following year, when the Court was presented with a case that paralleled *Bakke* in its particulars but concerned employment. In *United Steelworkers v. Weber* (443 U.S. 193 [1979]), a white employee named Brian Weber charged that his civil rights had been violated when his employer, Kaiser Aluminum, voluntarily reached a collective-bargaining agreement with the steelworkers' union to admit one black for each white admitted to a plant training program until the company labor force reflected the minority composition of the local workforce population. The case differed from *Contractors* and from *Griggs* in one significant way: no evidence was presented to demonstrate that Kaiser had discriminated against blacks in the past. Kaiser chose not to introduce such evidence because it might have resulted in a more severe remedial program than the one it had already negotiated. And Weber, of course, had no incentive to demonstrate that Kaiser had ever discriminated against blacks, because he was trying to prove that the discrimination was against whites.

In a sharply divided five-four decision, the Court upheld the agreement. In his majority opinion Justice William Brennan reasoned that if Congress had wanted to prohibit "all voluntary race-conscious affirmative action," it would have explicitly stated that position in the Civil Rights Act itself or in the legislative debates that surrounded it, and therefore affirmative action was permitted. Justice Rehnquist strenuously disagreed with this reading, arguing that if Congress had wanted affirmative action it would have said so. Their debate was reminiscent of Burger's focus on and interpretation of the verb "use" in the *Griggs* decision, concentrating as it did on the key word "require" (Eskridge and Frickey 1988).

Finally, in 1980 the Court agreed to consider the constitutionality of numerically explicit targets in *Fullilove v. Klutznick* (448 U.S. 448 [1980]), which challenged the set-aside provision in the 1977 Public Works

Employment Act. In another five-four split decision, the Court affirmed the program to set aside 10 percent of contracts for Minority Business Enterprises in local public-works programs. Burger's opinion was emphatic in stipulating that the program's acceptability was because Congress had demonstrated prior discrimination: "Congress had abundant historical basis from which it could conclude that traditional procurement practices, when applied to minority businesses, could perpetuate the effects of prior discrimination." In another section, however, the Court also stated, "As a threshold matter we reject the contention that in the remedial context the . . . Congress must act in a wholly 'color-blind' fashion" (482). While part of the justification for this position was a deference to Congress, it appeared to many observers that the Court had established a context in which comprehensive affirmative-action programs, complete with numerically specific targets, were constitutionally permissible.

1980–91: Retrenchment and Reversals

The election of Ronald Reagan to the presidency in 1980 promised to bring changes on many fronts, and civil-rights advocates were aware that affirmative-action and nondiscrimination policy would be among the earliest targets. Reagan had campaigned on a platform that promised a sharply reduced federal role and an assault on affirmative action, and from his first days he set about making both a reality. Even in the relatively unproblematic area of discrimination complaints, the Civil Rights Divisions of the Justice Department and the Department of Education sharply cut back their investigations and processing (Amaker 1988). So it might have been expected that when it came to more controversial issues such as affirmative action and fund cutoffs to discriminatory contractors, the Reagan administration would deviate from the practices established by previous administrations.

Reagan used the same initial approach to attack affirmative action as his predecessors had used to build it up, that is, through bureaucratic initiatives. But he also had the advantage of pending discrimination and affirmative-action cases before the Supreme Court. So opponents of the policies had two tracks by which to challenge the status quo without having to confront Congress, where the House was still controlled by Democrats.

Bureaucratic and Judicial Transformations of the Status Quo

The plans of the new administration were immediately apparent in the OFCCP, where the administration diminished enforcement in two ways.

The first was to cut back on the number of contractor debarments and administrative complaints filed by the agency. In addition, the OFCCP ordered nearly two-thirds less money in back-pay awards than the previous administration. Second, the agency attempted to change fundamentally the basic procedures of affirmative-action reporting. They advocated eliminating preaward reviews, raising the threshold of coverage, allowing medium-sized contractors to submit abbreviated affirmative-action plans, allowing companies to submit plans every five years rather than yearly, and relaxing the "goals and timetables" rules for contractors who were found to underutilize minorities and women (Amaker 1988).

The first instance for judicial intervention came in Reagan's first term, in the Court's decision in *Grove City College v. Bell* (465 U.S. 555 [1984]). The case had already attracted attention because the administration had abandoned the position the Justice Department had taken during Carter's presidency and adopted the opposite stance. The case involved the scope of the relationship between discrimination and federal funding. Grove City College had refused to file an Assurance of Compliance with the Office of Education, and the agency had sanctioned the college. Grove City contended that since the federal assistance at issue was student financial aid, only the financial-aid office should be targeted and not the entire institution. The appeals court had ruled in favor of the government, and the college appealed to the Supreme Court.

When the case was heard, the Reagan administration found itself in the unusual position of "attacking the very ruling its predecessors had sought and won" (Amaker 1988, 71). But its strategy paid off when the Supreme Court reversed the appellate-court decision. The Court rejected evidence that Congress had intended the category of federal assistance to encompass grants and loans and agreed with the administration's position that Title IX was intended to be program specific. Therefore, funding only for those programs that had been determined to be practicing discrimination should be terminated, and the rest of the school's funding should be continued.

This policy shift represented a major victory for those within and outside government who criticized excessive federal power and expansive federal civil-rights enforcement. It was not a new position; the acceptable extent of fund-cutoff provisions had been an important issue during the debates over the 1964 Civil Rights Act, and there had been a faction that had argued then and since that total fund cutoffs for partial discrimination were inappropriate. No administration had ever taken that position, however, and until 1984, neither had the Supreme Court. The *Grove City* decision represented a major blow to civil-rights supporters on two fronts. Most obviously, there was the defection of the executive and judicial branches from their previous support of broad nondiscrimination enforcement. While these defections were not unexpected, they represented a critical loss, since civil-rights and affirmative-action policy enforcement and implementation had been driven by support from the president, the agencies, and the courts. Without that support, enforcement could easily slow or even cease. Second, the civil-rights community had only one place to turn for help, to Congress, and up to now this had been their least reliable institutional resource. Congress was preferable to the other two branches because laws were more binding than statutes or court decisions, and because when Congress was committed to a policy it would put pressure on a recalcitrant bureaucracy to implement it effectively, as it did with HEW and southern school desegregation in the 1960s (Orfield 1969). But it had been difficult even under relatively favorable conditions to pass strong civil-rights policies in Congress, and at those times civil-rights bills had had presidential support.

Nevertheless, civil-rights proponents and their allies in Congress attempted to counter the ruling. The House Judiciary and Education and Labor Committees voted out bills that reversed *Grove City*. The language of the bills focused on the "recipient" of federal aid, stating that federal funds would be cut off to all of a recipient's programs if one or more of those programs was found to be in violation of federal regulations. In an attempt to make it difficult for supporters of affirmative action to vote for the bills, opposing members of the House attempted to introduce ad hoc amendments prohibiting federal funding of abortions for recipients of this federal aid, but one was voted down by the full House, 186–219, and the other amendment was ruled out of order. The bill then passed the House by the margin of 375–82, and the bill was sent to the Senate.

Here proponents' chances were much less bright. Republicans had gained control of the Senate in the 1980 elections, and the chairman of the Senate Labor and Human Resources Committee had changed from the liberal Democrat, Edward Kennedy, to the conservative Republican, Orrin Hatch of Utah, who was one of the champions of the new Republican effort to decrease Federal involvement in civil rights generally and affirmative action in particular. Not surprisingly, Hatch kept the bill bottled up in committee. Supporters attempted to circumvent this maneuver by having the bill put directly on the Senate calendar, but Majority Leader Howard Baker refused to call up the bill for debate until some type of compromise with the Reagan administration could be reached. Minority Leader Robert Byrd eventually forced the bill to be considered by the full Senate by introducing it as an amendment to an unrelated appropriations bill. When the Senate voted to find it germane, Baker added other controversial amendments, including gun control and busing, as well. The ensuing debate turned extremely acrimonious and threatened normal Senate conventions of operation (*CQ Almanac* 1986). Citing these conditions, Robert Packwood moved to table the Byrd amendment despite the fact that the Senate had voted to invoke cloture 92–4. Hatch and Baker then dropped their amendments. Civil-rights supporters felt betrayed by the liberal Republican Packwood, but there was nothing they could do, since liberal Republicans were their only hope in the Republican-dominated Senate, and it was clear that the leadership was unwilling to provoke a confrontation with its executive counterpart.

Modeling the Early Debate over *Grove City*

When we model this set of events, it becomes clear how much the preferences of some of the players in the game have changed and what a critical effect these changes have on policy outcomes. The institutional actors are the same as in the earlier models, but there are new individuals occupying these institutional positions, and they bring with them new preferences. The Judiciary Committee has changed from being chaired by a liberal Democrat to a conservative Republican (Orrin Hatch's ADA scores were generally ten or less), who won't release the bill from committee, while the Republican leadership of the Senate keeps bills off the floor until they have reached an agreement with the Republican president. Substantively, the Republicans are better off in terms of cohesive organization than their Democratic predecessors because they don't face a parallel to the southern Democrat problem. Their most difficult component is liberal Republicans, but these players have a strong allegiance to president and party.

The sequence of events in the *Grove City* case is straightforward. By siding with the plaintiffs, the bureaucracy had chosen to reverse its predecessors' position (Q) and establish a new status quo (Q*). The Supreme Court, which had also undergone critical changes in its composition and consequently in its preferences, could invalidate or uphold the bureaucracy, or it could make entirely new law. It voted to uphold the new status quo. This outraged the House (H), which passed legislation restoring the old status quo, which we place at the House ideal point. In the 1980 elections, Republicans had become the majority party in the Senate and therefore committees were now controlled by Republicans, so traditionally liberal committees like Labor and Human Resources could no longer be considered safe bastions of civil-rights support. And Ronald Reagan, who had campaigned on a conservative civil-rights and hostile affirmative-action platform, could be counted upon to veto civil-rights legislation that appealed to supporters.

When the Justice Department chose to change sides in the *Grove City* case, there was both consternation and outrage in the civil-rights community. But as figure 5.1 illustrates, the department was able to do so with considerable confidence that it would not be overruled by opponents.

Orrin Hatch has no incentive to allow new legislation to reach the Senate floor because it will be further from his ideal point than the *Grove City* decision. At the same time, supporters of the original status quo will have to override a presidential veto in order to establish a new status quo. Given the position of the veto point, this can only result in a bill that is at or near Q^*, so *Grove City* stands.

In the 1960s and 1970s, affirmative-action and civil-rights bills were supported by a majority of the institutional actors. In the Johnson years the Senate's cloture rule allowed a minority of that chamber to dictate the final policy outcomes, while in the Nixon era a veto capacity gave the president control over the shape of the final bill. Under Reagan, the combination of conservatives in the presidency and in control of the Supreme Court and Republican control of the Senate made reversals of existing affirmative-action policies almost a foregone conclusion.

Nevertheless, for the next two years, the House continued to introduce bills that would restore the pre–*Grove City* status quo. Hoping to overcome the debate that had arisen in 1984 over the use of the "recipient" of federal aid as the object of the legislation, the language was altered so that the focus of attention was limited to the "program or activity" in violation of civil-rights laws rather than the recipient, but this change proved insufficient to gain much new support. To complicate the debate further, the unrelated abortion riders that continued to give supporters of civil-rights enforcement and abortion rights trouble in voting for the bill reemerged to create cleavages on new lines (*CQ Almanac* 1986). And the Republican-controlled Senate continued to keep its version of the bill locked up in the Labor and Human Resources committee.

The Passage of the Civil Rights Restoration Act

Finally, in 1988, the bill's proponents were able to gain a significant victory despite the continuing opposition of the president. In the 1986 elections the Democrats had regained control of the Senate. In 1987 the Labor and Human Resources Committee, once again chaired by Edward Kennedy of Massachusetts, had reported out a bill to restore to previous status quo, but it had failed to reach the Senate floor. But Majority Leader Robert Byrd scheduled it for debate in January 1988. The abortion question was finally settled when two amendments were introduced to ensure that nothing in the bill would be construed to require or prohibit that fed-

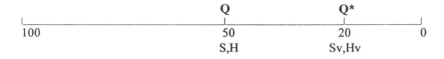

Fig. 5.1

eral funds be used for abortions. One of the amendments, John Danforth of Missouri's self-termed "abortion-neutral" amendment, passed by a slightly higher margin than the other, and the bill with his amendment was passed 75–14 and sent on to the House for its action (*CQ Almanac* 1988).

In the House the bill went straight to the Rules Committee, where it was reported to the floor with an unusual rule: there could be no amendments offered, but one Republican substitute was allowed. The ensuing substitute was easily rejected, while outraged Republicans protested that their rights of free speech and the power to amend were being denied on a civil-rights bill, and the bill passed the House 315–98 (*CQ Almanac* 1988). Thus, both houses of Congress passed the Civil Rights Restoration Act by margins that were large enough to override a potential presidential veto. Nevertheless, Reagan carried out his threat to veto the legislation, offering a weaker bill in its place. And, as was expected, the House and Senate both voted to override his veto, and the bill was written into law.

Modeling the 1988 Debate

Modeling these interactions reveals how civil-rights supporters were able this time to overcome the obstacles that had blocked them for four years. Both the House and the Senate became more liberal, and so did their veto points. The Senate Committee on Labor and Human Services was again headed by Edward Kennedy, whose ADA scores (regularly in the nineties) were the polar opposite of those of Orrin Hatch. The president and the bureaucracy remained conservative, but now a veto override was more likely. Nevertheless, the necessity to override meant that once again the veto points rather than the floor medians were relevant in establishing a new status quo. Figure 5.2 shows the policy outcome and the new status quo.

The model emphasizes the importance of the presidential veto in determining a policy outcome. Civil-rights proponents were able to overcome Hatch's obstructionist measures when Democrats regained the Senate, but they were still confronted with a much more conservative outcome than they would have obtained in a regular majority vote.

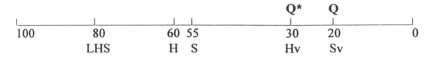

Fig. 5.2

The Supreme Court in the 1980s

During the second Reagan term the Supreme Court continued to issue decisions that suggested that it was becoming more conservative than it had been in the 1970s, although it was by no means uniform. As it continued to specify the condition under which affirmative action was constitutionally permissible, these conditions became increasingly stringent.

Some restrictions were not surprising because they concerned issues that had always fallen within the gray areas of affirmative-action policy. One of these was seniority. In *Wygant v. Jackson Board of Education* (476 U.S. 267), the Supreme Court struck down a layoff plan that protected minorities and laid off employees with seniority. The Jackson school board had been successful in increasing the number of minority teachers hired in recent years, but with cuts in school funds and decreases in enrollment they were forced to lay off teachers. If the usual last-hired, first-fired policy had been followed, minority teachers, who had been disproportionately hired after whites, would be disproportionately affected. Therefore, the board opted to lay off some more senior white teachers and retain more minority teachers.

The Court ruled in favor of the plaintiffs, the laid-off white teachers. In her opinion Justice O'Connor argued that while limited affirmative action in hiring could be justified because of increased minority representation, seniority was a more protected right and therefore policies that violated that right were subject to more stringent tests. By making this type of distinction, the Court demarcated levels of employment and different rights attached to those levels. The reasoning in *Wygant* proceeded from the assumption that being fired from a job imposed a greater hardship on an individual than not getting that job in the first place. It followed that since the hardship was greater, the conditions under which affirmative action could be imposed also had to be concurrently more severe, and the conditions of *Wygant* did not meet this test.

While *Wygant* represented a setback for proponents of affirmative-action policy, the Supreme Court had not completely eliminated the possibility that the scope of programs could continue to expand. In *Johnson v. Transportation Agency, Santa Clara County* (48 U.S. 616), the Court held that ignoring minor differences in test/interview performance in the hiring process did not constitute grossly unequal hiring practices in the name of affirmative action. In this case a woman was promoted to a skilled craft position that no other woman held even though her interview score had been slightly lower than the competing man's score. The Court, again in a five-four decision, maintained that such a small difference, determined in the subjective atmosphere of an interview, could be overlooked in the larger interest of achieving more equitable representation where prior discrimination had existed, especially since other tests had also been utilized and the affirmative-action candidate had done equally well on those. The case was noteworthy in two ways: first, the Court explicitly acknowledged that test results did not have to be followed blindly in all cases; and second, it extended affirmative action to cover women for the first time.

But while *Johnson* represented an important step forward for supporters of affirmative action, it was a rare bright spot for them, as the Court's shift away from its liberal approach in the 1970s became increasingly consistent. In *Croson v. City of Richmond* (488 U.S. 469), the city government of Richmond, Virginia, had chosen to institute a set-aside program for local contracts in which 30 percent of all contracts would be awarded to minority businesses. A nonminority business sued, and the Supreme Court supported the argument that the program was unconstitutional. The majority opinion held that there were insufficient grounds for the adoption of the set-aside program. No evidence of prior discrimination had been introduced, and inadequate justification for the 30 percent target figure had been presented. In other words, affirmative action was being introduced as a policy choice rather than as a remedy for a demonstrated prior history of discrimination. The case resembled *Weber* in that prior discrimination was not introduced as an issue, although the history of discrimination by Kaiser and United Steelworkers was clearer than in the immediate history of Richmond's contracts. But the Court refused to accept affirmative action unless it was introduced explicitly as a remedy for documented past discrimination.

Later in the same year, the Supreme Court issued opinions on a number of civil-rights cases that made it abundantly clear that more, not less, restrictions on affirmative-action and civil-rights issues more generally were going to be imposed. The most significant case was *Wards Cove Packing Co., Inc. v. Atonio et al.* (490 U.S. 642), a class action suit in which cannery employees in Alaska charged the packing company that employed them with discrimination in hiring practices. The workers argued that the disparity between nonwhite workers in cannery and "noncannery" jobs bore this out, since the cannery jobs were lower paying and few workers were promoted from one to the other. The workers lost in district court, but the court of appeals reversed on two grounds. First, the appellate court held that they had met the "disparate impact" standard introduced in *Griggs* and upheld statutorily since then. Second, since the disparate impact had been demonstrated, the burden of proof shifted to the company to prove that the practices that led to it were due to "business necessity," again as cited in *Griggs*. However, the Supreme Court reversed the Ninth Circuit on both grounds, significantly shifting the balance of legal power between the plaintiff and the defendant in affirmative-action cases.

Most civil-rights suits had traditionally been difficult to win because they required the individual bringing the suit to prove that the discriminating party was indeed at fault. Contract compliance, on the other hand, which operated in affirmative-action policy, required the contractor to prove that s/he was not discriminating in order to obtain the contract, effectively shifting the burden of proof from the victim to the perpetrator, and all OFCC implementation policies had possessed this property. Affirmative-action programs in accordance with the guidelines set down by the Supreme Court had to be based on demonstrated prior discrimination, but the rules of evidence placed the primary burdens on the employer.

In *Wards Cove,* the Court changed the balance of power between the litigants in three ways. First, it would now be up to the alleged victim of discrimination to demonstrate that discriminatory outcomes were directly traceable to company practices; disparate impact was not enough. Second, while the employer was still required to furnish proof of a business justification, it was up to the employee to "persuade" the court that this justification was baseless or insufficient. Finally, the Court relaxed the business necessity requirement of *Griggs* to a lesser one of justification, emphasizing that "there is no requirement that the challenged practice be 'essential' or 'indispensable' to the employer's business for it to pass muster (659).

Justice White's majority opinion acknowledged that "some will complain that this specific causation requirement is unduly burdensome on Title VII plaintiffs" (657) but dismissed this objection on the grounds that employer records were readily available. There was also a passing admission that the new interpretation of the burden-of-proof requirement reversed previous decisions, but White went on to state that those "earlier decisions [that] can be read as suggesting otherwise . . . should have been understood to mean an employer's production—but not persuasion—burden" (660).

These changes were welcomed by critics of the existing policy, and in invoking the innocent-until-proven-guilty proof requirements of criminal law, it seemed somehow to be abstractly just. But the practical effect of the decision was expected to be that discrimination suits would now be much harder to litigate, for a variety of reasons. First, many individuals were likely to be discouraged by the more stringent requirements even if they were victims of discrimination; even under existing conditions discrimination cases were difficult to win. They were also not costless, and the lower chances of success would make the prospect of employment retribution and the financial costs seem higher. Second, many instances of discrimination produced evidence that was compelling if the burden of proof were on the alleged perpetrator, but not if it were on the alleged target of discrimination.

The Congressional Response

Wards Cove produced outrage within the civil-rights community and among its congressional allies similar to that which had followed the *Grove City* decision. Initially there was some optimism that George Bush would prove to be more conciliatory on civil-rights legislation than Reagan had been, since Bush had directly appealed to the African-American vote during the 1988 election and he was perceived to be less ideological in general than his predecessor. Civil-rights advocates hoped that with a less ideological executive, their policies would stand a greater change of implementation or even restoration to their pre-Reagan status. But although Bush was not as personally committed to eradicating affirmative action, he took an equally strong programmatic stance against it, and his public pronouncements on affirmative action mirrored Reagan's in their equation of affirmative action with quotas. Given public opinion on affirmative action in the late 1980s, as shown in table 5.2, he may have considered this to be a fairly safe position.

The pattern of congressional response to *Wards Cove* mirrored the experience of *Grove City,* and initially with similar results. In 1990 companion measures in the House and Senate were unveiled with great fanfare at a press conference and then introduced in the Education and Labor and Labor and Human Resources committees. Labor and Human Resources was the first to report its bill, and after invoking cloture by a vote of 62–38, the full Senate passed the bill 65–34 over the objections of both Republican leaders and Bush's threat to use his veto power (*CQ Almanac* 1990). This veto threat was credible, because, despite the bill's large margin of victory, it was still two votes short of two-thirds necessary for a veto override.

Only slightly after the Senate had begun its deliberations, the House Education and Labor and Judiciary Committees reported out their bill, which was almost identical to that being considered in the Senate. The bill was passed by the House 273–154, which again was a large margin but twelve votes short of the two-thirds necessary to override a presidential veto. Both houses had attempted to placate the bill's opponents by adding matching amendments that stipulated that nothing in the bills could be construed to encourage or require quotas. In addition, the House had voted to amend the bill to provide a cap on punitive damages, which helped to shore up support among moderate representatives. The bill that emerged from the House-Senate conference retained both these amendments and added other provisions that would ease the burden of proof on employers (*CQ Almanac* 1990).

But these compromises proved to be insufficient to gain the votes necessary to override a veto. As promised, Bush vetoed the bill, and its backers set about trying to pick up more votes. But in the Senate only one member of the two that were needed was willing to change his position. Other senators who were more favorable to the bill after it emerged from the conference committee "said they did not want to abandon Bush during the difficult budget negotiations and ongoing trouble in the Persian Gulf" (*CQ Almanac* 1990, 473). Thus, just as in the Reagan years, party loyalty made it difficult to persuade Republicans to vote for civil-rights bills, even with a comfortable Democratic majority in both houses of Congress.

Modeling the 1990 Debate

Figure 5.3 shows the relative positions of the actors and the problems that backers of the bill faced. The Supreme Court established a new status quo (Q*) that was more conservative than the previous one (Q). The bill that emerged from conference committee (Q#) was further to the right than the original House and Senate bills, but it was still to the left of the congressional veto points, which allowed Bush's veto to be sustained.

TABLE 5.2. Attitudes toward Preferential Treatment for Blacks in Hiring and Promotion and Higher Education Admissions

	Hiring and Promotion		Higher Education	
	% in Favor	% Opposed	% in Favor	% Opposed
1986	23	77	38	63
1988	20	80	36	64
1990	25	75	37	63
1992	20	80	32	68

Source: National Eduational Survey data cited in Steeh and Krysan 1996.

Note: The NES asked separate questions about employment and education. The first asked, "Some people say that because of past discrimination, it is sometimes necessary for colleges and universities to reserve openings for Black students. Others oppose such quotas because they say quotas give Blacks advantages they haven't earned. What about your opinion—are you for or against quotas to admit Black students?" The second asked, "Some people say that because of past discrimination, Blacks should be given preference in hiring and promotion. Others say that such a preference in hiring and promotion of Blacks is wrong because it gives Blacks advantages they haven't earned. What about your opinion—are you for or against preferential hiring and promotion of Blacks?"

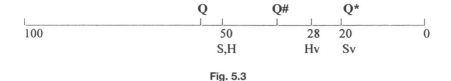

Fig. 5.3

It is probable that both the House and the Senate would have preferred to retain the original status quo based on the *Griggs* decision, because it was closer to their ideal points than either the *Wards Cove* decision or their compromise bill. But even though they were willing to move quite far from their ideal point to improve their outcome, they were unable to succeed. The model shows how critical it is for one actor to have the unilateral ability to change the status quo. Without the Supreme Court's decision, the president would have had no way to obtain a new status quo that was more favorable to him, because Congress would have had no incentive to initiate legislation that was bound to be further from their ideal points. But because the Supreme Court's verdict was on the other side of the president's ideal point, and the latter's veto power raised the effective cut point for the legislature from 50 percent plus one to two-thirds.

Wards Cove Redux and the Clarence Thomas Hearings

Especially in light of the closeness of the outcome, supporters were determined to try again to reverse *Wards Cove*. This time the House was ahead of the Senate, with the former's Education and Labor and Judiciary Committees reporting out a new bill in March 1991. The bill differed slightly from the previous year's failed attempt; most notably, it emphasized gender equality in addition to race. Its title, Civil Rights and Women's Equity in Employment Act of 1991, emphasized the new orientation. Despite Republican efforts to substitute the president's weaker bill, or at least to reduce requirements on businesses, the bill easily cleared the liberal-Democrat-dominated committees (*CQ Almanac* 1991).

This dominance did not, however, carry over to the House floor, where the reluctance of southern Democrats left the bill without strong support. To make the bill more appealing, and to gain enough votes to ensure a veto override, amendments similar to those of the previous year were included, in particular limits on damages and prohibition of quotas. In addition, amendments easing evidentiary rules for employers and tightening them for employees were added that brought the bill closer to the Bush version. But despite these compromises, sponsors were unable to pick up enough votes to stave off a veto. In fact, the final vote tally, in which the bill passed 273–158, fell short by three more votes than the previous year's bill. Bush's alternative and much weaker bill was defeated by almost as great a margin as the civil-rights bill was passed, 162–266, but this was small comfort to advocates of a new policy.

Meanwhile, the bill's backers in the Senate were encountering difficulties of their own. Edward Kennedy wanted a bill similar to the House bill, but his unlikely collaborator, John Danforth, pushed for a more moderate bill. With the conservatism of southern Democratic senators and the battle over the House bill, Danforth's weaker proposal began to prosper. Danforth's bill came closer to the administration's bill, further limiting compensatory damages, prohibiting punitive damages for women, and providing easier evidentiary rules on the justification of hiring practices for employers. But these compromises appeared to be inadequate to gain the single vote needed from the previous year to override Bush's promised veto (*CQ Almanac* 1991).

It was at this point that an exogenous shock tipped the balance away from the administration and toward Danforth. The Clarence Thomas confirmation hearings created a major battle, across party lines and to an extent within the Republican party as well. Danforth was the key Senate actor responsible for keeping the party together in the Senate and bringing about a favorable vote for Thomas, and his actions both earned the heightened respect of his colleagues and increased his political power. As Minority Leader Robert Dole remarked, "From our Republican standpoint, it's better to be in a position supporting a bill rather than going against Danforth" (*CQ Almanac* 1991, 256). Faced with this situation, the Bush administration compromised to the extent necessary to pass a civil-rights bill that would not be vetoed.

While the administration made greater compromises than Congress for the final bill, Bush's sustained opposition had provided him with several victories. The final bill returned the burden of proof on hiring practices to employers, where it had been before *Wards Cove,* but the courts (which were considerably more conservative than in the *Griggs* era) had greater discretion in determining how to evaluate that evidence. And the limits on punitive damages were pushed down even further, while employers with less than fifteen employees were exempt from damages altogether.

Modeling the 1991 Bill

The model shows the game essentially stayed the same as in 1990, with the House and Senate moving the 1991 bill (Q*) to the other side of the veto point. Figure 5.4 gives the policy outcome.

Since the Senate veto override fell short by only one vote, it is somewhat difficult to understand why the substantive compromise engineered

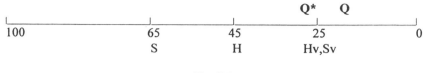

Fig. 5.4

by Danforth seems greater than might have been expected. The game cannot capture what was required to arrive at a successful compromise. Substantively, however, we can posit a couple of possibilities. Most obviously, that one vote could have required these compromises in order to switch. Or, given the House was fifteen votes short, it may have taken greater compromises than needed in the Senate to pick up those members.

The compromises made by those who wanted to restore the pre-*Wards Cove* status quo were an improvement over the status quo imposed by the Supreme Court with their 1989 decision, but the final outcome was considerably less favorable to plaintiffs of discrimination than the *Griggs* status quo had been. The changed preferences of the president and the court transformed the power relations between the branches, and this transformation gave opponents of affirmative action greater influence than they had ever possessed before. Until Ronald Reagan's election it had become highly unlikely that a president would veto a civil-rights bill. But the changed face of the Republican party, especially toward affirmative action, made it possible even for a relative moderate like Bush to do so and succeed politically.

Conclusion

The fortunes of affirmative-action policy development changed dramatically in the 1980s. At the beginning of the decade affirmative-action programs were strong, extensive, and appeared to be firmly in place. But by the beginning of the next decade, their conditions were much more tenuous. Enforcement had been curtailed, relations between plaintiffs and respondents in discrimination and affirmative-action cases had been almost reversed, and the specter of quotas was continually being equated with strong government activity. How can this transformation be explained?

An obvious and intuitively convincing answer is that the election of a conservative president whose antipathy to affirmative action was widely expressed and understood brought about these changes. Lending weight to this explanation is the fact that the American public has been consistently and firmly opposed to affirmative action since the early 1970s. For example, the number of Americans who support government intervention to guarantee school access for minorities declined from nearly half in 1964 to a quarter in 1978, while the number who supported government efforts to aid minorities to improve their social and economic position was less than one-fifth in 1980 (Schuman, Steeh, and Bobo 1985, 90–91). Therefore, it can be argued that Reagan's preferences reflected those of public opinion generally. With Reagan, Americans who opposed affirmative action and active civil-rights enforcement more generally had finally found an ally in government.

But while this argument sounds promising on its face, there are several problems with it. First, the public's antipathy toward affirmative action needs to be separated from its support for civil-rights policies. Schuman, Steeh, and Bobo make a distinction between policies of principle, like the Civil Rights and Voting Rights Acts, and policies of implementation, like busing and affirmative action (1985). Opponents are right to focus on quotas, because the public is overwhelmingly opposed to any programs that is said to feature them. But once that lightning-rod term is removed, attitudes are more diffuse. Page and Shapiro found that public opinion toward affirmative-action programs in industry and higher education was supportive at the level of 70 percent or higher if the question wording specified that "there are no rigid quotas" (1992, 97–98).

It can be argued, therefore, that while Reagan's policies reflected the opinions of a segment of the American public, it was by no means drawing support from a consensus. Nonetheless, his and his successor's focus on affirmative action as quotas, and the conflation of civil-rights enforcement with affirmative-action policies, was successful in arousing negative public attitudes. In 1990, Bush immediately and successfully termed the bill to restore the *Griggs* status quo a "quota bill" even though affirmative action had nothing to do with it (*CQ Almanac* 1990).

American attitudes toward affirmative action have remained fairly consistent over the last two decades, but policies have not. So the question arises, if Americans were opposed to affirmative action in the 1970s, why did programs continue to expand in scope and intensity? For the 1960s the argument might be made that the public was simply unaware of what was going on, since most of the programmatic innovations were being developed within the bureaucracy. But by the early and middle 1970s, programs were much more in the public eye and opponents were very effective at getting their objections heard and recorded.

This chapter offers an alternative explanation for why opponents of affirmative action were so much more successful in the Reagan and Bush presidencies than they had been before. As the games make clear, the relative positions of the actors changed critically during this time. The court and the president, and as a consequence of the latter the bureaucracy as well, became more conservative. And for a time, the Senate became more conservative as well. Given the institutional configuration and the need for more than one branch to agree in order for the status quo to be shifted, the balance shifted from one in which the actors supported affirmative action (in the 1960s and 1970s) to one in which a majority of the actors (not necessarily a majority of public opinion) opposed it.

I am not arguing that opponents were completely out of step with public attitudes. But the extent to which opponents were able to achieve their goals exceeded the extent to which the public wanted affirmative-action and civil-rights programs curtailed. Analogously, it is probably the case that proponents in the late 1970s went further in developing affirmative action than the American public would have supported in, say, a referendum. The reason for these asymmetries lies in the institutional makeup of American politics. The ability of a president to veto legislation means that if Congress and the president have opposing preferences, Congress needs two-thirds consensus rather than a simple majority to get its way. Similarly, if the president and the courts agree on a statutory interpretation, then Congress will need a two-thirds agreement in order to reimpose its own views (which may well have been passed by a 50-percent-plus-one majority). In the 1980s and early 1990s, opponents of affirmative action were represented by the president and the courts, and supporters were forced to overcome these preferences in order to achieve any further gains or prevent erosion of existing programs. This situation provided a mirror opposite to the 1970s, in which supporters were able to rely on sympathetic presidents and courts to push affirmative action well beyond the limits its opponents wanted to establish.

CHAPTER 6

Early Reservation Policy Development in India

In this chapter and the one the follows, I analyze the development of affirmative action, known as reservation policies, in India. The Indian experience diverges in several ways from that of the United States. The antecedents to the final policies began much earlier, at the beginning of the twentieth century. The policies initially targeted untouchables, but they later encompassed other disadvantaged groups as well. And their development spans the colonial period and the period after India gained independence from the British.

Nevertheless, I argue that the same combination of theory and empirical evidence used to explain affirmative action in the United States can explain reservation policy development in India. As in the U.S. case, policies were developed to make individual politicians and political parties appeal to specific electoral groups. The policies were debated, passed, and implemented by the same types of governmental actors. And the factors that affect the policy outcome are the same: the preferences of actors, the number of actors and the structure of their incentives, and the institutional structure in which actions are embedded.

While the types of actors, preferences, strategies, and actions found in India are the same as in the United States, the specific attributes of the policy process in India vary across time because of changes in the institutional structure and the relationships of the actors. As a result, the same model cannot be used for every situation. In the U.S. case, there was a single institutional framework, that of a democratic, separation-of-powers system, across the entire period being analyzed. In India, by contrast, there are two major types of institutional frameworks, that of a colonial political system and a federal parliamentary democracy, and within the latter there are differences in the types of party systems. The early years of democratic India featured a one-party dominant system, while the post-1971 era has featured growing multiparty competition.

To explain policy development in these different periods, I use a variety of models, all of which share the same assumptions about behavior but which capture the different institutional frameworks. In the colonial period, indigenous groups bargained with the British in a system that featured asymmetric power relations, so I employ an extended game in which players move serially and have a number of different strategies. In the postcolonial period there is a balance of power between government institutions who bargain over policies, so I employ single-dimensional models similar to those used in the U.S. case. During the periods following independence, actors select among policies that target different coalitions of electoral groups, so I use models that emphasize the trade-offs among these coalitions.

At the beginning of this book I asserted that a key factor common to both countries was that they were democracies. But I include in my discussion of India policy development under British rule. Obviously, this is not a democratic political system. However, the policies were developed and maintained with the critical participation of indigenous groups. These groups, especially the Congress, the Muslim League, and the leadership of the untouchable community, gained legitimacy with the British to the extent that they could show strong popular support. Therefore, in selecting among policy options they behaved in similar ways to vote-seeking politicians, and it is reasonable to model their policy choices as if they were actors in a democratic political system.

In this chapter I analyze the development of reservation policies during the colonial period and the early years of democratic government in independent India. The policies developed in the early part of the century were never intended to give Indians much power, but they introduced questions about the form of political representation that should be established. The British had two motives in encouraging groups within India to demand separate political representation. On the one hand, they wanted to protect those who had been their allies, especially the Muslims, while at the same time restraining the ambitions of the Indian National Congress, whom they correctly perceived to be a threat to their power.[1] But on the other, they also had a genuine belief that from a cultural point of view the religious, linguistic, and regional variations within Indian society naturally divided them into distinct and competing political groups.[2] The British felt that in time, as political sophistication and experience increased, Indians might be able to overcome these primordial identities, but until then they would dominate. These perceptions may have been derived from their own experience in Britain; when representation to Parliament increased in the sixteenth and seventeenth centuries, British interests were represented in terms of corporate groups (Kishlansky 1986; Ferejohn 1991). But whatever the reasons, British perceptions of India coincided neatly with their material interests.

The initial phases of Indian incorporation into the political process were completely at the discretion of the British. The Morley-Minto reforms of 1909, the Montagu-Chelmsford reforms of 1919, and the Simon Commission tour in the late 1920s all solicited the input of Indians, and in their reports they all acknowledged the demands put forward by different groups. During all of these reform efforts, the British consistently rebuffed the demands of the Indian National Congress while accepting many of the demands made by Muslims, Anglo-Indians, and untouchables, which makes the reluctance of the Congress to negotiate with the British and the eagerness of other groups to do so easy to understand.[3] The two options offered to Indians were to cooperate with the British and hope their demands were met, or to refuse to cooperate at all. By the late 1920s the Congress had opted to play the latter strategy, since it seemed probable that the British were unlikely to extend political liberalization in the new reforms to include dominion status for India and an increased role for Indians in governing their own affairs. Both of these demands had been basic elements of the Congress platform throughout the 1920s (*Report of the All Parties Conference* 1928)

By the 1930s, however, the Indian National Congress and untouchable leaders were able to negotiate between themselves and arrive at a compromise system of political representation. Untouchables agreed to give up separate electorates in return for reserved seats within the Congress fold. Somewhat surprisingly, these policies were not only maintained after India achieved independence, they were given legitimacy through their inclusion in the constitution. And in the years after independence, reservation policies in political representation were expanded to include government employment and higher education as well. During this period there was some discussion of incorporating non-untouchable low-caste groups, the OBCs, but these efforts met with little success. In the remainder of this chapter I focus on these developments under British and Congress rule.

Colonial Rule, the Transfer of Power, and the Entrenchment of Reservations

The refusal of the Indian National Congress to cooperate with the Simon Commission's fact-finding tour led the British to suggest a new form of negotiation to determine the shape the next wave of reforms would take. This departure is attributable to the accession to Parliament of a more sympathetic Labour government, as well as changing attitudes toward India within England and India's decreasing economic importance (and increasing political responsibility) (Moore 1974). These conferences, which were called the Round Table Conferences (RTC), consisted of representatives of major and minor Indian social and economic groups as well as representatives from the British government and the Liberal and Conservative parties. The expressed hope was that the conferences would produce an Indian constitution, but instead they revealed the deep divisions among the constitutional demands of the indigenous players.

Although they were ultimately unsuccessful, the RTCs helped to shape the contours of the political, social, and economic decisions that were eventually made. The first Round Table Conference, convened in late 1930, was inconclusive (Government of Britain 1931). Gandhi was in prison as a result of the civil-disobedience campaigns, and no Congress representatives attended the meetings. The British attempted to resolve the subject of an all-India federation with the Muslim League and the Princely States representatives, but the Muslim delegation refused to yield on separate electorates, and the Sikh representatives refused to accept the Muslim League's demands concerning the political apportionment of the Punjab. The question of princely representation in the federal legislature was also unresolved, as different groups of princes supported very different federal solutions (Moore 1974, 156–64).

The Round Table Conferences

When the representatives of the Muslim minority and the Indian National Congress assembled in London for the second RTC, there were grounds for optimism that a political compromise on electoral representation could be reached despite the fact that the public positions of Muslims and the Hindus were diametrically opposed. Coming into the conference, Muslims insisted that they should be allowed to vote in separate electorates; that is, only Muslims could elect representatives to political offices set apart for Muslims. Hindus, especially those representing nationalist and fundamentalist groups, took the converse view and asserted that undifferentiated electorates, in which all voters selected from the same slate of candidates and no offices were set apart for any groups, were the best solution.

But these publicly stated positions concealed the divisions that existed *within* each religious group. Among Muslims there was definitely a preference for separate electorates, but leaders with high standing both within the community and with the British had previously showed a willingness to compromise on joint electorates with reserved seats. Jinnah, the only Muslim Leaguer with a national reputation who was also recognized by the British, had previously expressed his willingness to entertain this possibility (Jalal 1985). The term *joint electorates* signified an undifferentiated electorate with reserved seats; political representation was guaranteed to Muslims through offices reserved for them, but all voters participated in the selection and election process.[4] For their part, Hindu nationalist representatives were staunchly opposed to separate electorates or even reserved seats, but the Congress had conceded separate electorates to Muslims in the 1928 Nehru Report (*Report* 1928), as had Gandhi on different occasions. When Gandhi and Jinnah arrived at the second RTC, it was not unreasonable to assume that they might be able to convince their allies to compromise on joint electorates and away from the prevailing status quo of separate electorates.

The British government had historically supported Muslim demands for electoral representation, but there were recent developments that suggested the Raj might be more favorably inclined toward Indian National Congress demands than usual (the usual strategy being the treatment of the Congress as a subversive and even terrorist organization). First, the Labour government of Ramsay MacDonald was led by the party with the least attachment to empire as an article of faith and the most willingness to treat the Congress as a legitimate organization (Moore 1974). Second, the government had initiated the idea of the conference in response to Indian hostility to the Simon Commission, and it pressed forward with the RTCs despite heavy opposition from Liberals and Tories. And finally, Gandhi, the most influential Congress leader at that time, had signaled a measure of confidence in British intentions by successfully negotiating with Viceroy Irwin the terms on which it would participate in the RTC (Brown 1977).

While the primary focus at the RTCs was on the Indian National Congress and the Muslim League, they were also instrumental in crystallizing the untouchable position on political representation. The two untouchable representatives, B. R. Ambedkar and R. B. Srinivasan, had not been decided on separate electorates at the outset of the first RTC. Rather, Ambedkar was most concerned with the establishment of adult suffrage, and he favored joint electorates with adult suffrage (Government of Britain 1931). Ambedkar was also opposed to communal representation in the cabinet. However, it became clear that the Muslim League would not yield on their demand for separate electorates, and Ambedkar and Srinivasan were reproached by a British Liberal MP Isaac Foot as being out of step with the rest of the Depressed Classes' "continual stress, for a separate electorate. Without that safeguard, they have said their interests cannot be secured" (1931, 87). While communal representation through separate electorates was by no means a unanimous choice of untouchables, various untouchable organizations had been demanding of the British government the same special protection awarded to Muslims since 1917 (Gupta 1985, 192–203). By the end of the meeting, the official untouchable position as announced by Ambedkar and Srinivasan favored adult suffrage with a limited period of separate electorates.

At the second RTC it became quickly apparent that all the minority groups except the Sikhs were in favor of separate electorates. Gandhi, representing the Indian National Congress delegation, spoke eloquently against separate electorates, indeed, against any kind of special treatment of minority groups, and his most vehement denial was reserved for the idea of special protection for untouchables.

> While the Congress will always accept any solution that may be acceptable to the Hindus, the Muhammedans, and the Sikhs, Congress will be no party to special reservation or special electorates for any other minorities. . . . I can understand the claims advanced by other minorities, but the claims advanced on behalf of the Untouchables, that to me is the "unkindest cut of all." . . . I claim myself in my own person to represent the vast mass of the Untouchables. . . . We do not want on our register and on our census Untouchables classified as a separate class. . . . It will create a division within Hinduism. (Government of Britain 1932)

In the face of this stalemate and the impending conclusion of the conference, Prime Minister Ramsay MacDonald, acting in his capacity as the chairman of the Minorities Committee, suggested that each committee member authorize him to settle the communal question and that his decision be binding upon all parties, and the Indian representatives agreed.

Modeling the RTC Stalemate

When these events are modeled, it is apparent that while certain aspects of the British-Indian game were changed at the RTCs, other important characteristics remained the same. The establishment of the RTCs was presented by the British as a major development, and it has often been accepted as such by historians (Moore 1974; Low 1977). But while it is true that the British decision to allow Indians seats at a negotiating table represented a departure from previous practice, its value was primarily symbolic rather than substantive. The RTCs were structured in the following way. The Indian groups and the British would meet and negotiate until they arrived at a consensually acceptable solution. The British positioned themselves as observers rather than as equal participants, but they set the terms of reference, or boundaries of negotiation, for the conferences, and they retained veto power.

Hypothetically, the Indians could have joined together and come up with a solution that fit within the terms of reference and the British would have been forced by their stated position to accept it whether they liked it or not. But this outcome was quite unlikely because the major partici-pants, that is, the Indian National Congress and the Muslims, had prefer-ences that were diametrically opposed to each other.[5] And the Muslims had very little incentive to negotiate, because in the past their demands had generally been granted by the British. Similarly, the untouchables, who were more willing to ally with the Congress, were encouraged by the com-ments of individuals within the British contingent to press for separate political representation.

Finally, by reserving veto power and by waiting for the Indians to move first, the British placed themselves in the position of being able to move last, when they had full knowledge of the positions the other players had taken. This had the potential to be a risky strategy, since a unanimous solution by the Indians could have put the British in the position of accept-ing an unfavorable policy or reneging on their commitment to accept any consensus decision, but given the divisions among the Indian groups it was worth taking.

Figure 6.1 displays the game in extended form. The Muslims are depicted as moving first (this is a somewhat arbitrary choice, but the out-come of the game is the same whether Muslims or the Congress moves first). The preferences and possible strategies of the Muslims and the Con-gress are known by all three players, but the Indians cannot be certain of British preferences, since the government's stated position (neutrality) is at odds with its policy history (favoring minorities, especially Muslims, in debates over representation). Muslims can be presumed to prefer separate electorates over joint electorates, and joint electorates over undifferenti-ated electorates. The Indian National Congress has exactly the opposite preference ranking. The stated British position is that they will accept any policy that is agreed to by all affected parties, and they may postpone any policy decision if agreement cannot be reached.[6]

Given these preferences and strategies, Muslims had a dominant strategy to insist on separate electorates. If the Congress agreed, then the British would adopt the policy, but even if the Congress did not, the British at worst would postpone the decision. History suggested that they would try to give Muslims what they wanted, since the British traditionally had done so each time policy was debated and changed. Congress also pre-ferred postponement to separate electorates, so they would never select separate electorates.

The events of the RTC were in accordance with the predictions of the model. The British postponed the decision and, with the consent of the Indians, undertook to break the deadlock. Their solution was all that the non-Congress groups could have wished. The British government announced its decision on the minorities question a few months after the

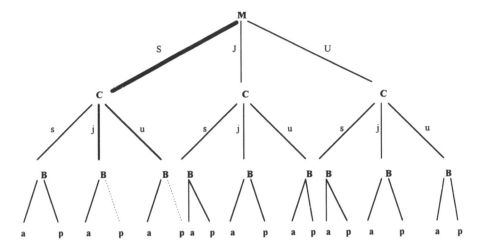

Muslims' preference ranking: S, J, U
Congress' pref. ranking: u, j, s

S: Strategy for M (Muslims): Play U
C: Strategy for Congress: If M play U, then u
                          If M play J, then j
                          If M play S, randomize between u & j
B: Strategy for British: If Uu or Jj or Ss then a
                          then a
                          Otherwise, p.
S = Separate electorates; U = undifferentiated electorates;
   J= joint electorates; a = accept; p = postpone

Fig. 6.1

end of the second RTC, in August 1932, in a proclamation entitled the Communal Award.[7] The Award granted separate electorates to Muslims and other minorities, but untouchables reaped the biggest benefits: they received voting rights in the general and their special electorates as well as reserved seats. This outcome followed earlier British choices in that it granted minority groups separate representation as they requested and ignored Congress demands that representation be unitary. And in awarding untouchables especially generous political benefits that separated them from caste Hindus, the British were driving a wedge into what the Indian National Congress considered to be its core coalition.

The Communal Award and the Poona Pact

Upon hearing the conditions of the Communal Award, Gandhi announced that he would fast until the government withdrew the benefit of separate electorates for untouchables. He had written to Sir Samuel Hoare, the secretary of state for India, from Yeravda jail in Poona, where he was being imprisoned by the Government of India, informing him of his proposed actions.

> From the newspapers which I am permitted to read, I observe that any moment H.M.'s Government may declare their decision. At first I had thought that if the decision was found to create separate electorates for the depressed classes, I should take such steps as I might then consider necessary to give effect to my vow. But I feel that it would be unfair to the British Government for me to act without giving previous notice. I feel that no penance that caste Hindus may do can, in any way, compensate for the calculated degradation to which they have consigned the depressed classes for centuries. But I know that separate electorate is neither penance nor any remedy for the crushing degradation they have groaned under.
> I therefore respectfully inform H.M.'s Government that in the event of their decision creating separate electorate for the depressed classes I must fast unto death. . . .
> I am painfully conscious of the fact that such a step whilst I am a prisoner must cause grave embarrassment to H.M.'s Government and that it will be regarded by many as highly improper on the part of one holding my position to introduce into the political field methods which they would describe as hysterical, if not much worse. All I can urge in defense is that for me the contemplated step is not a method, it is part of my being. It is a call of Conscience which I dare not disobey, even though it may cost whatever reputation for sanity I may possess.[8]

The British had kept Gandhi's communication in mind, but they appeared to be skeptical about his resolve. In the internal telegrams between London and the viceroy that preceded the announcement of the Communal Award, Secretary Hoare wrote,

> You will remember Gandhi's threat in the event of our deciding for separate electorates for the Depressed Classes. No doubt our scheme is only half as bad as he was expecting. Nevertheless, I imagine it is possible that he will carry his threat out. I think it would be well to make up our minds in advance what to do in this event and I should be glad to know what you and Sykes contemplate. I think that we can enlighten public opinion on the issue of separate electorates for the Depressed Classes sufficiently to prevent his action having embarrassing consequences outside India, if he acts for this reason.[9]

Gandhi began his "epic fast" on September 20, 1932 (Tendulkar 1952). In response, MacDonald informed Gandhi that the British government could not unilaterally rescind any part of the Award (despite the fact that it had been unilaterally introduced). He reiterated that

> In response to very general request from Indians after they had failed to produce a settlement themselves, the Government very much against its will undertook to give a decision on Minorities question. They have not given it and they cannot be expected to alter it except on conditions they have stated. I am afraid therefore that my answer to you must be that Government's decision stands.[10]

MacDonald went on to say that there was only one way that the Award could be altered:

> only the agreement of communities themselves can substitute other electoral arrangements for those that Government have devised in a sincere endeavour to weight conflicting claims on their just merits.

As soon as Gandhi began his fast, Indian National Congress leaders began to mobilize efforts to find a solution to the problem. Several leaders went to Yeravda jail to try to persuade Gandhi to give up his crusade, while in Bombay the Hindu Leaders' Conference that was taking place addressed the issue of electoral representation for untouchables. The Congress members in Poona found that Gandhi was willing to compromise and allow joint electorates to be provided for untouchables. But in Bombay, Ambedkar was unwilling to give up separate electorates unless untouchables received "a much larger number of total seats than the Prime Minister's award had given them" (Tendulkar 1952, 207).

Ambedkar was persuaded to meet Gandhi in person to arrive at a compromise acceptable to both sides, and he journeyed to Yeravda. There, after two days of negotiation with the participation of other Congress and untouchable leaders, the two agreed on a system in which joint electorates would be introduced for untouchables; all voters could participate in the general election, but the panel of candidates for the primaries would be chosen by untouchables only. The Communal Award had originally provided a total of 71 reserved seats for untouchables in separate electorates. In joint electorates Ambedkar initially demanded 197 seats, but he compromised at 147 total (Tendulkar 1952, 210). This solution, which came to be known as the Poona Pact, was presented to the British, who accepted it and modified the Award accordingly.

The Poona Pact resembled the negotiations conducted at the Round Table Conferences, but there were differences that were critical to determining the successful outcome of the former. Just as the British implemented their preferences through the Communal Award, they could have maintained separate electorates for untouchables if Gandhi and Ambedkar had been unable to agree. But unlike the case at the RTCs, the Congress and untouchables had grounds for compromise even though their first preferences were opposed. Although the British were skeptical that Gandhi would starve himself to death,[11] Indians were more convinced that Gandhi was quite capable of carrying out his threat. Ambedkar was probably more skeptical than the Congress leaders, but he could not afford to be wrong, since Gandhi's death would be attributed to his unwillingness to compromise. At the same time, while Gandhi was willing to die for his principle of keeping untouchables within the Hindu fold, he was apparently ready to acknowledge caste Hindu responsibility for the untouchables' plight (Brown 1977),[12] which made joint electorates an understandable compromise.

Both Gandhi and Ambedkar had good reason to compromise, Gandhi to achieve his stated goal of abolishing separate electorates and Ambedkar to keep Gandhi alive while increasing the total seats to be reserved under the joint electorate system. Correspondence between the Government of India and London reveals that at least the British were under the impression that Ambedkar hoped to use the Poona Pact negotiations to increase untouchable political representation. On the day before Gandhi began his fast, Viceroy Willingdon wrote to Hoare that "both Rajah and Ambedkar seem to think that they are going to get a great deal out of this business."[13] The two sides thus presented the British with a consensual solution that the latter could only have ignored at the cost of adverse reputational effects. And the British really had no reason to do so; the principle of some sort of distinction in electorates was not only maintained by sanctioned by the most popularly revered Indian leader.

During the first half of the twentieth century, India was still a colony of Britain, but the British government was allowing an increasing level of participation by Indians in the political process. In order to receive recognition as indigenous leaders deserving of official recognition as spokesmen, elites had to mobilize mass support. The Indian National Congress claimed to represent all Indians regardless of religion or caste affiliation, the Muslim League claimed to represent Indian Muslims, and B. R. Ambedkar claimed to be the preeminent spokesman for the untouchable community. The British correctly perceived the Indian National Congress to be their greatest threat, and so they encouraged the aspirations of minority elites to dilute its power. Therefore, the Congress was competing not only with other groups, such as the Muslim League, they were also competing against the policies offered by the British. They were never able to gain the allegiance of sufficient Muslims or of the Muslim League to overcome the separate electorates granted by the British, but they compromised with the untouchable leadership to grant reserved seats within joint electorates. Both groups had an incentive to compromise when Gandhi began his fast; the Congress because they wanted to keep untouchables within their political fold, and untouchable leaders because Gandhi was venerated in their community.

Separate Electorates and Reservations in the Constituent Assembly Debates

With the policy of joint electorates and reserved seats established with great fanfare in the Poona Pact, preferences for untouchables were settled for the remainder of the independence period. They arose again only when all policies were being reviewed during the debates that accompanied the drafting of a constitution for newly independent India, during the constituent assembly of 1947–50. At the end of World War II Clement Attlee's newly elected Labour government announced that it would hold national elections in India with a view toward establishing a constituent assembly that could draft a constitution for India's self-governance. The outcome of provincial elections held in December 1945 had determined the distribution of seats in the constituent assembly and the Congress party's electoral victories had given it over two-thirds of the total seats available (Austin 1966).

Initially the Muslim League had boycotted the constituent assembly, justifiably fearing that since they were so outnumbered they would be forced to accept unpalatable political choices. But the partition of India and the creation of Pakistan rendered this problem moot, as most of the Muslim League departed for the new state, and Muslim representation was reduced accordingly. As a result, the Congress's dominance increased even more, to more than 80 percent. Minorities were still represented, but with the exception of Muslims, their representation was through the Congress. The truncated Muslim League was reduced to twenty-eight representatives, out of a total of thirty-three Muslim members, and there were only sixteen other non-Congress, non–Muslim League representatives. The total scheduled-caste representation was thirty-three, but only one member was elected from outside the Congress (Austin 1966, chap. 1).

Granville Austin has argued that despite the overwhelming dominance of the Congress at the constituent assembly the body was representative of the social and religious diversity of the country because of "the unwritten and unquestioned belief that the Congress should be both social and ideologically diverse and of a deliberate policy that representatives of various minority communities and viewpoints should be present in the

Assembly" (1966, 10). He cites party directives and policy to support his contention that "the minority communities were fully represented in the Constituent Assembly, usually by members of their own choosing" (13). But this argument, while accurate in one sense—there was certainly some diversity in the religious and cultural backgrounds of the representatives— misses a more important point. In a supremely political setting, the overwhelming majority of participants belonged to the same party.

Some of this homogeneity was mitigated by the fact that the Congress, as Austin points out by quoting Nehru, "has within its fold many groups, widely differing in their viewpoint and ideologies" (1966, 15). Nonetheless, it could not reasonably be expected to include within its fold enough opponents of its core positions to make passage of its platform and programs uncertain. So it incorporated some diversity of opinions and groups, but not too much. One result of this process was that minority positions that were not within the diverse Congress tent were excluded. Minorities were represented, but they were generally pro-Congress minorities; anti-Congress positions held by minorities could only be represented through other parties, but the latter numbers for these latter groups were tiny.

Adding to Congress's control and further limiting any concrete effects of diversity was the dominance of what Austin calls the "Oligarchy." This group was made up of the most influential leaders within the Congress, including Nehru, Sardar Vallabhai Patel, Maulana Azad, Rajendra Prasad, and others for a total of about twenty. These leaders ranged along a spectrum, from the conservative Patel to the socialist Nehru, but they shared common positions on many important political issues. In the same way that they controlled the Congress, they controlled the constituent assembly: "Either Nehru, Patel, or Prasad chaired each of these [major] committees, and in many cases the other two or Azad were also present" (Austin 1966, 18). By controlling the committees, they were able to control the shape of reports, recommendations, and amendments that came to the floor of the assembly.[14]

It is not surprising, therefore, that most issues of political representation were decided in ways that were compatible with Congress preferences, and that the discussions of alternatives had a pro forma quality to them. The Minorities Subcommittee of the Advisory Committee, chaired by Patel, overwhelmingly rejected separate electorates for all groups but recommended that joint electorates with reserved seats be provided for some groups (*Constituent Assembly Debates [CAD]* 8:313–15). The Advisory Committee concurred and sent the subcommittee's report to the full assembly for debate. In his opening remarks, Patel noted that there had been "a considerable change in the attitude of the minorities themselves . . . the vast majority of the minority communities have themselves realised after great reflection the evil effects in the past of such reservation on the minorities themselves, and the reservations should be dropped" (*CAD* 8:270), with one exception: scheduled castes. The next day Nehru, whose opposition to reservations was of long standing, added his reluctant support to the extension of the policies for scheduled castes only, but on economic rather than religious or caste grounds.

> Frankly I would like this proposal to go further and put an end to such reservations as there still remain. But again, speaking frankly, I realise that in the present state of affairs in India that would not be a desirable thing to do, that is to say, in regard to the Scheduled Castes. I try to look upon the problem not in the sense of a religious minority, but rather in the sense of helping backward groups in the country. I do not look at it from the religious point of view or the caste point of view, but from the point of view that a backward group ought to be helped and I am glad that this reservation also will be limited to ten years. (*CAD* 8:331)

Despite Patel's presentation of the abolition of separate electorates and reservations for Muslims as a consensual decision, there was vocal opposition on the floor. One representative reminded the assembly, "The Muslim League, which still is the representative organisation of the Muslim community, has more than once within this year not only expressed a definite view in favour of reservation of seats, but has also urged the retention of separate electorates" (*CAD* 8:277). Another demanded, "if it is said that many members have said that they do not want it, let us take the majority view of the Muslim members present here. If the majority of the members say that they do not want it, I will be the first person to bow to the opinion of the majority" (*CAD* 8:305). But these dissenting voices were drowned out by supporters of the Congress position, and their claims to representativeness were undermined by Congress-allied Muslims, who spoke out against reservations: "Therefore I am strongly of opinion that there should be no reservation of seats for anyone and I, as a Muslim, speak for the Muslims. There should be no reservation of seats for the Muslim community [Hear, hear]" (*CAD* 8:333).

The constituent assembly's decision to abolish separate electorates completely is consistent with the Congress's preferences, but the decision to continue the policy of reserved seats for scheduled castes requires explanation. The Congress was the Raj's most implacable and ultimately most successful opponent, and reservations were a direct consequence of separate electorates, which the Indian National Congress had fought bitterly since the 1920s. Most untouchables were strong supporters of the Congress despite Ambedkar's efforts to wean them away. They would probably have remained in the fold even if reservations had been scrapped, and certainly there were numerous political grounds to justify such an action. So why did the Congress retain preferences and even provide in the constitution for their expansion to other groups and other arenas?

The answer to this apparent paradox lies in the structure of incentives faced by the Congress and the interests of its political coalition. The Congress had two goals in this area: it wanted to establish a system of political representation in which all groups voted in a single electorate, and it wanted to include as many groups as possible in its electoral coalition. Separate electorates were out of the question, and they were far from necessary to appeal to Muslims, since most of the Muslim League had gone to Pakistan. Moreover, the Congress had never agreed to such a system; Muslims had received them from the British. Untouchables, however had been granted reserved seats by the Congress, and by Gandhi's actions, no less, so they were a Congress-approved policy. If they were abolished, the Congress might be more vulnerable to Ambedkar's hitherto ineffective accusation that the Congress, especially after Gandhi's death, did not represent the true interests of untouchables.

This risk was seemed especially unnecessary to run given that reservation policies were not that unpopular with caste Hindus at the time. Gandhi's "Harijan Uplift" campaign had neither abolished untouchability nor made untouchables universally accepted, but it had increased caste Hindu awareness of the oppression they faced, and it made reservation policies less problematic than they might have been. In addition, there were few practical negative aspects for caste Hindus in reservation policies. Their own share of representation had not diminished, untouchables were still so badly off and relatively unaware politically, so they were not seen as a threat to caste Hindu power even with preferential treatment. Therefore, the nontargeted part of the Congress's coalition was at worst indifferent to reservations, while untouchables perceived them as important. It made strategic sense for them to be continued in independent India.

Reservation Policy Development in Independent India

With the enshrinement of untouchable reservations in the constitution, independent India began with two distinct types of reservation policy. At the national level were reservations in political representation for untouchables, or scheduled castes, while at the state level there continued to be preferences in place for low castes in Mysore and Madras. During the colonial period, the Congress had been in continual competition with the

British government for control of the political agenda. After partition and independence, the Congress appeared to be the only political power in India. But its ability to make policy was almost immediately challenged by an institution of its own creation.

Parliament and the Supreme Court

During the constituent assembly debates, representatives had agreed that they wanted a strong Supreme Court that would protect the constitution, and they accordingly provided it with the explicit power of judicial review. But in two early critical cases, and to the great consternation of Congress leaders, it ruled that while the government was empowered to provide benefits for backward *classes,* caste could not be used as a substitute. In *State of Madras v. Champakam Dorairajan* (S.C.R. 226 [1951]), a student challenged the reservation policy implemented by the state of Madras after the constitution came into effect. The state had decreed that places in medical colleges be distributed according to castes and classes; for example, for every fourteen seats, six should go to non-Brahmin Hindus, two to "backward" Hindus, two to Brahmins, and so on (Galanter 1984, 365). A Brahmin student who exceeded the quota but would have been admitted if only merit requirements were being used sued on the grounds that the policy violated article 29(2) of the constitution:

> No citizen shall be denied admission into any educational institution maintained by the State or receiving aid out of State funds on grounds only of religion, race, caste, language or any of them.

The court ruled in favor of the student, finding that her denial was solely on the basis of her caste. In its opinion, it held that "the right to get admission into any educational institution of the kind [covered by article 29(2)] is a right which an individual citizen has as a citizen and not as a member of any community or class of citizens" (S.C.R. 226).

The Indian National Congress had championed the rights of individuals during the independence period, but it was not pleased by the restrictions on state action that the Supreme Court clearly believed that these rights entailed. Within two months of the decision, the Congress-controlled Parliament voted overwhelmingly to amend article 15 to include a new section,[15] 15(4), which provided that

> Nothing in Article 15 or Article 29(2) . . . shall prevent the State from making any special provision for the advancement of any socially and

educationally backward classes of citizens or for the Scheduled Castes or Scheduled Tribes. (*Constitution of India* 1985)

Modeling the *Champakam* Debate

If we model this series of events, we can see more precisely the role that the court could play in the policy process. The Indian Supreme Court's powers are in practice less sweeping than those of its U.S. counterpart, even though its enumerated powers are greater (Baxi 1980). For the Indian Supreme Court, judicial review is an explicitly granted responsibility, not one it had to carve out. But while the court can invalidate parliamentary acts, it cannot easily prevent Parliament from rewriting the constitution to bring it into accord with previously invalidated legislation. The only constraint on Parliament is that if it changes the constitution too much, it will undermine the document's legitimacy, which may in the long run be detrimental to party or parliamentary interests. In this case, however, the court's interpretation clearly ran afoul of the Congress party's and Parliament's intention to implement expanded reservation policies. Figure 6.2 uses a single-dimensional model to show the policy outcome of the debate.

The constituent assembly (CA), which had been dominated by the Congress party, had set the status quo, Q, where it wanted. The Supreme Court (SC) then found Q unconstitutional and established a new status quo, Q*, at its ideal point. Parliament (P), which was controlled not only by the same party, but by the same individuals in that party, then amended the constitution to make Q explicitly constitutional, which removed the basis for the Supreme Court's objection and restored the original status quo. The Supreme Court had played its most powerful card, declaring a policy unconstitutional. But Parliament trumped this card with a constitutional amendment, so the court was then forced to accept the constitutional amendment and interpret policies on these new terms.

Balaji and the Limits to Reservation Policy

But while the amendment cleared the way for the state and central governments to extend reservation policy as they saw fit, politicians were still somewhat constrained by the court's interpretation of the constitution. The latter's determination to balance the rights of individuals against those of groups surfaced again in the 1960s, when the state of Mysore's reservation policies came under scrutiny.

As discussed earlier, the princely state of Mysore, after urging from non-Brahmins in the early twentieth century, had developed and imple-

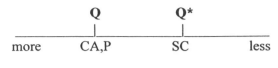

Fig. 6.2

mented preferences for non-Brahmins (including untouchables) in education, employment, and government service. In 1947 these policies had been in effect for twenty-five years, and the representation of non-Brahmin groups in the civil services had increased from 39 percent of gazetted and 30 percent of nongazetted posts to 51 and 62 percent respectively.[16] Similarly in education, scholarships and other assistance programs helped middle and lower castes improve their representation in primary, secondary, and higher education (Chandrasekhar 1985). Dominant castes, notably Lingayats and Vokkaligas, benefited more than lower status and less politically powerful groups, but many more groups were represented than would have been without preferences. Indeed, it might be argued that a stronger bias existed in favor of urban over rural residents rather than of particular caste groups, since most schools and universities were concentrated in the major cities and largest towns (Manor 1977).

By the time India gained independence in 1947, Mysore's preference policies had become well entrenched, and non-Brahmin groups had had ample opportunity to appreciate their benefits. The political legitimacy of the policies was unquestioned, and the benefits they provided were great enough to ensure a strongly supportive constituency. Preferential benefits were available to 96 percent of the population (Dushkin 1974), and the standard of backwardness continued to be English literacy. In the 1950s and 1960s, the issue facing Mysore was not the introduction and development of preference policies, as it was in so much of India, but the reconciliation of existing policies with the rights and liberties codified in the new Indian constitution. Mysore was in the unusual situation of having to *decrease* its benefits for designated backward classes in order to conform with constitutional mandates. This proved to be extraordinarily difficult to achieve because of the political expectations created by the existing system of preferences.

The debate between the Mysore government and the courts began with the States Reorganization Act of 1956. Under the terms of this act, Mysore, as the newly renamed state of Karnataka, incorporated districts from five other previous provinces and princely states, with Mysore as its major component, and each had its own lists of backward communities and preferential benefits. The Karnataka government's attempt to extend princely Mysore's criteria for backwardness to the population in the newly incorporated areas was struck down twice, first by the Mysore High Court in 1958 and then by the Supreme Court in 1959. In January 1960, the government appointed a Backward Classes Commission, under the chairmanship of Nagana Gowda, to establish an acceptable list of eligible groups. In 1961, the government order based on the commission's report was struck down by the Supreme Court in the landmark *Balaji v. Mysore* case. The court cited Mysore's use of caste as the sole determinant of backwardness and the reservation of more than 50 percent as reasons for its decision (Galanter 1984).

The court's *Balaji* decision upset the foundation on which the long-established south Indian coalition on reservation policy rested. Before independence the issue of individual versus group rights was raised on occasion, but individual rights had not yet been codified in a constitution. Congress party leaders could not easily change the criteria for eligibility to caste alone, especially since the constitution had abolished it. And if the party passed amendments explicitly to allow greater than 50 percent reservations, then they were subject to the charge by nontargeted groups that too many merit positions were being sacrificed. At the same time, however, a reduction in the percentage of seats reserved in education and employment to the 50 percent level mandated in *Balaji* would lead to a political nightmare in south India.

The political leadership of the Congress-controlled government arrived at a compromise policy that on its face complied with *Balaji* while maintaining the political status quo. A new test for backwardness was adopted, one that used income and occupation as eligibility criteria rather than caste. Under this system, parents' income was limited to Rs. 1,200 per year and had to be in a specified range of occupations. While this new standard placated many of the Brahmin litigators, "it proved itself eminently manipulable by those who had the effective power in society" (Dushkin 1974), as Brahmins, Lingayats, and Vokkaligas monopolized the reserved positions and benefits through the use of false income certificates (Galanter 1984).

Modeling the *Balaji* Debate

If we model this series of events, we see that the government was able to achieve an accord that slightly restricted the policies but still accomplished their political goals (their substantive policy goals were another matter). The bureaucracy implemented a program at point Q that the Supreme Court found unconstitutional, and the court established a new status quo at Q*. The state government (P) then passed legislation changing the eligibility criteria (Q#), which on its face accepted much of the new status quo. Figure 6.3 shows the outcome.

The model suggests that the Supreme Court was able to draw the new policy closer to its ideal point by threatening an even more stringent one. What the model is unable to show is that the new status quo was brought about by a policy that reduced the number of recipients who were most needful. Instituting an income ceiling for eligibility allowed the government to reduce the percentage without alienating the dominant castes, because false income certificates were easy to obtain.[17] The actual policy outcome was indeed closer to Q* than to Q, since the practical effect of this policy was to make nondominant low castes compete with dominant castes, usually unsuccessfully. But while the general result was the exclusion of the presumably more deserving from taking advantage of reservation policies, there were few negative political repercussions, since the disadvantaged lower castes had little political influence of their own.

The model does, however, illustrate that the party and the state of Karnataka went along with the Supreme Court because it was in their interests to do so, not because the Supreme Court was able to exert power over them. For reasons quite apart from the court, the Congress could not afford politically to pass a new amendment to overturn the court's *Balaji* decision, as they had done in the *Champakam* case, because the *Balaji* policy was a peculiarly south Indian solution. It would not have been acceptable to north Indian middle and upper castes, who were much more numerous, organized, and politically powerful than their south Indian counterparts. Therefore, the Congress accepted the court's decision and found a way to work around it. Thus, the court was able to impose its view of the constitution in this case, but its success was due to the political incentives faced by the Congress party rather than the court's institutional power.

Expanding Reservations at the Center

Efforts to facilitate or curtail the expansion of reservations to other arenas and groups were not limited to the judicial arena. The divergence between north and south India's policies regarding the scope and extent or reservations led to efforts to expand reservations to OBCs throughout India soon after independence. The president of India, at the request of Parliament, appointed a special commission, chaired by retired judge Kaka Kalelkar and packed with other respected jurists and academics, to consider the issue. The main terms of references given the commission were to determine which groups could be classified as backward, determine what steps

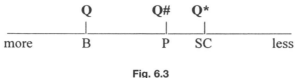

Fig. 6.3

should be taken to improve their conditions, and present their recommendations to the president (Government of India 1955).

The commission immediately discovered how difficult their directives would be to carry out when its members realized that there was no straightforward way to gather statistics on caste. When caste was abolished in the constitution, it was also abolished as a category in the census. Sardar Vallabhai Patel put the reasons for this decision succinctly.

> Formerly their used to be elaborate caste tables which were required in India partly to satisfy the theory that it was a caste-ridden country, and partly to meet the needs of administrative measures dependent upon caste division. In the forthcoming Census this will no longer be a prominent feature. (Government of India 1981, 1:9–10)

Census data on scheduled castes and tribes, Anglo-Indians, and religious groups continued to be collected, but general caste information became taboo. The commission resorted to old census data and "the general impressions of Government offices, leaders of public opinion and social workers" (Government of India 1981, 1:8). But there was considerable debate over who could be considered backward. In a poor country with severe stratification, there were few groups who did not feel they had been taken advantage of by rich high-caste groups, including poor high-caste groups, and any division was guaranteed to create discontent among the nontargeted. Inclusive efforts came up with OBC percentages of up to 70 percent, while exclusive measures created considerable unhappiness among politically active groups. In the south, with its absence of middle castes, everyone who was not Brahmin was considered an OBC, which meant over 90 percent of the population. In the north and west, where castes were more evenly distributed, middle castes and economically disadvantaged upper-middle castes in particular felt themselves squeezed between potentially newly privileged OBCs and traditionally powerful high castes.

The commission considered its terms of reference to indicate that caste was the primary criterion of eligibility (Government of India 1955).

It included other criteria, such as lack of educational advancement, inadequate or no representation in government service, and low representation in trade, commerce, and industry. But the main unit being analyzed was the caste group, not the individual, region, or state. This strategy, while understandable, was bound to cause controversy because the fit between caste hierarchy and economic standing was less strong than it was for scheduled castes and scheduled tribes and therefore more open to criticism.

The commission delivered its recommendations in a report to the president in 1955, but their potential influence was undermined by the multiple dissents from commission members that comprised the third volume of the report. These signs of internal conflict were damaging, but the final blow was probably struck when Chairman Kalelkar repudiated the commission's final report and cited its reliance on caste as a measure of backwardness as a primary reason (Galanter 1984).

The report was discussed in Parliament, but there was little agreement over its findings and even less over its recommendations. The Congress party, whose coalition was extremely diverse, stood much to lose from a debate over which groups should be accorded OBC status, and Nehru's opposition to caste as a criterion for anything was well known. The parliamentary debate was relatively perfunctory and the issue was tabled (Galanter 1984).

Despite (or perhaps because of) the lack of support it received, the Kalelkar Commission was the sole bureaucratic or parliamentary attempt to consider the issue of reservations for backward classes at the national level for over two decades. Only when Congress dominance had been shattered by the breakup of Nehru-era coalition and the first non-Congress party occupied the central government did OBC reservations once again become the object of a commission's investigations.

Conclusion

Reservation policy in India emerged as a by-product of British colonial rule, after separate electorates were given by the British to minorities who asked for them. This policy allowed the Raj to bargain with social groups separately and created a disincentive for diverse interests to band together in challenging colonial rule. The Indian National Congress was steadfastly opposed to separate electorates from its inception and maintained this position through partition and independence, but it was unable to keep minorities from bargaining with the British if they could not get their first preferences in negotiation with the Congress.

In this climate, reservations were a compromise that the Congress reached with untouchables to stave off separate electorates. The Congress's acceptance of the principle and practice of reserved seats in the Poona Pact occurred because the party leadership felt that they needed to keep untouchables within their political coalition if they were to be persuasive in their argument that they were the sole party that represented all Indians. But since untouchables could obtain separate electorates by demanding them from the British, the Congress had to provide them with a reason to settle for reserved seats. Gandhi's popularity, and his apparent willingness to sacrifice his life in this effort, helped the Congress to achieve its goal. But in gaining the untouchable community as allies, it was forced to legitimate reserved seats as a policy.

The Poona Pact's outcome resonated during the constituent assembly debates, where reserved seats for untouchables were the only form of preferential representation to survive the colonial period. Nehru was as opposed to them as ever, but other Congress leaders, such as Sardar Vallabhai Patel, were willing to retain them in order to ensure that untouchables stayed loyal to the Congress. Gandhi's assassination had removed the Congress leader most identified with the abolition of untouchable oppression, and while Ambedkar's attempts to form a political party to compete with the Congress had been unsuccessful, the abolition of reservations might provide the impetus his fledgling party needed to convert untouchables to his cause. And since reservations for untouchables did not engender much animosity within the rest of the Congress coalition, the advantages of retaining them outweighed the disadvantages at the time.

The Supreme Court challenges to reservation policy foreshadowed the conflicts that were to arise beginning in the 1970s, when the policy was extended to OBCs, but in the 1950s and 1960s the Congress's dominance of the political landscape, especially through the parliamentary institutional structure that made it difficult for other governmental actors to oppose it, allowed reservation policies to expand and become entrenched as policy options.

The models and the empirical evidence emphasize the effect of institutional configurations on the policy process. In the United States, the separation and balance of power between different branches of government constrains the ability of each actor to impose policy preferences on the others. The general result is to pull policies toward the status quo. In India, by contrast, in all the periods considered there are actors who have the institutional ability to act unilaterally. During the colonial period, quite obviously the British could introduce policies with which indigenous elites were then forced to work. But even after the end of colonial rule, the practical ability of the Congress to dominate as the primary political party combined with the concentration of power in a parliamentary system created a political arena in which policies supported by the Congress were subject to very little institutional constraint.

The Supreme Court, as the official guardian of the Indian constitution, was given the explicit power of judicial review of parliamentary legislation. But while this power appears to give it the capacity to challenge Parliament if it considers a law unconstitutional, the analysis above reveals that the likelihood of this challenge being successful is dependent on Parliament's capacity to amend the constitution. Since the amendment procedure is relatively simple, especially if the governing party has a solid majority, the court is more constrained in its capacity to sustain its preferences over those of Parliament than its enumerated powers would suggest.

However, the fact that Parliament has considerable undivided power does not mean that there are no conflicts, and that interest groups cannot be represented. The locus of the struggle for power has not disappeared, but it has moved. As the dominant force in a one-party democracy, the Congress was made up of diverse social groups, and conflicts were negotiated and managed within the party organization. By the time policies were introduced in Parliament they had been largely worked out. But the reason the Congress was able to dominate Indian politics for decades was twofold: the strength of its organization and the stature of its leaders, particularly Gandhi and Nehru. After Nehru died, followed shortly by his successor, there was no consensus over who should lead the Congress. The power struggles that followed had ramifications for the way power was distributed across institutions, and reservation policies were transformed into a major tool to increase the power of individuals and parties.

CHAPTER 7

Reservation Policies under Party Competition

As long as Nehru was alive, his popular appeal and political power transcended factional conflicts within the Congress party and ensured that resolutions would be found to conflicts that had the potential to be damaging. After his death, however, the diversity within the Congress, which had been one of its greatest assets, began to present grave problems. The party leadership was well aware that after Nehru there would be a vacuum at the top; not only was he by far the most powerful Congress leader, there was no other individual within range of him. Nevertheless, the party itself still maintained a formidable organization and was seen by the majority of the Indian public as the primary, if not the only, legitimate party to govern the nation. In 1964 the party's elite agreed on a successor to Nehru: Lal Bahadur Sastri, a longtime Congress leader who was respected and esteemed by both party members and the Indian public.

Sastri's respect and popularity helped to dampen conflicts over political transitions in the post-Nehru era, both within and outside the Congress. Had his tenure as prime minister been longer, the various factions that were poised to struggle for power might have been able to work out their differences as they always had, within the party and therefore outside both the electoral process and the public limelight. But Sastri died suddenly and surprisingly after negotiating an importance peace agreement with Pakistan in 1966, in Tashkent in the Soviet Union. So two years after Nehru's death Congress party leaders were once again forced to choose a successor, and this time there was no easy consensus choice.

The leadership offered the prime minister's post to Nehru's daughter, Indira Gandhi, believing that her family heritage would make her a favorite with the Indian public and her political inexperience would make her dependent on their expertise. They were correct in their first supposition, but spectacularly wrong in the second. Gandhi had little formal political experience, but she had grown up in an intense political environment, she was both intelligent and strong willed, and she learned quickly. It was not long before she was chafing against the role in which she had been cast, and by the late 1960s the disagreements between the old guard and those who backed Gandhi were becoming impossible to resolve. Eventually the Congress party split, with the two main contenders being the Congress-O (for organization), which retained the traditional, more conservative leadership, and the Congress-I, which comprised Indira Gandhi and her emerging political coalition.

The ensuing national and state elections confirmed the continuation of the Nehru family dynasty and the disintegration of the Nehru-led Congress. Indira Gandhi swept to power as prime minister in her own right on the strength of her father's name and her new electoral base, the latter symbolized in her election slogan, "Garibi hatao" (abolish poverty). When the party split, much of the high-caste elite base remained with Congress-O. Gandhi explicitly set out to court the other end of the party's electoral spectrum, the scheduled castes, minorities, and especially the political group that had begun to be mobilized in the 1960s, the OBCs.

The breakup of the Congress party and the emergence of a new political coalition led by Indira Gandhi had ramifications for many aspects of Indian politics and society, among which were reservation policies. As discussed in the previous chapter, Nehru's Congress party was able to take advantage of the existence of reservations without encountering any serious liabilities. In the south, where reservations were overwhelmingly popular, the party supported extensive reservations for scheduled castes and OBCs that exceeded the Supreme Court's constitutional limits. In the north and west, where reservations were disliked by elite and middle castes, the party refrained from introducing reservations for groups beyond scheduled castes and tribes. And at the national level, the party tabled OBC reservations when it became clear that there were both practical and political difficulties involved in their formulation and implementation.

In the new era of party competition and the rise of Indira Gandhi's Congress-I party, however, these accommodations could no longer be sustained. Her victory had been achieved in part through the mobilization of low castes and minorities directly, not through traditional elite channels, and her campaign rhetoric had stressed equality and the introduction of policies that improved conditions for the poor and disadvantaged. Reservation policies were a high-profile, expected component of this program. But until now their development had been undertaken in ways that would not alienate traditional elite and middle castes. From the 1970s on, however, the increasing political awareness of low castes and politicians who needed to court their votes made reservations both more important and politically more volatile. It is difficult to state categorically whether the expansion of reservation policies was generated from a grassroots movement or by the top-down mobilization of new groups; most probably it was a combination of these two factors. The rise of competition between Congress factions created incentives for them to mobilize new electoral banks, but these efforts would have been much less successful if democratic politics had not made these group more politically aware over the course of the preceding decades.

I continue the analysis in this chapter using the same method of embedding a rational-choice theoretical framework within a detailed historical context. In the post-Nehru era, the institutional structure remained the same, but the structure of incentives changed as parties began to compete with each other for votes. In this changed environment debates over policies took place less often between branches of government than they did within a ruling party's electoral coalition. Therefore, the models in this chapter depict the electoral groups ("vote banks" in Indian political parlance) captured by specific policies. Since these policies have high electoral salience, they correlate quite highly with expected votes in elections.

When the Congress was the dominant party and elites mobilized less advantaged groups through clientelist ties, there was no incentive to offer reservations to OBCs in nonsouthern states, since high-castes who disliked reservation policy could still deliver their votes. But once politicians and parties began to be competitive, there were incentives to appeal to OBCs directly. Moreover, they had become more politically aware in the decades since independence, so their votes could not be taken for granted. Reservation policies were a way for politicians to show their commitment to these increasingly important electoral groups.

In order to show the variety of ways in which reservation policies played a role in the political process, I have selected three exemplary cases. The cases are substantively different, but the structure of incentives offered the actors is similar. In each context, politicians needed to develop strategies to solidify coalitions, and OBCs constituted a large and fluid vote bank. The southern state of Karnataka illustrates how reservation policy changed after the 1960s in southern states. The south was the least problematic area in India for reservations, but even in the south the modification of reservations to incorporate the truly disadvantaged among the non-Brahmin castes has created difficulties for whichever party is in power. The western state of Gujarat illustrates the problems that accompanied the introduction of OBC reservations outside south India and the incentives and constraints faced by politicians. The northern and western states have been the arenas of severe and enduring conflict over reservation policies, but their political importance in mobilizing emerging backward-caste groups makes it impossible for any party to forswear them completely. And finally, the debate at the national level demonstrates how the incorporation of new political groups and the rise of authentic party competition has led central governments finally to introduce reservations for centrally controlled employment and education, despite the conflict these initiatives have engendered.

Karnataka

The collapse of the unified Congress party and the struggle for power that ensued was decisively won by Indira Gandhi in Karnataka. In 1971 her Congress-I party swept to power on the slogan "abolish poverty," and one of her allies, Devraj Urs, was elected chief minister of the state. In common with other states, the Congress-I coalition in Karnataka was made up of newly mobilized lower and middle castes, untouchables, and Muslim minorities. Urs had to work with the dominant non-Brahmin elites, the Lingayats and the Vokkaligas, but he set out to incorporate the core of his coalition into politics and patronage as well. This included, in addition to nondominant lower castes, sections of the dominant castes who were poorer and consequently less economically and politically powerful than their elite-caste brethren.

As a self-styled "pragmatic populist" (Manor 1977), Urs fused caste and class issues. He proclaimed an explicit commitment to the poor, and he expanded resources and opportunities to previously excluded groups. But he also handled high castes shrewdly, knowing that an alliance between the dominant castes against him could threaten his power. To forestall this possibility Urs extended benefits to poorer Vokkaligas, attempting to drive a wedge through the Vokkaliga community and between disadvantaged Vokkaligas and Lingayats in general. In this way Urs used both class and caste distinctions to create his political base. One of the key policies in his arsenal was Karnataka's reservation policy, which was one of the most important in terms of symbolism, although somewhat less so in substance.

Urs declared the existing reservation policy to be unjust and appointed a new Backward Classes Commission to be chaired by L. G. Havanur. The chief minister sought a new standard of backwardness that would be more beneficial to those castes that had been harmed by the 1963 government order.[1] The 1975 Havanur Commission report recommended reservations for backward classes totaling 32 percent, with the standard of backwardness being determined by a combination of factors, including level of education, caste, and economic status. In addition to the backward classes and communities, a reservation of 5 percent was set aside for a "special group" whose eligibility was determined by an income and occupation formula (Government of Karnataka 1975). Of the two dominant non-Brahmin castes, Lingayats and Vokkaligas, the latter were included and the former excluded.

In 1975 the government accepted the majority of the commission's recommendations, but it increased the total backward classes and communities reservation to 50 percent, part of which was due to an increase in the "special group" category from 5 to 15 percent.[2] This special category had many of the same requirements for eligibility as the 1963 preference policy and was widely seen as a concession to the elite castes, most importantly the Lingayats, who were excluded from the general schedules of castes.[3] Including the constitutionally mandated reservations for scheduled castes and scheduled tribes, this brought the total number of reservations to 68 percent.

Lingayats refused to be placated by the special category and almost immediately challenged in the courts the government order providing for these reservations.[4] The policy was very likely to be invalidated by the Supreme Court, because it clearly exceeded the 50 percent ceiling that the court had established in *Balaji* and reinforced in later decisions. The government staved off this likely outcome by informing the Supreme Court that it would appoint a new Backward Classes Commission to develop a more satisfactory system, and in 1983 a new commission was constituted under the chairmanship of T. Venkataswamy.

Modeling the Debate over the Havanur Report

When we model these events, it becomes clear how shifts in the electoral coalition led to a shift in reservation policy. Urs had risked alienating the Lingayats by removing them from the targeted groups, but he expected to more than make up for this loss through the addition of hitherto unmobilized poor backward castes. However, he neglected to take into account the pivotal role of the Supreme Court. Figure 7.1 depicts the policy outcomes that result from specific coalitions. The graph is two-dimensional because reservations in Karnataka politics target both OBCs and dominant castes. The y-axis shows dominant-caste groups and the x-axis shows OBC groups.

The Urs coalition abandoned Lingayats to include a larger group of poor and backward castes. This policy increased the number of voters targeted, but it also moved well beyond the Supreme Court's policy space, and by filing suit the Lingayats gave the court the opportunity to change the policy to fit their preferences. The government, anticipating that the court's actions might be worse than they could politically tolerate, preempted a decision by appointing a new commission.

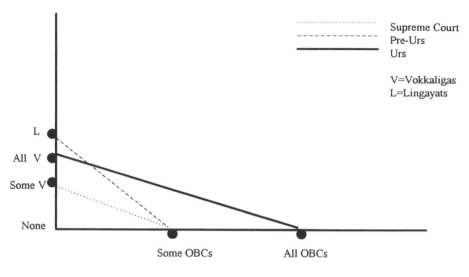

Fig. 7.1

The Venkataswamy Solution

In 1986 the Venkataswamy Commission delivered its report. This report took into consideration many of the same factors as the Havanur Commission over ten years before, but it encompassed more of the population and imposed economic ceilings on the caste groups.[5] Using stricter criteria, the commission reduced the number of eligible groups from 69 to 35, abolished the "special group" category, and instituted a Rs. 15,000 ceiling on all recipients (Government of Karnataka 1986a). The percentage of reserved seats for backward groups was reduced from 50 percent to 27 percent, bringing the total with scheduled castes and scheduled tribes to 45 percent, well under the Supreme Court recommendation of 50 percent. Among the groups excluded from the new lists were the Vokkaligas, who now joined the Lingayats in being defined as "forward."

The commission's report was delivered to a new government. Urs, who had split from Indira Gandhi in 1979 and been replaced by the spectacularly incompetent Congress hack Gundu Rao, had died in 1983. The Gundu Rao regime, after demonstrating its complete inability to govern the state, had been defeated by the Janata party in the 1983 state elections. Janata, whose core coalition consisted of the old elites, including the Lingayats and the remnants of the 1960s rival to Congress-I, Congress-O, had formed an alliance with Urs's party, the Kranti Ranga in 1983, and they formed the first non-Congress government in the state since independence.[6]

The Janata government's political coalition included more elite groups than had Congress-I under Urs, but because of its alliance with the old Urs political base, it also had to take into account the interests of lower and non-dominant castes and classes.[7] This was a difficult coalition to manage at best, but in the specific arena of reservation policies the problems were particularly acute, as events soon confirmed. Public reaction to the commission's report was swift and vehement. Leaders from the excluded castes denounced it, and their supporters took issue with the quality of the data gathered and the scientific validity of the measures used to determine backwardness.[8] One Vokkaliga leader went on a hunger strike, and several other leaders threatened to do so. Excluded-caste groups organized to protest the report, and as the agitations commenced, several of the chief minister's party members threatened to leave his legislative coalition.[9]

In the face of this opposition, the chief minister, Ramakrishna Hegde, convened a meeting of his cabinet to determine what course of action to pursue. His government was composed of a fragile coalition of Brahmins, Lingayats, Vokkaligas, and lower castes, with Lingayats and Vokkaligas representing the largest bloc and the Venkataswamy Commission's report recommended reducing or eliminating reservations for his core constituency.[10] It came as no surprise to observers when, three weeks after the commission's report was submitted and made public, the chief minister announced that the government "cannot accept the Venkataswamy Commission report in its present form" and would modify it to ensure no injustice was done to any caste group (Government of Karnataka 1986b).

Hegde ordered that a new commission be appointed and, until that commission's report was received, an interim solution be implemented. This interim plan included both Lingayats and Vokkaligas, as well as 221 other castes and communities. With 46 percent reservations for backward classes, 18 percent for scheduled castes and scheduled tribes, and 28 percent for Lingayats and Vokkaligas, the total percentage of the population eligible for reservations was increased to 92 percent. The total percentage of reserved seats in education and employment was returned to 68 percent.[11]

Modeling the Debate over the Venkataswamy Report

Figure 7.2 models these events. Hegde's coalition was more dependent on Lingayats and Vokkaligas than Urs's Congress party had been, and the Venkataswamy Commission recommendations were far to the left of his coalition's ideal policy. But at the same time, the poor and backward classes that had been mobilized by Urs had become too politically aware

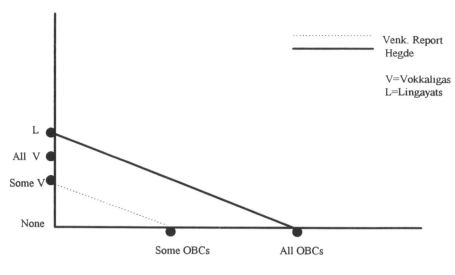

Fig. 7.2

to be ignored as they had been in the pre-Urs days. The only answer was to incorporate the Lingayats while still retaining the truly disadvantaged groups, which meant that almost every Karnatakan was part of the eligible population.

This policy solution, while politically necessary, was clearly outside the acceptable bounds set by the Supreme Court, and the government preempted the inevitable suit and unfavorable court opinion by appointing yet another commission.

The Chinappa Reddy Commission

The new commission, headed by the respected justice Chinappa Reddy, delivered its report in late 1992. Its recommendations vindicated the Venkataswamy Commission, and especially its chairman, a quiet career civil servant whose integrity was as unquestioned as his lack of political savvy, and who had been excoriated in the press, the government, and political circles generally when the report was being debated. The Reddy commission report upheld the Venkataswamy recommendation that privileged groups be excluded from reservation policy benefits, but the method of doing so was much less politically volatile. The report argued that administrative safeguards could be set in place so that elite members of targeted social (and especially caste) groups could not be the beneficiaries.

A combination of social and economic factors should be taken into account so that, for example, the children of professionals, or current high-level civil servants, or landowners, could not be beneficiaries. In this way the "creamy layer" of the disadvantaged groups, who had benefited so greatly from reservations in the preceding decades, would no longer monopolize reserved seats to the disadvantage of their more deserving community members.

The Chinappa Reddy solution implicitly acknowledged the political problems inherent in designing a reservation policy that excluded any part of the government's electoral coalition. By the time the commission had finished its work, the Janata government had been replaced by a Congress government, but both relied on similar political configurations: a combination of traditional dominant and ruling castes and the more newly mobilized backward castes. This combination is inherently unstable when it comes to reservation policies, because dominant groups demand to be included as they always have been, but "the backward castes and other groups cannot be ignored anymore" (Kohli 1990, 97). If both are included, the reservation percentage is certain to exceed the 50 percent ceiling and trigger a Supreme Court intervention. But if the elites are not included, the government's survival is threatened.

Gujarat

If the Karnataka dilemma is that too many groups consider themselves eligible for reservation policies, the state of Gujarat reveals the problems of implementing strong policies in a state with a balance between elite, middle, and low castes. Gujarat is located in the western part of India. The home of Mahatma Gandhi, Gujarat was, along with the United Provinces (renamed Uttar Pradesh at independence), a major base of the Indian National Congress, and during the independence movement was the site of several major protests, such as the salt march and the Bardoli satyagraha. Under Gandhi's influence, the Harijan Uplift movement, with its advocacy of improvement of conditions for untouchables and the abolition of caste restrictions toward them, was a major social issue; the ashram founded by Gandhi to embody nonviolence, service, and tolerance is located just outside Ahmedabad, the original capital city. Politically, Gujarat was the western half of the "Ahmedabad-Allahabad nexus" that had originally given birth to the Indian National Congress (Seal 1971), and its urban and rural elites were strongly represented in the Congress both before and after independence. Sardar Vallabhai Patel, a major Gujarati leader, was one of the most powerful leaders in India until his unexpected death in 1950, and Morarji Desai, another Gujarati who helped to form the Congress-O party after the split in 1967, eventually became prime minister during the Janata government of 1977–79.

Gujarat was formed by the division of Bombay state into Gujarat and Maharashtra during the linguistic reorganization of the states in 1960 (Brass 1971). Historically, although much of what is now Gujarat state was part of the Bombay Presidency, Ahmedabad was relatively neglected by the British and allowed to flourish on its own. As a consequence Gujarati merchants and traders were largely able to continue their thriving businesses and develop new industries as well, and by the late nineteenth century Ahmedabad was a strong commercial center financed primarily by indigenous capital (Gillion 1968). At the same time, fertile lands, progressive agricultural techniques, and enterprises such as cooperative dairy farming created a thriving agricultural economy as well. Thus, economically as well as politically, Gujarat has been one of India's most developed and prosperous states.

In Gujarat, as in much of northern India, Brahmins are more numerous than in Karnataka and the rest of south India, and social and economic power is not concentrated in their hands. Instead, there are several high castes that have political and economic (although not ritual) power in competition with Brahmins (Weiner 1967). They include Banias, who rank just below Brahmins and comprise much of the commercial, urban, and merchant population of Gujarat; Kshatriya Rajputs, who are descended from princely families but occupy a much lower position in the caste hierarchy today; and Patidars (often referred to generally as Patels), who control much of the agricultural and rural areas. Lower castes and untouchables comprise a substantial proportion of the population but are less numerous than their counterparts in Karnataka. These lowest groups are diverse; one untouchable caste, the Vankars, who are weavers by tradition, profited by the textile boom and obtained work in urban areas, while Bhangis and Chamars are among the lowest scheduled-caste groups and have not improved their positions.

Gujarat's traditions of political sophistication, social activism, and emphasis on cooperative development did not manifest themselves through the development of preference policies for socially and educationally backward groups. During the British colonial period, the Bombay Presidency, which was under direct British rule, had established some special benefits in education and government service for depressed classes, but these benefits ceased at independence (Mehta and Patel 1985). Until the 1970s, the only groups covered by preference policies were scheduled castes and tribes, whose benefits were determined by the central government (Galanter 1984). The failure to develop preference policies for backward classes in Gujarat is not surprising, because politics was controlled by Brahmins, Banias, and elite Patidars, who were able to command electoral support through "modern" patronage and "traditional" socioreligious ties (Weiner 1967).

The split within the Congress party after Nehru's and Sastri's deaths may have had the most acute state-level repercussions in Gujarat. Morarji Desai was one of the leaders of Congress-O, and his power base within the state meant that he was able to keep much of the traditional high-caste leadership within his wing of the party, but Indira Gandhi appealed to groups that had been locked out of this relationship. When Congress-I swept to victory in 1971, the old guard was swept out and replaced by a new political generation that was short on organization but long on ambition and attachment to Gandhi. As in Karnataka, reservation policies became a way for the new government to cement its political base and incorporate new groups into its coalition. But unlike Karnataka, in the social context of Gujarat, with its less polarized and more evenly distributed caste hierarchy, the process was fraught with greater conflict, as upwardly mobile middle- and upper-middle-caste groups saw their opportunities to improve their status through education being taken away.

In 1972, a commission chaired by retired Gujarat High Court judge A. N. Baxi was formed to inquire into the conditions of low-caste groups, to report which groups should be considered to be backward, and to determine which benefits currently offered to scheduled castes and tribes should be extended to those groups. The Baxi Commission submitted its report in 1976 (Government of Gujarat 1976). It identified 82 castes as backward and deserving of special benefits. In the area of higher education, the commission did not recommend the extension of scholarships and fee remissions, which were available for scheduled castes and tribes, to the other backward classes. It did, however, recommend reservations in colleges and in residential hostels, as well as the creation of a Board of the Backward Classes to oversee backward-class policies and programs. Reservations of 10 percent were proposed for the most competitive colleges, that is, medical, technical, and engineering (Government of Gujarat 1976).

The government did not immediately take up the commission's recommendations; the imposition of a state of emergency by Indira Gandhi had pushed most other political issues from the stage. In 1978, however, Congress-I was defeated by the coalition Janata party, which accepted and began to implement the recommendations of the Baxi Commission report. The Janata coalition's political base was more conservative than that of Congress-I, both in Gujarat and nationally, but in an attempt to woo some of the Congress-I vote banks, it adopted reservation policy development as a strategy. The policy was challenged in the court almost immediately, but the Supreme Court ruled against the plaintiffs and allowed the new policy to go forward.

With the 7 percent reservations for scheduled castes and the 14 percent reservations for scheduled tribes that were already in place through central government policies, the total percentage of seats reserved came to 31 percent. These provisions were not particularly generous, even by north Indian standards, as both Bihar and the neighboring state of Maharashtra had already implemented higher percentages of reserved seats for backward classes alone at 24 percent and 40 percent respectively (Mehta and Patel 1985). In addition, the relatively slight relaxation of academic requirements made it unlikely that students from disadvantaged groups would be able to utilize their full quotas.

Nevertheless, students from medical colleges in Gujarat immediately promised to protest. The new reservations took effect in June 1980, the beginning of the academic year. In December 1980, severe antireservation agitations broke out. Medical students demanded that the government reduce the number of reservations at the postgraduate level, abolish the policy of carrying forward unoccupied reserved seats to the next year, and abolish the roster system, which rotated reserved seats among different postgraduate medical specializations. Within two weeks, the government conceded the carry-forward system and increased the number of unreserved seats, but this proved to be insufficient. The medical students went on a strike, soon joined by other college students, and then demanded the abolition of all backward-class reserved seats. In retaliation, the government closed down all medical colleges in Gujarat for six months and all schools and colleges in the main city of Ahmedabad.[12]

The decision of members of nontargeted groups to engage in protest is attributable to at least two factors. First, having exhausted legal options and failed to win a favorable opinion from the Supreme Court, the only way opponents of reservation policies could have the policies revoked was to persuade the government. If the government had still been the Janata, this might have been possible, since elite and high-middle castes were the bedrock of the party coalition. But in the state elections of 1980 Congress-I had won, just as Indira Gandhi had once more taken control of Parliament in 1979. Congress-I was significantly less committed to the group most affected by the extension of reservations to OBCs, the poorer of the Patidar, or Patel, caste. Moreover, the new chief minister, Madavsinh Solanki, had no personal or political roots among the Patidars. Thus, the agitations had a twofold purpose: to reverse the reservation policies and to threaten the Solanki government and make it more responsive to Patidar interests.[13]

By the end of January, the antireservation protests had exploded into a much larger agitation encompassing religious and caste conflicts, and over fifty people were killed. As conditions in Gujarat drew national attention, leaders from Delhi pressured their local supporters to defuse the tensions. By the middle of April, the medical students and their supporters ended their protest. The Gujarat government agreed to appoint a new commission to examine the reservations issue, and as the protests ceased, a second commission was appointed under the chairmanship of retired Gujarat High Court judge C. V. Rane.[14] The Rane Commission had two charges: to evaluate whether any castes should be added to the 82 already stipulated as backward under the Baxi report, and to consider whether seats should be reserved in proportion to the backward-class population, rather than the flat 10 percent then in effect.[15] Meanwhile, the policy in effect was a very conservative 10 percent reservation for all OBC groups together.[16]

The Rane Commission submitted its report in October 1983, and it quickly became apparent that the commission had gone beyond the terms of reference of its directives. Instead of reviewing the Baxi Commission's list of backward classes, it stated that "no useful purpose would be served by retaining the list of OBCs prepared by the Baxi Commission" (Government of Gujarat 1983), and went on to prepare a new list using different criteria of backwardness. The most notable divergence from the Baxi method was that the Rane Commission completely rejected caste as a measure of backwardness. Using income and occupation, it arrived at a list of 63 "classes" to be specified backward. With respect to reservations, the commission recommended that the percentages be made as close to the backward-class population proportion as possible. In order to stay within the 50 percent limit, backward-class reservations were to be set at 28 percent, which when combined with the 21 percent allotted to scheduled castes and tribes would bring the total reservation percentage to 49 percent. In addition, the commission recommended that admission to colleges not be contingent on achieving a specific number of marks in the entrance examination, but be evaluated by more flexible (as yet unspecified) criteria.[17]

When the report was delivered, Solanki suppressed it, refusing to make public its recommendations. Finally, in January 1985, with state elections only two months away, he announced that he would accept the recommendations, albeit with his own modifications. The report was still not being disseminated publicly and could not be purchased through the Government of Gujarat Printing Office, where most official documents were easily available. Solanki approved the Rane Commission's recommendation of an increase in reservations from 10 to 28 percent, but he rejected the new list of eligible groups on the grounds that it was beyond the terms of reference of the commission.[18] Therefore, the new Rane percentages would go into effect, but the Baxi list would be retained. The response from opposing groups was immediate and intense.

Opponents of reservation were infuriated by Solanki's actions on two counts. First, they bitterly opposed the 180 percent increase in reserved seats. And second, they were insistent that if there were to be reservations, they should be class rather than caste based, arguing that under the caste-based system castes that were economically disadvantaged but ritually higher, such as the powerful Patels, were denied the opportunity to improve their status through education.[19] Solanki's decree combined the two aspects of reservations these antireservationists most disliked and feared: high percentages and caste as the primary criterion. And, as a final affront, the timing of the announcement made it evident that Solanki had written off the middle- and upper-caste voters in favor of backward classes and scheduled castes.[20]

It is apparent that there was considerable truth to Solanki's opponents' charges. Solanki's electoral support was derived from the KHAM (Kshatriya, Harijan, Adivasi [scheduled tribes], Muslim) coalition put together by Indira Gandhi and the Gujarat Congress-I in the 1970s, but a major provider of vote banks had withdrawn his allegiance to Solanki just before the new reservations were announced.[21] Solanki was taking a risk in increasing reservations almost threefold, given the strength of the opposition and its potential for violence, but if he could not keep his KHAM vote bloc together, he stood little chance of being reelected.

Modeling the Debate over the Rane Report

When we model these events as shown in figure 7.3, it is evident that Solanki adopted much the same tactic as Urs had done a decade earlier in Karnataka, with similar problems. In Gujarat, only OBCs were targeted by reservations, so a single-axis model is used.

The KHAM strategy incorporated more low-caste and minority groups, but it both eschewed and alienated middle and high castes more than had previous governments. Solanki needed the assure himself that the entire KHAM contingent would be delivered. When one of the political allies instrumental to this process defected, he turned to reservation policies to secure the votes of that constituency. The new policy appealed to a larger coalition and incorporated the groups whose votes had become uncertain through the defection. But the new policy shrank the role of the nontargeted groups even further, and they responded by protesting.

Solanki and Congress-I won the state elections, but the price was high. Antireservation protests broke out once more in Ahmedabad and

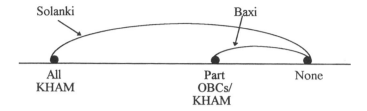

KHAM: The Kshatriya, Harijan, Adivasi, Muslims coalition

OBCs: Other Backward Classes

Solanki: Interpretations of the 1983 Rane Report by the Chief Minister of Gujarat, Madavisinh Solanki

Baxi: Baxi Commission Report, submitted in 1976

Fig. 7.3

the larger college towns in Gujarat, as students and teachers called for an examination boycott, and it soon escalated beyond even the 1981 unrest. Nearly three hundred people were killed, schools and colleges were shut down for the better part of a year, and the old quarter of Ahmedabad was torn apart with religious conflict. Several cities remained under curfew for months, and business and industry lost hundreds of millions of rupees as people were unable to get to work.[22] Solanki withdrew the proposals in March 1985, but by that time the unrest was fueled by a dynamic beyond the reservation issue. The agitation finally began to diminish after Solanki resigned and was replaced as chief minister.

In July 1985 an agreement was reached between the Gujarat government and the leaders of the antireservation movement. The government agreed that there would be no increase in the percentage of seats reserved for backward classes until a "national consensus" had been reached on the issue, that is, some decision about backward-class reservations had been made at the center. A new commission would be appointed to review the schemes currently in place and to recommend whether the 10 percent reservations should be continued beyond March 31, 1988, when the government resolution based on the Baxi report was scheduled to expire (Solanki's proposal had never been formally implemented as a government resolution).

The new commission was chaired by a sitting high-court judge, R. C. Mankad.[23] The date of expiration for the government resolution passed while data were still being gathered, so its term was extended until the Mankad Commission's report could submitted and considered.[24] The commission was not empowered to consider increasing the percentage of reserved seats from the current 10 percent, but it could review any other aspects of the program in deciding whether to recommend extending it in its current or modified form (Government of Gujarat 1987).

In 1990, before the Mankad Commission had finished and delivered its report, another conflict over reservations erupted, this one with the potential to incite serious conflict in Gujarat. The central government of V. P. Singh announced that it would implement the recommendations of the long dormant Mandal Commission report, which provided for OBC reservations at the central level in the civil service and in centrally administered colleges and universities. The first instances of violent opposition came in Bihar, a state in which conflicts over policies and politics were frequently played out in the streets. But the violence did not stop there, spreading to Uttar Pradesh, Orissa, and even Delhi, which was usually quiescent on this issue. Surprisingly, however, the violence did not spread to Gujarat. Those who had been at the forefront of the 1985 agitation attempted to rally their supporters, but they were unsuccessful, and the government promised to deal swiftly with any public conflict that arose.[25]

The reasons for this change of pace are fairly apparent. The government in 1990 was not a Congress government led by Solanki or one like him, with a political base limited to the KHAM alliance that aroused hostility in the traditional elites and Patidars. This Congress government was led by a new chief minister, Chimanbhai Patel, who had brought his splinter faction of Janata into the Gujarat Congress party, and with it Patidar interests and votes. The Patels had multiple reasons to resort to violent agitation in 1985, hoping to destabilize both reservation policies and Solanki. But now they had access to power and influence, and instability was more likely to jeopardize these resources than to increase them. Therefore, while other states in India experienced conflict and upheaval in 1990, Gujarat stayed relatively calm.

Modeling Chimanbhai Patel's Policy Solution

Figure 7.4 models these relationships. Like the Hegde government in Karnataka, the Patel government's electoral base was among the middle and high castes who were opposed to reservations. The government could not completely abandon reservations, because low castes had become a neces-

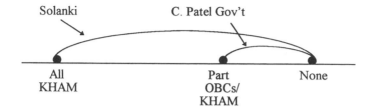

KHAM: The Kshatriya, Harijan, Adivasi, Muslims coalition

OBCs: Other Backward Classes

Solanki: Interpretations of the 1983 Rane Report by the Chief Minister of Gujarat, Madavisinh Solanki.

C. Patel Gov't: Implementation of policies by C. Patel Government.

Fig. 7.4

sary component of any party that expected to win elections, but it could (and did) move reservation policy to a more restrictive level, the original Baxi report solution that had been in place before Solanki.

Moreover, the fact that it relied more strongly on middle- and high-caste vote banks meant that it was less likely to pursue aggressive implementation even of those policies it supported, so nontargeted groups were reassured. A change of government was unlikely to improve substantially these groups' positions, and their situation could easily become worse if the new government was more reliant, as Solanki had been, on the KHAM coalition.

Despite changes in government, this compromise has continued well into the 1990s. With the demise of the KHAM strategy and the accession to power of Chimanbhai Patel, there was no party that specifically appealed to OBCs in Gujarat. After Patel's death in 1993 the Congress became even weaker, and it lost to the Bharatiya Janata party in the 1995 state elections. But the campaign was almost silent on the issue of reservations. In the 1990s, unlike the 1980s, electoral competition in Gujarat focuses on attracting OBCs by paying lip service to reservations and concentrating on other policies.

Reservations at the Center

After tabling the Kalelkar Commission report, the central government did not again consider reservations for over two decades. The pro-poor movement that swept Indira Gandhi into power in 1971 did not return the subject to prominence at the central level, in part because of the difficulties inherent in providing central reservations and in part because Gandhi thought that state-level reservation policies would be just as effective politically without incurring the same problems. Somewhat surprisingly, the next initiative was undertaken by the Janata coalition party, which was victorious over Congress-I in the elections that followed the state of emergency.

The Janata was composed of parties that succeeded the old Congress-O, conservative parties like the Jana Sangh, and regionally strong parties (Baxter 1969; Hardgrave 1980). As such, its electoral base was more conservative, and it might have been expected to eschew policies like reservations. But Morarji Desai, the leader of the Janata coalition and the new prime minister, knew that their election was as much (if not more) a protest against Indira Gandhi's excesses during the emergency as it was a vote of confidence in his coalition, and so the new government set about finding ways to woo away Congress-I voters.

One of its early actions was to appoint a new commission along the lines of the Kalelkar Commission to study once again the OBC reservation question. The new commission was appointed almost immediately upon the Janata coalition's accession to power; it was chaired by a retired civil servant named B. P. Mandal and featured distinguished scholars as its members. The terms of reference of the Mandal Commission were much like those given Kalelkar: to determine criteria for defining socially and educationally backward groups, to recommend policies for their improvement, and to consider whether to reserve positions within the government and higher education for them to increase their representation and ultimate advancement (Government of India 1981).

By the time the Mandal Commission delivered its recommendations in 1980, the Janata government had been dissolved and Indira Gandhi and her Congress-I party were once more in power. Mandal had faced many of the same problems as its predecessor and made similar recommendations. It had attempted to improve on Kalelkar's efforts by sampling two villages and one urban block in each district in the country, but for national figures on caste it was forced to fall back on the 1931 census for enumeration, with the 1971 census used to extrapolate to the relative percentage of the population. Unlike the Kalelkar Commission's range of reservation percentages, however, the Mandal recommendations were limited to a flat 27 percent for government positions and higher education alike.[26]

The political and social environments were relatively receptive for this commission. Indira Gandhi's party and government were much less committed to secular-appearing policies than Nehru had been, and the OBCs had become a politically powerful electoral force in the twenty-five years since the Kalelkar Commission had delivered its report. But perhaps because it was a commission established by one government and reporting to another, Mandal operated under a handicap, and its recommendations were accepted and then ignored. Indeed, for most of the 1980s it was impossible even to obtain a copy of the report, which quickly went out of print at the government publishers. It seemed likely that the report and its policies would simply fade away, until in 1990 it was resurrected by V. P. Singh's minority National Front government.

V. P. Singh came to power in 1989 after Rajiv Gandhi's Congress government was defeated in national elections. Singh's Janata Dal party did not command an absolute majority, but he was able to gain support from the Hindu-nationalist Bharatiya Janata party (BJP) and form a government. His majority, however, was still slim, and it was dependent within his National Front coalition on the continued cooperation of ambitious regional political leaders who had previously led smaller parties of their own. Singh's initial decision to implement the long-dormant Mandal Commission recommendations were almost certainly motivated by the loss of Devi Lal, an important north Indian leader who commanded strong voter support.[27]

Devi Lal brought into the National Front a critical and highly sought after vote bloc: lower-caste small-scale farmers in north India. He had been a difficult coalition partner, because he had aspirations to be prime minister himself. But he was necessary because of his demonstrated ability to deliver his vote banks. When Devi Lal defected, there was no leader, either within the National Front or outside the party and co-optable, who could take his place. V. P. Singh himself was an aristocratic north Indian who commanded respect but lacked the personal appeal or background characteristics that might appeal to Devi Lal's constituency. Implementation of the Mandal Commission report offered a concrete way to demonstrate his commitment to that electoral group.[28]

There were no initial indications that V. P. Singh's decision would precipitate a major crisis for the government and for the country. All major parties had consistently included support for the commission recommendations in their platforms, so the prime minister may not have anticipated the political firestorm that erupted after he announced on

August 7, 1990, that the government would immediately begin implementing the Mandal recommendations on OBC reservations. However, the reactions across northern India that were unprecedented in their scope and intensity. The initial violence, which began in Bihar, was somewhat to be expected given Bihar's history of violent response to previous attempts to extend reservation policies. But conflict spread from Orissa in the east to western Uttar Pradesh and into New Delhi. And in addition to riots and destruction of property, which had occurred in similar circumstances before, it also took uncommon forms, including mass student strikes and acts of self-immolation by college students. These protests, which continued for over two months, severely undermined the strength and credibility of the government and contributed to its fall later in the year.[29]

The other members of the coalition government, notably the BJP and members of Singh's own party, were in an awkward position. They could not denounce the idea of OBC reservations because they all depended on the vast OBC vote and they all supported implementation of the Mandal recommendations in their platforms. So they were left with various contradictory responses. Rajiv Gandhi condemned Singh's action in Parliament, but the Congress party as a whole failed to repudiate it. The BJP contended that Singh had not consulted with them before making such an important policy decision and that therefore while they did not disagree with the principle of OBC reservations, they opposed the specific instance and the way the policy had been chosen. Individual political and other critics drew on expert opinion and argued that while *some* OBC reservations might be acceptable, the specific recommendations of the Mandal Commission were flawed because the data-gathering techniques and data analysis were not up to social-science standards; therefore there should be no implementation.[30]

In the face of sustained protests and strikes by students within the capital city, V. P. Singh withdrew the plan for implementation of OBC reservations in higher education and limited them to central government employment. This concession was not enough to bring the unrest to an end, however, and the tenor of the conflict took on a horrifying new aspect as teenagers and college students began to burn themselves alive and cited the Mandal policy as their motivations. The extent to which Mandal was the true reason for their actions is debatable, but the connection was widely accepted. At the same time the Indian press, which is arguably the best in the developing world, continued their unrelenting opposition to V. P. Singh's actions.[31] Finally, the BJP, which had been particularly outraged by V. P. Singh's policy decision, retaliated. Perceiving the Mandal policy as cutting across its own attempt to unite Hindus regardless of caste, the party sought to mend the caste cleavages it had revealed. The

BJP announced that it would make the demolition of a mosque at Ayodhya, in Bihar, a major priority. It was contended that a Hindu temple had been destroyed in order to build the mosque, and there had been periodic conflicts between Muslims and Hindus over the legitimacy of the mosque. That the supposed destruction had taken place hundreds of years ago carried little weight with the militant Hindus; they contended that the land was holy for Hindus and therefore must be reclaimed. The additional conflict generated by this new crisis proved to be too much for the frail National Front government. Bereft of its BJP support, Janata Dal was unable to hold its coalition together, and V.P. Singh lost a no-confidence vote in Parliament. He was replaced by a former ally, Chandra Sekhar, who had led sixty Janata Dal MPs in a breakaway and who made a pact with Rajiv Gandhi's Congress party so that he could achieve his ultimate goal: to be prime minister. Meanwhile, the Mandal policy was put before the Supreme Court, which could rule, as *India Today* noted at the time, in a matter of months or a matter of years.[32]

Modeling the Mandal Debate

This policy conflict differs from those modeled earlier in the chapter, because unlike the Gujarat and Karnataka cases, the events took place across a coalition of parties that formed a government rather than within a single party. Since these parties are balanced relative to each other in terms of power, a single-dimensional model with different governmental actors is appropriate to show the preferences of the different members of the coalition. These relative positions and the policy outcome are shown in figure 7.5.

The National Front with Devi Lal (NF*) in it commanded a vote bank of lower-middle- and low-caste groups, and it depended on the BJP and its high-caste Hindu base to provide a governing coalition in Parliament. This was an inherently unstable combination as far as reservation policies were concerned, because it contained groups that both demanded and abhorred reservations. But the National Front was able to circumvent potential problems by simply ignoring the Mandal report, as several governments before it had done. Once Devi Lal defected, however, V. P. Singh was at NF, and since he could no longer be sure of his OBC electoral support, he turned to reservations to signal his commitment to them. But this move was anathema to the BJP, which could not publicly repudiate Mandal but which supported efforts to destabilize the government, especially during the Delhi riots.

It would be inaccurate to say that reservation policies brought down the V. P. Singh government. The National Front agreed only on defeating

Fig. 7.5

the Congress party, much like the Janata party before it, and once it occupied the government the differences within the coalition became more difficult to ignore. Devi Lal's defection made V. P. Singh's position more tenuous, and the Ayodhya mosque conflict was the final straw in a series of events. But while reservations were only one of many factors leading to the government's failure, they were undoubtedly a crucial one.

The Supreme Court Decides

The Supreme Court handed down its decision on Mandal in late 1992, and V. P. Singh was in large part vindicated. The court held that the government's plan was constitutionally valid, and that caste could be taken into consideration as one of a number of factors when targeting groups for reservations (Government of India 1993). The party in power at the time, which was the Congress, and the prime minister, Narasimha Rao, who had succeeded Rajiv Gandhi as party leader after the latter's assassination, announced their intention to comply with the Supreme Court decision and implement the Mandal report as soon as was practical.

Although there had been anticipation of conflicts in New Delhi and several state capitals, widespread opposition never materialized. Some leaders of the 1990 riots called for protests, but they were unable to generate much support, and the issue faded from newspapers' front pages fairly quickly. There are several possible reasons for this lack of enthusiasm for confrontation. First, the Supreme Court's imprimatur took away some of the protesters' ideological justification; if the commission report could stand the scrutiny of the highest court in the land, then opponents' claims that the policies were unconstitutional lost much of their force. Second, the ruling Congress party was prepared for the court's opinion and had already determined that they would follow it, which made protests seem less likely to sway them. The minister for social welfare, Sitaram Kesri, who would be responsible for implementation, had immediately announced his intention to implement the report and had been one of the few Congress leaders who had supported the report during V. P. Singh's administration, and Kesri was very powerful within the party. And finally, the natural constituency for opposition, the BJP, was preoccupied with the upcoming confrontation at the Ayodhya mosque. And as events soon proved, in Ayodhya they found an issue that became even more explosive and threatening to the Congress and other rivals than reservations had been.

Conclusion

Reservation policies since the breakup of Nehru's Congress party have become both vitally important and politically volatile for many Indian parties. They are vitally important because they are among the most powerful signals available to make emerging electoral blocs realize that parties are interested in them. But their power leads to their political volatility, because the policies spring from the enduring inequalities generated by the caste system. Like other policies that focus on individuals' and groups' ascriptive characteristics, reservations create strong attachments in the groups they target and hostility in the groups they ignore.

During the period of Congress dominance under Nehru and Sastri, reservations were unproblematic for two reasons: first, Congress party hegemony made it difficult for individual groups to break whatever policy consensus had emerged; and second, the groups that were to make reservations problematic had only just begun to mobilize as distinct political entities. The compact over reservation policies in the south had been set by the early 1920s, and the extension of reservations to scheduled castes was accomplished by the 1930s. Between that period and 1970, there were no substantial policy changes, and attempts at reform, like the Kalelkar Commission, were abandoned as soon as their controversial aspects became evident.

The rise of party competition after the breakup of the Congress party combined with increased political mobilization to disturb this stability. Since neither wing could depend on winning a majority, they were forced to appeal to numerous vote blocs. The Congress-O, which was more conservative, stuck to its traditional methods of appealing to high-caste groups and hoping these elites would bring their hierarchical dependents with them. But Indira Gandhi played a different, much more successful strategy: she appealed to the low castes and minorities directly, rather than through their caste superiors, and she offered them benefits in order to demonstrate why breaking traditional ties could be in their interests. Reservation policies were a key aspect of this process. It was not completely top-down; disadvantaged groups had been mobilizing since the independence movement. But the organizational efficiency of the old Congress party and the regularity of democratic elections sped up the development of political awareness and sophistication, and the emergency of competitive party politics created the conditions under which to tap them.

The expansion and implementation of reservation policies have led to circumstances in which they are seen as necessary to ensure support by OBCs, but their inclusion in party platforms leads to inherently unstable coalitions. Few parties can afford to abandon the still-powerful traditional high- and middle-caste elites, on whom they depend for expertise and financial resources as well as votes. But they also need the huge electoral blocs delivered by less expert and poorer groups. It is possible to combine the two, as Indira Gandhi and, for a short time, the Bharatiya Janata Party did. But both were dependent on other factors, the former on her formidable personal appeal and the latter on a backlash against other parties and a desire for more efficient government. But when these factors vanish parties lose their advantage, as the Congress party did after Gandhi's assassination and the BJP did after it proved to be no more effective at governance than its rivals. The cases discussed in this chapter show that despite demographic, historical, and political differences, reservation policies are adopted across India precisely because they represent a way to solidify electoral support, and in spite of the controversy they engender.

Substantively, Gujarat and Karnataka appear to be contrasting cases, whether the subject is political violence, attitudes toward reservations, or north-south comparisons. But theoretically they are very similar; as the models show, the essential issue is one of forging and maintaining vote blocs through political coalitions. The evidence offers conditions under which we can predict the interjection of reservations into the political calculus: when a political party or leader loses a significant electoral group, at either end of the spectrum but especially toward the low-caste end, in trying to rebuild its coalition it has strong incentive to use reservation policies to target that group (if it is OBC) or a new one (if the defector is non-OBC), presumably because OBCs remain a fairly fluid vote bank susceptible to policy-based appeals. And this incentive appears to exist regardless of the actor's knowledge of the consequences. V. P. Singh may not have known what he was risking, but Solanki and Urs certainly did.

Given this structure of incentives and the preferences of OBCs for reservations, reservation policies are difficult to give up, and the political decisions that parties have made in the 1990s reflect this reality. No party has disavowed reservations completely, and even the BJP, which was least dependent on OBC votes in the 1990 debate, has begun to support reservations, albeit gingerly, as it expands its electoral base to include targeted groups. The Supreme Court's decision has provided a protective layer of legitimacy for all political parties, and no doubt it has dampened the enthusiasm of opponents to pursue strategies of protest and violence. As even high castes have discovered, the electoral benefits of backing reservations are simply too great to ignore.

CHAPTER 8

Conclusion

At the beginning of this book I set forth three goals for this analysis. The first goal was to gain a greater understanding of the politics and process of affirmative-action policy development in the United States and India. Affirmative action is part of a class of policies, which might be termed ascriptive policies, that generate considerable conflict but endure, even in democratic countries. By comparing two otherwise quite different countries it was hoped that reasons for this endurance might be discovered and explained.

The second goal was to expand the range of comparisons acceptable in social-science research beyond the limits currently set forth. Theories of comparative analysis limit comparisons according to whether enough independent variables can be held constant to explain variation on the dependent variables or if variation on the independent variables can explain convergence on the dependent variables. If key independent variables cannot be held constant when the dependent variable diverges, as in similar-systems analysis, and if the dependent variable does not converge sufficiently to be held constant, as in different-systems analysis, then the results of that comparison cannot be trusted.

The third goal was to generate, in the process of acquiring substantive knowledge, generalizable insights to inform the study of policymaking more broadly. Theoretically, it is preferable to develop parsimonious theories that explain more rather than fewer cases. But from a substantive point of view as well, a theory that can explain policies besides affirmative action in countries other than the United States and India would have much to offer. For example, ethnic and nationalist ideologies and the policies based on them have experienced a resurgence in recent years, and social scientists have been at something of a loss to account for this development. A theory that can be generalized successfully to these cases might help us to understand similar phenomena in very different countries.

In order to achieve these goals, factors from two methodological approaches were combined to create a new theoretical framework. Aspects of comparative historical methodology were used to construct an analysis of policy development that was sensitive to historical, cultural, and political contexts in the two cases, since policies are not developed in a vacuum, and the timing and content of their development can rarely be traced to a single cause. Comparative historical methods direct attention to contextual factors that play a role in policy development. At the same time, however, comparative historical methodology is of limited use in theory construction, and so tools from rational-choice methodology were used to develop theoretical models that spanned countries and contexts to find common elements from which generalizable theories might be developed.

Assessing the Approach

Studying affirmative action comparatively across the United States and India has led to useful substantive insights. But are there generalizable propositions that can help to explain other policies in other contexts? In order to answer this question, a number of factors need to be considered. At a minimum, there must be a way to analyze the case that transcends the differences and locates common explanatory factors across them. If this condition is met, then these explanatory factors need to be generalizable to other settings.

The first condition has been met in this analysis. Although there were important differences in the historical, cultural, and political factors leading to the development and implementation of affirmative action, models drawn from rational-choice methodology were fruitfully used to explain the relationship between preferences, institutions, and policy outcomes across the United States and India. The models themselves varied, because the interactions were not always identical, but they are comparable because they were based on the same sets of assumptions and modeled the same types of relationships between the actors.

This combination of divergent models and convergent assumptions and explanations is especially apparent in the Indian case. In India, reservation policies were initiated under colonial rule, expanded during the drafting of the Indian constitution, maintained during one-party-dominant democratic conditions and then expanded under democratic party competition. It is therefore not surprising that the same model could not capture every important policy shift. During the colonial period a three-person serial game was modeled and solved through backward induction. During the 1950s, when the Congress party dominated, a single-dimensional spatial model was used. And during party competition a model that captured the policy outcomes of different electoral coalitions was used. But all three of these models delineated and solved the policy outcomes by focusing on the preferences of the actors, their relationships to each other, and the institutional means by which power was distributed between them.

In the United States, a single-dimensional spatial model could be used because the actors and the institutional structure in which they operated remained constant across time. It is apparent, however, that the ability of each actor to achieve his or her preferences depends on the way that other actors and their preferences are distributed across the spectrum. No single actor can achieve his or her preference unilaterally, and an actor's abilities to reach his or her ideal points is dependent on how his or her preferences relate to those of the other actors in the game. Once again, power is relational.

When we examine the information provided by these models, it becomes clear that there are common processes at work that appear to be critical in determining policy outcomes. Simply put, the shape that affirmative-action policies have taken in the United States and India has depended on the structure of incentives each actor faces, the preferences of the actors, the nature of the political coalitions, and the institutional structures present in each country at the time the policies were being considered. In the United States, affirmative-action programs were developed and implemented under two sets of conditions. First, when presidents and agencies chose to do so and had the unilateral ability, they implemented their preferences. This was the case during the early years of affirmative action, during the tenure of the PCEEO and the early years of the OFCC. However, given the separation of powers in the U.S. government, these policies were relatively limited and weak. In order to develop stronger policies with greater enforcement capacities, at least one of the other branches of government had to be included.

Under these conditions, however, the original player loses the unilateral ability to implement his or her preferences, and therefore affirmative-action policy outcomes are determined by the relative preferences of the different actors. During the Reagan and Bush administrations, the president and the Supreme Court were more conservative than the Congress, and they together were able to roll back existing policies, although not all the way to the president's ideal point. Congress had sufficient power to keep affirmative action from being completely gutted, but it could not impose its own preferences because they were far more liberal than either the Court's or the president's.

These outcomes are shaped in important ways by the structure of the institutions in which policies are determined. In the United States, the distribution of power among three branches of government results in policies that are almost always the result of compromise, and the tendency is for policies to approach the preferences of the more moderate actor. In India, by contrast, where the parliamentary institutional structure concentrates power, when compromises became necessary, they were usually effected outside formal government, unless a coalition controlled Parliament. During the colonial period, the British government had veto power over policies and was able to impose its preferences in most cases. Those indigenous groups whose preferences came closest to British preferences did the best, as can be seen in the case of Muslims, who were never forced to compromise with the Indian National Congress. Untouchables, whose interests were allied with but somewhat divergent from the Congress, were able to force compromises on the latter because the Congress knew that the British would compete with Congress offers.

The Indian case makes clear, however, that a parliamentary system does not mean a unilateral imposition of preferences, but means instead that the locus of negotiation and compromise is shifted. In these cases the policy outcomes are determined by the types of coalitions that exist within a party. The Poona Pact was negotiated because the Congress and untouchables had incentives to form an alliance, and reservations were the compromise policy that emerged from the actors' first preferences of no policy and separate electorates, respectively. During the constituent assembly debates, the broad range of Muslim interests was not represented, and Muslims were accorded no reservation benefits. During party competition in the 1980s, reservations were expanded as the OBC members of the party coalitions became critical and competitive.

The use of rational-choice methodology has led to the development of theoretical insights that are generalizable to cases beyond the ones studied here. However, it depends on the empirical contributions of comparative historical methodology in order to do so. In this study, the models are not abstract; instead, they are based on empirical data from the United States and India, and this data is collected according to the procedures specified in comparative historical analysis. Abstract rational-choice models are useful for extending theory, but they have difficulty linking theory to specific cases. In addition, comparative historical methods provide explanations for why specific policies are chosen from the vast range of potential choices. Chapters 2 and 3 offer insights into why affirmative action would arise as a policy option, but these insights come from using the comparative historical approach, not rational-choice methods.

The successful application of the theoretical framework introduced in chapter 1 achieves the second and third goals stated there. Despite the incompatibility of existing comparative methods with the cases being studied here, the comparative study of the United States and India yielded insights that shed light on their own histories as well as suggesting theoretical extensions to other policies and cases. The limitations imposed by existing theories of comparative analysis can be transcended and should not prevent apparently odd sets of cases from being studied in tandem. And the ability of a parsimonious theory to explain complex events over time makes it possible to test the theory across a broad spectrum of alternative scenarios.

Nevertheless, while these advantages are well worth gaining, there are some aspects of comparative historical analysis that are sacrificed. Perhaps most importantly, the comparative historical method offers the potential to discover insights about one case precisely through the study of a second, carefully selected one. In research on the development of the welfare state, for example, learning about Britain has highlighted what features are unique or idiosyncratic to the United States. Indeed, the entire debate over American exceptionalism is one that is driven by the tenets of qualitative comparative research. Such an analysis might be possible with a more parsimonious theoretical approach like the one here, but because it concentrates on a narrow range of factors and treats the rest as context, it cannot provide the richness of a comparative historical analysis.

Despite these trade-offs, this theoretical framework, which might be called the analysis of strategic choice within context, provides a superior alternative to purely abstract models as well as to empirically rich findings that are difficult to extend beyond the cases being analyzed. It provides the ability to explain individual cases with some depth and subtlety, while generating generalizable theories that can be used to explain other outcomes in other cases.

Theoretical Implications

The analysis suggests intriguing insights about the relationship between ascriptive policies and democratic institutions. In both the United States and India, the requirements of democratic politics led to the development of affirmative-action policies. In the United States, as African-American voters became incorporated into the political system, competing parties and politicians sought ways to appeal to them and capture those votes, and affirmative action provided an effective signal of good intentions. Similarly in India, even before the development of truly democratic political procedures, the Indian National Congress needed to show it was representative of all Indians, and it competed with British efforts to woo groups into its coalition. Reservation policies became a signal of its commitment to improved conditions for untouchables.

It seems evident that the choice of policies was not accidental. Ascriptive policies, despite their obvious problems and potential for controversy, signal as do few other policies a recognition by ruling elites that bedrock characteristics of groups are recognized and valued. And for newly mobilizing groups, ascriptive features are often the most easily targeted to create a sense of community and political cohesion.

In the 1970s, the study of ethnic and other ascriptive identities was characterized by a debate over whether these identities were primordial and unchanging or instrumental and politically manipulated. In the 1980s, when ethnic issues were neglected in favor of other social phenomena, the debate subsided, but it has reemerged since the breakup of the Soviet Union and the civil war in the former Yugoslavia. This study reveals how misguided is a debate based on this dichotomy. In both the United States and India, ascriptive identities are important for practical and symbolic reasons. African-Americans and untouchables were oppressed because of their ascriptive characteristics, and their social and political identities were shaped by these experiences. No political appeal or policies based on ascriptive characteristics could be successful unless they were salient for the targeted group. But these factors are also strategically useful to politicians because they provide an easy way to mobilize groups into cohesive electoral blocs. Therefore, it is best to see ethnic policies as a result of the interplay of strategic and substantive issues and interests.

The relationship between democratic politics and the development of ascriptive policies has a second intriguing component. The policy experiences analyzed here suggest that authentic democratic politics increases the controversy associated with ascriptive policies. In the United States, affirmative action was propelled by the incorporation of African-Americans into the policy process, and its rollbacks increased as opponents became aware of the policies and mobilized against them. In India, reservations became more important as more groups were brought into the political system. This suggests a paradox: as groups become politically active, which is desirable in a democracy, ascriptive policies both spur them to participate and exacerbate separations between them and other groups that do not share these ascriptive characteristics. This paradox arises because politicians are constantly seeking new votes, and ethnic, religious, or racial identities are among the most basic social categories. Their meaning is somewhat transformed in the political arena, as the Rudolphs' classic study of the modernity of caste demonstrated. But a political reliance on them keeps them from fading away or being replaced by other identities.

Finally, the study raises questions about the relationship between institutions and democratic politics that might be examined across cases.

In the United States and India, the political systems are quite different, but the same issues of power relations and coalition building arise, albeit in different forms. This suggests that the key variable in explaining policy-making is the distribution of power within political coalitions rather than the institutional structure. Clearly the institutional structure affects the contours of policymaking; for example, the ability of losers to affect policy outcomes is greater in a separation of powers system than in a parliamentary system. But the passage of a policy is dictated by the coalitions for and against it more than by the institutional structure from which it emerges.

In the United States, the institutional separation of power between different branches of government who can exercise checks on each other result in policies that do not easily move far from the status quo. Essentially, all three branches have to be in agreement about a policy to bring about a major shift, and this rarely happens. The New Deal and the Great Society are singled out as cases of such convergences, but even then the Court in the 1930s and conservative legislators in both eras were able to limit the scope of policy innovations.

In India, the parliamentary structure is seen as providing a more hospitable forum for rapid policy change, and there is clearly evidence to support such a claim. In the 1950s and 1960s, the Supreme Court attempted to curtail reservation policy development, but the Congress party was able to use its dominance in the Parliament to amend the constitution and override the Supreme Court. Clearly, when one party dominates a parliamentary political system and amending powers are liberal, then it will be able to enforce rapid change at the government level. What this argument assumes, however, is that the party is both dominant and cohesive. Nehru's Congress party and the early Congress-I of Indira Gandhi had these characteristics. But once parties were less able to control the groups within their coalitions, as happened in the 1980s and 1990s at the central and state levels, they were confronted with conflicts within their coalitions that made it difficult to use policies gain new votes without suffering any losses within the existing coalition.

These findings suggest intriguing avenues of research on the relationship between parties, institutions, and power. The ability of a party of dominate a government will depend on the institutional structure of the government and the cohesion of the party. In the United States, the Democratic party has always been heterogenous, which makes it difficult for the party to undertake major policy shifts. In India, the institutional makeup of the government aids strong parties; it does not really hinder weak ones. Therefore, it might be argued that party cohesiveness is as important to the development of strong policies as institutional structure. While this study cannot determine such a result with certainty, it suggests how we might undertake such a task.

Assessing the Cases

United States

In the United States, affirmative action arose in a context in which the historical oppression of African-Americans was finally addressed through the development of civil rights to ensure greater equality of opportunity. Affirmative action was not an explicit component of the policies that were popularly known as civil-rights policies; instead, it developed on a parallel track in part to address demands that were not being met by the emphasis on formal legal equality. Affirmative action emerged as a policy choice in part because of specific historical, cultural, and political conditions. They created an environment in which compensatory or preferential policies were an important means of signaling a commitment to a previously excluded group. But these policies also arose because of the requirements of democratic politics: the incentive to signal came from the increasing political power of African-Americans.

Before the mid–twentieth century, it would have seemed inconceivable that there could ever be sufficiently compelling reasons to initiate affirmative-action policies for African-Americans. Race has been called the defining cleavage of American politics, and the legacy of bitterness engendered by conflicts over race relations made even egalitarian policies difficult to support. The Supreme Court did not explicitly affirm that segregation was unconstitutional until 1954, and until 1957 the only civil-rights legislation Congress was able to pass was pushed through Reconstruction legislatures in which the South had no genuine representation.

However, the victories won by segregationists and racists in the eighteenth, nineteenth, and early twentieth centuries created the conditions for affirmative action by structuring the terms of the debate. Before the Civil War, the South refused to accept any northern interference with its practices relating to slavery; the only concession it made was to agree that new states would be divided evenly between slave and nonslave. After the Civil War, when slavery had been abolished, southern elites set about reconstructing segregationist policies as soon as they were allowed to govern themselves after Reconstruction. And perhaps most importantly, in the twentieth century, while nonsouthern attitudes toward African-Americans were being transformed, southern positions on Jim Crow and civil rights remained unwavering. This intransigence created a situation in which compromise was almost impossible to achieve, so it is not surprising that when civil-rights proponents were able to gain political power, they were determined to make up for years of frustration. And given the uneven application of existing equal-rights policies, especially in the South, unenforced declarations of nondiscrimination seemed inadequate.

The early years of policy development reflect this desire to develop policies that were active in bringing about not just the abolition of discriminatory policies, but that also incorporated affirmative measures to integrate African-Americans into employment and education. In the early 1960s, Kennedy's unwillingness to challenge Congress on civil-rights legislation led to the creation of affirmative-action policies in the executive branch so that he could assure the civil-rights constituency that some action was being taken. In the Johnson administration, compromises with southern Democrats and conservative Republicans were necessary to achieve passage of the Civil Rights Act. These compromises shaped the decision to keep civil-rights programs that included affirmative action within the executive branch and the agencies. Because pro-civil-rights presidents had to coexist with more conservative legislatures, they had incentives to develop civil-rights policies on two tracks and in two different locations: Enforcement of formal legal equality was overseen by Congress, and affirmative action remained the province of the Department of Labor.

The continuing development of affirmative action during the first Nixon administration is less straightforward. Kennedy and Johnson were both liberal Democratic presidents for whom African-Americans and the larger civil-rights lobby were key allies, but Nixon's 1968 presidential campaign drew on an explicitly conservative platform with regard to civil rights. A number of factors contributed to this apparent paradox. First, Nixon's public pronouncements exaggerated the extent of his anti-civil-rights position. Nixon, and to an even greater extent his appointees, came from the liberal Republican tradition in which civil rights was an important issue and African-Americans were a constituency worth courting. Second, retaining affirmative-action programs within the agencies and making them more effective accorded with other goals of the Nixon administration: to rationalize government and to concentrate as much power as possible in the executive. Third, affirmative-action policy drove a wedge into the standard Democratic coalition, and in particular pitted some liberal groups against others, a situation that Nixon sought politically and enjoyed personally. And finally, and perhaps most important, as a Republican president who was moderate to liberal on many civil-rights issues, Nixon was able to build a coalition that eluded his more liberal Democratic predecessors. Party loyalty was high among Republicans, especially after eight years of Democratic domination in the executive and legislative branches. Nixon was able to tap this loyalty on many policy issues including affirmative action and to use it to induce all but the most conservative to vote with his administration. Liberal and moderate Democrats joined the coalition despite their antagonism toward Nixon because they favored the policies. Kennedy and Johnson, by contrast, were unable to draw any but the most liberal Republicans without major concessions, and party loyalty was an insufficient inducement for southern Democrats when it came to civil rights and affirmative action. It is ironic, given the distribution of preferences across the Republican and Democratic parties in the 1960s and 1970s, that a moderate Republican, even one who ran on a southern-strategy election platform, was more effective at expanding affirmative action than any Democratic president except Johnson in the landslide years of 1965–66.

The Reagan and Bush presidencies reiterate how important this distribution of preferences is and introduce a new factor: public opinion about affirmative-action policy. By the 1980s, liberal Republicans had become an almost extinct species, and civil rights was no longer a competitive party issue; instead, it was seen as the exclusive province of the Democrats. But while southern Democrats were becoming less adamant in their opposition to civil-rights issues as their electoral dependence on African-Americans increased, civil rights as an issue was becoming more problematic politically for Democrats in general. Until the 1970s, affirmative action was developed outside the public limelight, and few Americans had strong opinions. By the end of that decade, affirmative action had become a lightning rod, with opponents citing it as an embodiment of how civil rights had been perverted and supporters pointing to the need for affirmative action because of the limitations of earlier civil-rights programs.

The Reagan administration demonstrated to perfection how to exploit this conflict and use it to roll back affirmative action farther than the median voter probably wished. Reagan was firmly toward the conservative end of the ideological spectrum, but presidential veto power gave him the ability to require that any civil-rights bill have the support of two-thirds of both the House and the Senate. An increasingly conservative Supreme Court provided no relief for civil-rights supporters, and the controversy that affirmative action aroused among whites, and even among a few vocal African-Americans, made many legislators uncomfortable with taking strong positions in its favor.

But while Reagan and Bush were able to reverse the trend set by their predecessors in affirmative-action policy, they were not able to do away with it entirely, a move that Reagan might well have favored. Although the

Supreme Court limited the scope of affirmative-action programs, it did not rule them unconstitutional as long as they were presented as remedies for demonstrated prior discrimination. By the late 1980s, Congress was able to muster the two-thirds needed to override Reagan's veto of the Court's most constraining civil-rights decision, *Grove City v. Bell.* And it repeated this feat in 1992, when it overrode a Bush veto of a bill designed to restore some of the affirmative-action provisions the Court had removed in *Wards Cove.* By the end of the Bush administration, the boundaries of affirmative-action policy had been fairly well established. Programs had been rolled back from their high-water mark during the Nixon and Carter administrations, but they overcame repeated attempts to weaken them to the point of total ineffectiveness. It seems reasonable to conclude that there is a stable consensus around a limited application of affirmative-action policies by the government. Any attempts to completely eradicate them are likely to fail, but so are attempts to expand their scope significantly.

India

Affirmative action in the United States can be characterized as a policy push beyond formal legal equality for African-Americans. In India, by contrast, reservations developed as a compromise policy for minority groups, first and most notably for untouchables. The gradual introduction of indigenous political representation and political participation under colonial rule was inevitably quite different than the introduction of these institutions would have been in a democratic system, and not surprisingly, they gave rise to different policies. When the British began to allow Indians to take part in government, they were concerned with keeping Indian society divided into separate groups in order to reduce the threat of successful challenges to colonial authority, and one of the earliest tools in this process was the development of separate systems of political representation. Indian Muslims, especially those in the United Provinces who had comprised the ruling elite under Mughal and early British rule, welcomed the possibility of separate political electorates as a way of maintaining their standing in the face of an increasingly strong and mobilizing Indian National Congress.

As other groups began to become more politically aware, the British incorporated them into political-reform efforts as well, but always with the potential to remain separate from the Indian National Congress. By the 1930s, when the British invited Indian representatives to London to draft a new Government of India Act at the Round Table Conferences, the British were willing to offer every non-Congress group separate electorates, and the Congress was just as determined to avoid fragmentation. Given the British position, it was ultimately impossible to convince the Muslim leaders to compromise on separate electorates, since they could exert more power and autonomy if they stayed apart from the Congress. But untouchables were a different story. Many untouchables wanted to be considered a valued part of Hindu society, and they revered Gandhi, especially when he begin to espouse the abolition of untouchability and initiated the Harijan Uplift campaign. Therefore, they were willing to give up greater autonomy in favor of a compromise that would give them a preferential position within the Indian National Congress fold. Reservations, as codified in the Poona Pact, represented this compromise.

Although most leaders in Congress were not particularly fond of reservations, they were willing to keep them, to the extent of writing them into the Indian constitution and retaining them as policies once India gained independence. Unlike Nehru, most leaders did not have strong and principled objections to reservations, and they were well aware of their advantages. In the south, political parties had to support reservations for non-Brahmins if they expected to be electorally viable. In the north, untouchable reservations did not arouse much opposition among caste Hindus, and OBCs were not yet sufficiently mobilized as a separate group to demand them and cause conflicts with high- and middle-caste electoral blocs. Therefore, the Congress party was able to forge a political coalition that included untouchables, high-caste Hindus, Muslims, and southern non-Brahmins, without any of the potential instabilities of this combination coming to the fore.

This equilibrium broke down, however, when the Congress party factionalized and split into different wings in the late 1960s. At that point party competition began to develop and factions could no longer take for granted any group's vote, so they developed programmatic appeals. OBCs, who were mobilizing on their own and becoming more politically sophisticated, and whose clientelist ties were weakening in terms of electoral loyalty, became the new targets for many politicians. Indira Gandhi, whose name recognition and family legacy were especially strong among the poor and historically oppressed, solidified these advantages by promising to develop policies that were aimed specifically at them. Reservations were a key part of this new policy thrust, and they were successful both in attracting newly mobilizing groups and in mobilizing potential new vote blocs. But while Gandhi was able to expand her electoral base to incorporate some of the same inherently contradictory interests as her father had done, her allies, who lacked her family appeal and her personal strength, were less able to avoid conflict.

The experiences of Urs and Solanki are illustrative. Urs came to power on Gandhi's coattails and with a specific mandate to increase representation for OBCs. Accordingly, he repudiated the existing reservation policy and formed a commission to develop new criteria that would incorporate more disadvantaged groups. Urs, who was an extremely savvy politician, attempted to drive a wedge through the dominant caste elites who had benefited so greatly from the existing policies by including some and not others in the new scheme. But he was ultimately unsuccessful, and he compromised by expanding the total percentage of eligible groups, keeping the elite groups as targeted recipients but expanding the constituency downward in the population. This solution, while politically sensible, has been deemed constitutionally invalid. But neither Urs nor any of his successors, regardless of party, has been able to come up with a solution that is both constitutionally acceptable and politically feasible. The equilibrium solution, which involves continually promising the Supreme Court that an acceptable policy is just a commission away, may also run out of time politically. As the poorer and more disadvantaged groups become more politically active and powerful, they will challenge the disproportionate benefits elite OBCs have been receiving. And the elite OBCs will not give up without a fight, so Karnataka in the future may eventually come to resemble Gujarat in the present.

In Gujarat, Solanki had little choice and a more volatile situation that the one Urs confronted. The introduction of OBC reservations greatly angered middle castes, who saw themselves as traditionally suppressed by high castes and newly squeezed out by rising OBC groups. When their protests were unsuccessful, they took to the streets and shut down major cities for months at a time. But Solanki could not afford to do away with reservations, because OBC groups, as part of the KHAM coalition, were an integral part of his political base. This dependence was illustrated dramatically in 1985, when the defection of a major OBC leader from Solanki's coalition led to the unilateral imposition of higher reservation quotas just before state elections. As Solanki must have expected, the quotas were greeted with protests that developed into violent and sustained riots, but he maintained them until forced to back down by the party high command in Delhi.

The problem with Gujarat's policies is different from the Karnataka case in that the Supreme Court is not a player; Gujarat's reservations have never come close to the Supreme Court limits established in *Balaji v. Mysore,* much less exceeded them. The animosity of high and middle castes keeps reservation quota percentages well below the targeted groups' population percentages. There is a similarity in the two cases, however, in that increases in percentages trigger negative responses that have to be addressed. In Karnataka, the negative responses come from Brahmins, dominant-caste elites, and the Supreme Court. In Gujarat, they come from middle castes who take to the streets. In both cases, the political solutions are essentially the same. Commissions are convened to reconsider policy choices, thus placating the Court and the middle castes, and in the meantime the policies are implemented according to the former status quo.

Political parties were able to keep these disputes at the state level until the 1980s, when the assassinations of Indira and then Rajiv Gandhi removed the Nehru dynasty's comparative advantage and increased party competition. This change increasingly took the form of coalitions in which inherently contradictory groups were forced to coexist in order to form a government. As long as these coalitions stayed intact, reservation policies could be avoided. But in 1990, when a major deliverer of OBC votes defected from the ruling party's coalition, the prime minister resorted to announcing that a long-dormant commission report on reservations would be implemented. This decision touched off riots throughout India, angered his coalition partners, and contributed to his government's dissolution less than six months later. But it is easy to understand why this action was taken. The OBC vote bank had to be ensured if the government was going to last, and reservation policies were the clearest and most powerful signal with which to appeal. Their value can be seen by the way the next government treated the issue: as long as the Supreme Court was deliberating, reservations were put on hold, but once the Court ruled in favor of their implementation, the government announced that it would follow the Court's dictate, and within a year had done so. Even the BJP, which is probably the most dependent of the major national parties on high-caste votes, has always supported the implementation of reservations in its party platform.

Policy Implications

In both the United States and India, affirmative action emerged as a political response to appeal to historically oppressed groups who were development into electorally important constituencies. For political parties and individual leaders, they signaled a commitment that went beyond formal legal equality, which was often viewed as insufficient or ineffective by these groups, to concrete assurances that African-Americans and low-caste Hindus would be represented in politics, government employment, and education. When these policies were initiated, they provoked little hostility, especially when compared to the benefits they provided to parties. But over time, as nontargeted constituencies became aware of them, a backlash developed in each country, and affirmative action became highly controversial.

Despite these controversies, however, affirmative action could not be abandoned. It continued to represent a powerful appeal for the groups it targeted, and most parties needed to gain these groups' votes. The result, in both cases, is an uneasy compromise in which policies are subject to expansions and contractions depending on the political preferences of the parties in power. In India, the parliamentary structure tends to make these swings quite pronounced, whereas in the United States the separation-of-powers system offers minority groups several opportunities to block policies and therefore mitigates against sharp swings.

Policy development over the last two or three years confirm the importance of the relationship between parties' electoral interests, public opinion, and policy changes. In India, the national riots touched off in 1990 by the prime minister's decision to implement the Mandal report and the BJP's reaction to these events led observers to theorize that reservation policies might not withstand many more years. But the sheer numbers of citizens targeted by the policies and the importance they assign to reservations has mitigated against such a trend. The BJP's behavior is perhaps the most unexpected. As the party has become more hopeful of capturing power at the national level, it has muted its previous vocal opposition to reservations. This change is not due to an ideological transformation, but because the BJP has realized that it cannot win Parliament without at least some OBC support. Reservations are not its primary policy weapon; instead, it relies on relief work and a form of Hindu nationalism that embraces all castes equally. But the party leaders are becoming increasingly aware that these policies are symbolically very meaningful to their prospective voters, and they cannot afford to ignore those preferences.

The result is that in current Indian politics reservations are accepted even by their opponents as a policy choice that is here to stay. It may well be that as more and more OBCs are able to take advantage of the opportunities offered, divisions will increase within the targeted groups. Or, as resources become even more contested, the deprivations felt by the middle and upper castes will grow more intense and jeopardize the present equilibrium. But unless parties can develop an even more salient policy or targeted groups abandon their attachment, reservations will remain a part of the Indian political landscape.

India's experiences are worth keeping in mind when observing current U.S. debates about affirmative action. At present the policies are as embattled as they have ever been, including the ebb period following *Grove City* during the Reagan presidency. The Republican party appears to be relatively comfortable abandoning much of the African-American vote, and many Democratic party politicians are silent on the issue. Electorally, the impetus for supporting affirmative action seems less strong than it does in India. The targeted population is smaller and there exists a small but highly visible minority within it that opposes the policy. Public opinion appears to be solidly opposed, making support costly for politicians, although the subject's sensitivity to question wording makes a clear reading difficult.

Nevertheless, there are several reasons to think that predicting the demise of affirmative action would be premature. When Americans are asked directly if they want affirmative action to be abolished, only about 25 percent say yes (Steeh and Krysan 1996). The rise of minority middle-class groups and the decline of overt racism has made the original compensation argument used to justify the policy choice less compelling, but the enduring poverty and lack of opportunity for many minority-group members continues to provide a strong rationale. Public opinion suggests that Americans object to any policy that privileges candidates chosen solely on the basis of ascriptive characteristics over other equally or more qualified candidates who are assumed to have benefited from privileges conferred by race. But they are more supportive of policies that rectify demonstrated wrongs. Put more simply, Americans want to know that preferences are used sparingly and in carefully chosen situations; in this attitude they mirror some of the choices made by the Supreme Court. If proponents of affirmative action are able to show that they are taking these concerns into account, support may well rise.

Affirmative-action policies originated to solve social inequalities that have undergone important transformations in the years that followed. In India, the electoral calculus provides the stark reality that maintains them even when they are suboptimal in terms of social outcomes. In the United States the calculus is less straightforward, and both proponents and opponents need to persuade voters on the other side for their positions to carry the day. If the policies are to be retained, they will have to be transformed so that skeptics are convinced that they answer today's social issues, not those of fifty years ago. Even the most central of society's symbols undergo changes in order to remain relevant.

Notes

Chapter 1

1. The policies studied in the book are known as affirmative action in the United States and reservation policies or reservations in India. Unfortunately, there is no term that adequately covers both sets of policies and conveys the same meanings in both countries. Throughout this book I use the term *affirmative action* when discussing policies in both countries and in the United States, and the terms *reservations* or *reservation policies* when discussing the Indian case alone.

2. See the Department of Labor (DOL) records for this period in the National Archives (EEO Files, NN-370), especially Wirtz 1962.

3. DOL records, Wirtz 1965, 1966, 1967.

4. Affirmative-action policy did not surface on the public agenda until the early 1970s. See for example, Schuman, Steeh, and Bobo (1985), and Page and Shapiro (1992) for the emergence of public opinion.

5. Galanter (1984) provides an overview of the development of reservation policies. Irshick (1969) discusses the development of representation for non-Brahmins in Madras in the early twentieth century.

6. This is not the first study to attempt such a synthesis. Bates (1981, 1989) and North (1981) pioneered this type of combination, and others have followed in recent years. However, most of these studies emphasize one approach over another, using either sophisticated models and sketchy secondary data, or extensive primary data with rational choice as a heuristic. In this book I have attempted a more balanced approach.

7. For the United States, Graham (1990) provides an excellent description of the early processes. Sundquist (1968) refers in passing to the executive action of the early 1960s. For India, Moore (1974) provides the most careful overview, but the subject is taken up from different perspectives in Zelliot (1969), Brown (1977), Dushkin (1974), Irshick (1969), and Galanter (1984).

Chapter 2

1. The Court neglected to mention that the state of Massachusetts had outlawed school segregation six years after that court decision. See Kluger (1975, 77) for a discussion.

2. See, for example, the correspondence in the Lansdowne Collection about representation in the India Office Library and Records (IOLR), MSS.Eur.D.558/5.

3. Government of Britain (1861), Lansdowne Collection, MSS.Eur.D.558/5.

4. Morley Collection, MSS.Eur.D.573/34.

5. This view is not universally held across the subcontinent; in Indian history textbooks Akbar is usually held up as an ideal king and Aurangzeb is depicted as a corrupt religious fanatic, whereas in Pakistan Aurangzeb is the hero and Akbar draws mixed reviews.

Chapter 3

1. Under the rules of the Senate, any bill could be debated for as long as at least one senator wished to speak, and the only way to end debate was by a two-thirds majority vote. In practical terms, this meant that bills often need the support of two-thirds of the Senate.

2. Lansdowne Collection, Mss.Eur.D.558/5, No 20.

3. Lansdowne Collection, MSS.Eur.D.558/5, No 20.

4. Morley Collection, MSS.Eur.D.573/34.

5. These are the 1892 reforms (MSS.Eur.D.558/5), 1909 reforms (MSS.Eur.D.573/34), 1918 Reforms (Government of Britain 1918).

6. The marquess of Lansdowne's papers provide an insight into this type of British civil servant. An intelligent and insightful viceroy, he also happened to be a cousin of Queen Victoria (MSS.Eur.D.558/5).

7. Lansdowne Collection, MSS.Eur.D.558/5.

8. Morley Collection, Mss.Eur.D.573/33.

9. Morley Collection, Mss.Eur.D.573/33.

10. Backward classes are defined as those groups who rank above untouchables and below the twice-born in the caste hierarchy. In north India there are many non-Brahmin, twice-born caste groups, but in south India there are few castes between Brahmins and non-twice-born castes. This has created a social situation in which caste groups can be quite powerful politically and economically but have little social and ritual power.

11. Some small communities, such as Indian Christians and Mudaliars, who did not meet the language requirement, were also included.

12. Morley Collection, MSS.Eur.D.573/33.

Chapter 4

1. See Rosenthal (1990) for an excellent review.

2. Kheel report, Wirtz 1962, Box 15.

3. The positions of the House, Senate, and their committees are calculated by determining their median ADA scores, obtained from the ICPSR database at the University of Michigan. The position of other actors are approximated through the use of other empirical sources, such as public speeches, internal memos, etc.

4. The memo is unsigned, but it was probably commissioned by and directed to

the secretary of labor, Willard Wirtz, who had succeeded Goldberg in 1962 (Wirtz 1964, Box 155).

5. Wirtz 1964, Box 155, memo, p. 12.

6. Wirtz 1964, Box 155, memo, p. 14.

7. Wirtz 1964, Box 155. memo, p. 15.

8. Wirtz 1965, Box 251, Roosevelt letter.

9. Wirtz 1965, Boxes 247, 251.

10. Wirtz 1965, McCreedy to Taylor, 5/28/65, Box 246.

11. Wirtz 1965, Katzenbach to Wirtz, 10/29/65, Box 251.

12. Wirtz 1965, McCreedy to Taylor, 9/13/65, Box 247.

13. Wirtz 1965, McCreedy to Taylor, 9/13/65, Box 247.

14. Wirtz 1965, McCreedy to Taylor, 5/28/65, Box 246.

15. Wirtz 1965, Humphrey memo, 9/17/65, Box 247.

16. *New York Times,* April 10, 1966, p. 1.

17. Wirtz 1966, Memo on Downing meeting, Box 360.

18. Wirtz 1967, Gardner to Wirtz, 7/26/67, Box 61.

19. Wirtz 1967, Rothermund to Wirtz, 12/19/67, Box 61.

20. Wirtz 1967, Macaluso to Dunn, 12/15/67, Box 61.

21. Wirtz 1967, Wirtz to Dunn, 12/26/67, Box 61.

22. See Page and Shapiro (1992), Schuman, Steeh, and Bobo (1985). 23. Wirtz 1966, Wirtz to contracting agency heads, 1/10/66, Box 360.

24. Wirtz 1968, *DOL News,* 5/26/68, Box 54.

25. Wirtz 1968, Sylvester to Wirtz, 5/9/68, Box 54.

26. Shultz 1969, Shultz testimony, 8/11/69, Box 52.

27. Shultz 1969, Packard to Shultz, 2/13/69, Box 68.

28. Shultz 1969, Box 67.

29. See, for example, the DOL file letters on Cleveland (Wirtz 1967, Box 61).

30. Shultz 1969, 6/27/69, Box 67.

31. Staats to Shultz, 8/5/69, Box 67.

32. Staats to Shultz, 8/5/69, Box 67.

33. 42 U.S.C. 2000e-2(j).

34. Shultz 1969, 12/20/69, Box 67.

35. Shultz 1969, Press conference, 12/20/69, Box 67.

36. Shultz 1969, Press conference, 12/20/69, Box 67.

37. Hodgson 1969, Box 8.

38. Hodgson 1969, Box 8.

39. Hodgson 1969, Order No. 4, 11/20/69, Box 8.

40. Hodgson 1969, Order No. 4, p. 11.

41. Hodgson 1969, Order No. 4, p. 14.

42. Silberman 1972, quoted in Henaghan memo, 7/19/72, Box 1.

43. Silberman 1972.

Chapter 5

1. After nearly two decades, the appointment of William Rehnquist to the Court broke a tradition of unanimous votes supporting school integration through

busing. By 1976, the Court had shifted enough in personnel and ideology to bring court-ordered busing to a virtual halt with its *Milliken* decisions.

Chapter 6

1. See the correspondence in the Lansdowne Collection, MSS.Eur.D.558/44, IOLR.

2. Lansdowne Collection, MSS.Eur.D. 558/44, Copeland (1945).

3. Morley Collection, MSS.Eur.D.573/35, Government of India (1918, 1930).

4. A second variant of joint electorates allowed only Muslims to vote in a primary to select Muslim candidates, from whom a winner would be chosen by all voters in the general election.

5. *Report of the All Parties Conference* (Nehru Report) (1928), Government of India (1932), Templewood Collection, MSS.Eur.E.240/65.

6. These preferences have been drawn from public and confidential statements in archival materials, especially the Templewood Collection, MSS.Eur.E.240/1, and the RTC *Proceedings.*

7. Templewood Collection, MSS.Eur.E.240/11(b) and (c).

8. Templewood Collection, MSS.Eur.E.240/16, pp. 10–11.

9. Templewood Collection, MSS.Eur.E.240/11(b) and (c), p. 253.

10. Reading Collection, MSS.Eur.F.115/1, p. 53.

11. The viceroy was less skeptical than London; see the correspondence between Willingdon and Hoare, MSS.Eur.E.240/11 (b) and (c).

12. After the Poona Pact was announced, Gandhi immediately began a campaign to abolish untouchability and allow untouchables into places, like temples, from which they had historically been prohibited.

13. Templewood Collection, Mss.Eur.E.240/6.

14. This strategy of controlling committees, and through them policy agendas, is consistent with theories and empirical evidence for the structure of committees in the U.S. Congress (Gamm and Shepsle 1989).

15. Constitutional amendments are generally easier to effect in India than in the United States. Most simply require a two-thirds vote of those present and voting in both houses of Parliament.

16. Gazetted and nongazetted posts are analogous to the distinction between commissioned and noncommissioned posts in the military.

17. Interview with M.A.S. Rajan, Bangalore, April 1988.

Chapter 7

1. Interview with L. G. Havanur, Bangalore, April 1988.

2. Interview with M. A. S. Rajan, Bangalore, April 1988.

3. Interview with Mumtaz Ali Khan, Bangalore, April 1988.

4. Interview with M. A. S. Rajan, Bangalore, April 1988.

5. Interview with T. Venkataswamy, Bangalore, April 1988.

6. Interview with M. S. Rao, Bangalore, April 1988.

7. Interview with M. S. Rao, Bangalore, April 1988.

8. Government of Karnataka 1986b; interviews with M. A. Khan, M. A. S. Rajan, T. Venkataswamy, Bangalore, April 1988.

9. Government of Karnataka 1986b; interview with M. S. Rao, Bangalore, April 1988.

10. Interview with S. Basulingappa, Bangalore, April 1988.

11. Interview with S. Basulingappa, Bangalore, April 1988.

12. This chronology is drawn from Yagnik and Bhatt (1984).

13. Interview with Achyut Yagnik, Ahmedabad, March 1988.

14. Interview with T. D. Soyanter, Ahmedabad, March 1988.

15. Interview with R. C. Mankad, Ahmedabad, March 1988.

16. Interview with M. Subha Rao, Ahmedabad, March 1988.

17. Interview with M. Subha Rao, Ahmedabad, March 1988.

18. Interview with Indubhai Jani, Ahmedabad, March 1988.

19. Interview with Shankarbhai Patel, Ahmedabad, March 1988.

20. Interview with Indubhai Jani, Ahmedabad, March 1988.

21. Interview with Indubhai Jani, Ahmedabad, March 1988.

22. Interview with Anil Bhatt, Ahmedabad, March 1988.

23. Interview with R. C. Mankad, Ahmedabad, March 1988.

24. Interview with M. Subha Rao, Ahmedabad, March 1988.

25. Interview with Achyut Yagnik, Ahmedabad, December 1992.

26. Interview with Achyut Yagnik, Ahmedabad, December 1992.

27. Interview with Sitaram Kesri, New Delhi, December 1992.

28. *India Today,* September 1, 1990.

29. *India Today,* November 15, 1990.

30. *India Today,* September 15, 1990.

31. *India Today,* September 15, 1990.

32. *India Today,* November 15, 1990.

Bibliography

Primary Sources

India

India Office Library and Records, London

Lansdowne Collection, MSS.Eur.D.558.
Templewood Collection, MSS.Eur.D.240.
Morley Collection, MSS.Eur.D.573.
Haig Collection, MSS.Eur.F.115

Official Printed Sources

Government of Bombay. 1930. *Report of the Depressed Classes and Aboriginal Tribes Committee, Bombay Presidency.* Bombay: Government Press.
Government of Britain. 1861. *Despatches Relating to the Constitution of Councils in India.* Cd. 307, Parliamentary Papers: LXIII.
———. 1918. *Report on Indian Constitutional Reforms.* 06.18.90. Cd. 9109, Parliamentary Papers VIII.
———. 1930. *Report of the Indian Statutory Commission.* Vols. 1-XVI. London: HMSO.
———. 1931. Round Table Conference, 12 November 1930–19 January 1931: Proceedings of the Sub-Committees. Vol. 2. London: HMSO.
———. 1932. *Round Table Conference,* 7 September 1931–1 December 1931, Proceedings. Cd. 3997.
Government of Gujarat. 1976. *Report of the Socially and Educationally Backward Class Commission.* (A. R. Baxi, Chairman.) 2 Vols. Gandhinagar, Gujarat: Government Press.
———. 1983. *Report of the Socially and Educationally Backward Classes [Second] Commission.* (C. V. Rane, Chairman.) 2 Vols. Gandhinagar, Gujarat: Government Press.
———. 1987. "Resolution No:SSP-1086–997-A." (Commission to Review the Scheme Now in Force for Socially and Educationally Backward Classes.) Social Welfare Department, Sachivalaya, Gandhinagar.

Government of India. 1948–49. *Constituent Assembly Debates.* Vol. 8. Delhi: Government Press.
———. 1955. *Report of the Backward Classes Commission* (Kaka Kalelkar, Chairman). 3 Vols. Delhi: Manager of Publications.
———. 1981. *Report of the Backward Classes Commission* (B. P. Mandal, Chairman). 7 Vols. (in 2). New Delhi: Controller of Publications.
Government of Karnataka. 1975. *Karnataka Backward Classes Commission Report.* (L. G. Havanur, Chairman.) 2 Vols. Bangalore: Government Press.
———. 1986a. *Report of the Second Backward Classes Commission.* (T. Venkataswamy, Chairman.) 2 Vols. Bangalore: Government Press.
———. 1986b. *A New Deal for Backward Classes in Karnataka.* Bangalore: Government Press.
(Nehru Report) *Report of the All Parties Conference.* 1928. 3 vols. Allahabad: All India Congress Committee.

Periodicals

Frontline. Bombay, 1986.
India Today. Bombay, 1986–92.

Interviews

Anil Bhatt, Ahmedabad, March 1988.
Indubhai Jani, Ahmedabad, March 1988.
R. C. Mankad, Ahmedabad, March 1988.
Shankarbhai Patel, Ahmedabad, March 1988.
T. D. Soyanter, Ahmedabad, March 1988.
M. Subha Rao, Ahmedabad, March 1988.
S. Basulingappa, Bangalore, April 1988.
L. G. Havanur, Bangalore, April 1988.
Mumtaz Ali Khan, Bangalore, April 1988.
M. A. S. Rajan, Bangalore, April 1988.
M. S. Rao, Bangalore, April 1988.
T. Venkataswamy, Bangalore, April 1988.
Sitaram Kesri, New Delhi, December 1992.
Achyut Yagnik, Ahmedabad, December 1992.

United States

National Archives, Washington, D.C.

Department of Labor Records (EEO Files, NN-370):
Wirtz 1962, 1964–68
Shultz 1969
Hodgson 1969
Silberman 1972

Periodicals

New York Times, 1966.
Congressional Quarterly Almanac, 1969, 1984–92

Secondary Sources

Alt, James E., and Kenneth A. Shepsle. 1990. *Perspectives on Positive Political Economy.* New York: Cambridge University Press.
Amaker, Norman C. 1988. *Civil Rights and the Reagan Administration.* Washington, D.C.: Urban Institute Press.
Amenta, Edwin. 1991. "Making the Most of a Case Study: Theories of the Welfare State and the American Experience." *International Journal of Comparative Sociology* 32:172–94.
Amenta, Edwin, Elisabeth Clemens, Jefren Olson, Sunita Parikh, and Theda Skocpol. 1987. "The Political Origins of Unemployment Insurance in Five American States." In *Studies in American Political Development,* vol. 2., ed. Karen Orren and Stephen Skowronek. New Haven: Yale University Press.
Amenta, Edwin, and Theda Skocpol. 1988. "Redefining the New Deal: World War II and the Development of Social Provision in the United States." In *The Politics of Social Policy in the United States,* ed. Margaret Weir, Ann Shola Orloff, and Theda Skocpol. Princeton: Princeton University Press.
Anderson, J. W. 1964. *Eisenhower, Brownell, and the Congress.* Case Study 80, Inter-University Case Program Series. Kingsport, Tenn.: Kingsport Press.
Austin, Granville. 1966. *The Indian Constitution: Cornerstone of a Nation.* Oxford: Clarendon Press.
Bailyn, Bernard. 1967. *The Ideological Origins of the American Revolution.* Cambridge: Harvard University Press.
Bardach, Eugene. 1977. *The Implementation Game.* Cambridge: MIT Press.
Bates, Robert H. 1981. *Markets and States in Tropical Africa.* Berkeley and Los Angeles: University of California Press.
———. 1989. *Beyond the Miracle of the Market.* New York: Cambridge University Press.
Baxi, Upendra. 1980. *The Indian Supreme Court and Politics.* Lucknow: Eastern Book Company.
Baxter, Craig. 1969. *The Jana Sangh: A Biography of an Indian Political Party.* Philadelphia: University of Pennsylvania Press.
Bayly, C. A. 1988. *The New Cambridge History of India.* Vol. 2, no. 1: *Indian Society and the Making of the British Empire.* Bombay: Orient Longman Press.
Bellah, Robert N., Richard Madsen, William M. Sullivan, Ann Swidler, and Steven M. Tipton. 1985. *Habits of the Heart: Individualism and Commitment in American Life.* New York: Harper and Row.
Bennett, William, and Terry Eastland. 1979. *Counting by Race.* New York: Basic Books.
Benokraitis, Nijole V., and Joe R. Feagin. 1978. *Affirmative Action and Equal Opportunity: Action, Inaction, Reaction.* Boulder, Colo.: Westview Press.

Beteille, Andre. 1983. *The Idea of Natural Inequality and Other Essays.* Delhi: Oxford University Press.

Binmore, Ken. 1992. *Fun and Games: A Text on Game Theory.* Lexington, Mass.: D.C. Heath.

Bouton, Marshall, and Philip Oldenburg. 1993. *India Briefing.* New York: Asia Society.

Brass, Paul R. 1971. *Language, Religion, and Politics in North India.* New York: Cambridge University Press.

Brown, Judith M. 1977. *Gandhi and Civil Disobedience.* Cambridge: Cambridge University Press.

———. 1985. *Modern India: The Origins of an Asian Democracy.* New York: Oxford University Press.

Burk, Robert Frederick. 1984. *The Eisenhower Administration and Black Civil Rights.* Knoxville: University of Tennessee Press.

Burstein, Paul. 1985. *Discrimination, Jobs, and Politics.* Chicago: University of Chicago Press.

Carmines, Edward G., and James A. Stimson. 1989. *Race and the Transformation of American Politics.* Princeton: Princeton University Press.

Carter, Stephen. 1991. *Reflections of an Affirmative Action Baby.* New York: Basic Books.

Cates, Jerry. 1983. *Insuring Inequality: Administrative Leadership in Social Security, 1935–54.* Ann Arbor: University of Michigan Press.

Cawelti, John G. 1965. *Apostles of the Self-Made Man: Changing Concepts of Success in America.* Chicago: University of Chicago Press.

Chandra, Bipan. 1979. *Nationalism and Communalism in Modern India.* Delhi: Orient Longman.

Chandrasekhar, S. 1985. *Dimensions of Socio-Political Change in Mysore, 1880–1930.* Delhi: Allied.

Constitution of India. 1985. Delhi: Eastern Book Company.

Copeland, Reginald. 1945. *The Constitutional Problem in India.* Vol. 1. London: Oxford University Press.

Cox, Gary W., and Mathew D. McCubbins. 1993. *Legislative Leviathan: Party Government in the House.* Berkeley and Los Angeles: University of California Press.

Dalfiume, Richard M. 1969. "The 'Forgotten' Years of the Negro Revolution." In *The Negro in Depression and War,* ed. Bernard Sternsher. Chicago: Quadrangle Books.

Danziger, Sheldon H., and Daniel H. Weinberg, eds. 1986. *Fighting Poverty: What Works and What Doesn't.* Cambridge: Harvard University Press.

Darnell, Alfred T. 1995. "Exploring the Boundaries of Feasible Sets: The Role of Cultural and Temporal Constraints." Vanderbilt University. Unpublished paper.

Davis, David Brion. 1975. *The Problem of Slavery in the Age of Revolution, 1770–1823.* Ithaca, N.Y.: Cornell University Press.

Denzau, Arthur T., and Robert J. MacKay. 1983. "Gatekeeping and Monopoly

Power of Committees: An Analysis of Sincere and Sophisticated Behavior." *American Journal of Political Science* 27:740–61.

Derthick, Martha. 1979. *Policymaking for Social Security.* Washington, D.C.: Brookings Institution.

Dumont, Louis. 1980. *Homo Hierarchicus.* Rev. English ed. Chicago: University of Chicago Press.

Dushkin, Lelah. 1974. "The Non-Brahman Movement in Princely Mysore." Ph.D. diss., University of Pennsylvania.

Ellwood, David T. 1988. *Poor Support.* New York: Basic Books.

Elster, Jon. 1989. *Nuts and Bolts for the Social Sciences.* New York: Cambridge University Press.

Enelow, James M., and Melvin J. Hinich. 1984. *The Spatial Theory of Voting: An Introduction.* New York: Cambridge University Press.

———, eds. 1990. *Advances in the Spatial Theory of Voting.* New York: Cambridge University Press.

Eskridge, William N., Jr. 1990. "Overriding Supreme Court Statutory Interpretation Decisions." *Yale Law Journal* 101:331–456.

Eskridge, William N., Jr., and Philip P. Frickey. 1988. *Legislation: Statutes and the Creation of Public Policy.* American Casebook Series. St. Paul: West Publishing.

Ezorsky, Gertrude. 1991. *Racism and Justice: The Case for Affirmative Action.* Ithaca, N.Y.: Cornell University Press.

Fenno, Richard F., Jr. 1978. *Home Style.* Boston: Little, Brown.

Ferejohn, John. 1991. "Rationality and interpretation: Parliamentary Elections in Early Stuart England." In *The Economic Approach to Politics: A Critical Reassessment of the Theory of Rational Action,* ed. Kristen Renwick Monroe. New York: HarperCollins.

Ferejohn, John, and Charles Shipan. 1990. "Congressional Influence on Bureaucracy." *Journal of Law, Economics, and Organization* 6:1–27.

Fiorina, Morris. 1977. *Congress: The Keystone of the Washington Establishment.* New Haven: Yale University Press.

Fishel, Leslie H., Jr. 1969. "The Negro in the New Deal Era." In *The Negro in Depression and War,* ed. Bernard Sternsher. Chicago: Quadrangle Books.

Foner, Eric. 1988. *Reconstruction: America's Unfinished Revolution, 1863–1877.* New York: Harper and Row.

Franklin, John Hope. 1980. *From Slavery to Freedom: A History of Negro Americans.* 5th ed. New York: Alfred A. Knopf.

Fredrickson, George. 1971. *The Black Image in the White Mind.* New York: Harper and Row.

Fullinwider, Robert K. 1980. *The Reverse Discrimination Controversy.* Totowa, N.J.: Rowman and Allanheld.

Galanter, Marc. 1984. *Competing Equalities: Law and the Backward Class in India.* Berkeley and Los Angeles: University of California Press.

Gamm, Gerald, and Kenneth Shepsle. 1989. "Emergence of Legislative Institutions: Standing Committees in the House and Senate, 1810–1825." *Legislative Studies Quarterly* 14:39–66.

Gely, Rafael, and Pablo Spiller. 1990. "A Rational Choice Theory of Supreme Court Statutory Decisions with Applicatiosn to the *State Farm* and *Grove City* Cases." *Journal of Law, Economics, and Organization* 6:263–300.

Gibbons, Robert. 1992. *Game Theory for Applied Economists.* Princeton: Princeton University Press.

Gilligan, Thomas, and Keith Krehbiel. 1986. "Rules, Subjurisdictional Choice, and Congressional Outcomes: An Event Study of Energy Tax Legislation." Social Science Working Paper No. 594, California Institute of Technology.

Gillion, Kenneth L. 1968. *Ahmedabad: A Study in Urban History.* Berkeley and Los Angeles: University of California Press.

Glazer, Nathan. 1987. *Affirmative Discrimination: Ethnic Inequality and Public Policy.* Rev. ed. Cambridge: Harvard University Press.

Goldman, Alan H. 1979. *Justice and Reverse Discrimination.* Princeton: Princeton University Press.

Gopal, Sarvepalli. 1983. *Jawaharlal Nehru: A Biography.* Cambridge: Harvard University Press.

Graham, Hugh Davis. 1990. *The Civil Rights Era.* New York: Oxford University Press.

Gupta, S. K. 1985. *The Scheduled Castes in Modern Indian Politics: Their Emergence as a Political Power.* New Delhi: Munshiram Manoharlal.

Gustafson, D. R. 1968. "Mysore 1881–1902: The Making of a Model State." Ph.D. diss., University of Wisconsin.

Hanson, Russell. 1985. *The Democratic Imagination in America.* Princeton: Princeton University Press.

Hardgrave, Robert L., Jr. 1980. *India: Government and Politics in a Developing Nation.* 3d ed. New York: Harcourt Brace Jovanovich.

Hardy, Peter. 1971. *The Muslims of British India.* Cambridge: Cambridge University Press.

Hartz, Louis. 1955. *The Liberal Tradition in America.* New York: Harcourt, Brace, and World.

Heclo, Hugh. 1974. *Modern Social Politics in Britain and Sweden.* New Haven: Yale University Press.

Heesterman, J. C. 1985. *The Inner Conflict of Tradition.* Chicago: University of Chicago Press.

Heidenheimer, Arnold J., Hugh Heclo, and Carolyn Teich Adams. 1983. *Comparative Public Policy.* 2d ed. New York: St. Martin's.

Higgs, Robert. 1987. *Crisis and Leviathan: Critical Episodes in the Growth of American Government.* New York: Oxford University Press.

Hirschmann, Albert O. 1977. *The Passions and the Interests.* Princeton: Princeton University Press.

Holderness, T. W. 1911. *Peoples and Problems of India.* London: Williams and Norgate.

Hunt, Lynn. 1984. *Politics, Culture, and Class in the French Revolution.* Berkeley and Los Angeles: University of California Press.

Irschick, Eugene F. 1969. *Politics and Social Conflict in South India: The Non-*

Brahmin Movement and Tamil Separatism, 1916–1929. Berkeley and Los Angeles: University of California Press.

Jalal, Ayesha. 1985. *The Sole Spokesman: Jinnah, the Muslim League, and the Demand for Pakistan.* Cambridge: Cambridge University Press.

Katznelson, Ira. 1981. *City Trenches: Urban Politics and the Patterning of Class in the United States.* New York: Pantheon.

Kaufman, Herbert. 1960. *The Forest Ranger.* Baltimore: Johns Hopkins Press.

Keohane, Robert. 1983. "Associative American Development, 1776–1860: Economic Growth and Political Disintegration." In *The Antinomies of Interdependence: National Welfare and the International Division of Labor,* ed. John Gerard Ruggie. New York: Columbia University Press.

King, Gary, Robert O. Keohane, and Sidney Verba. 1994. *Designing Social Inquiry.* Princeton: Princeton University Press.

Kishlansky, Mark. 1986. *Parliamentary Selection: Social and Political Choice in Early Modern England.* New York: Cambridge University Press.

Krehbiel, Keith. 1991. *Information and Legislative Organization.* Ann Arbor: University of Michigan Press.

Kreps, David M. 1990. *Game Theory and Economic Modelling.* New York: Oxford University Press.

Kluger, Richard. 1975. *Simple Justice.* New York: Alfred A. Knopf.

Kohli, Atul. 1990. *Democracy and Discontent: India's Growing Crisis of Governability.* New York: Cambridge University Press.

Laver, Michael, and Norman Schofield. 1990. *Multiparty Government.* New York: Oxford University Press.

Laver, Michael, and Kenneth A. Shepsle. 1990. "Coalitions and Cabinet Government." *American Political Science Review* 84:873–90.

Lawson, Stephen F. 1976. *Black Ballots: Voting Rights in the South, 1944–1969.* New York: Columbia University Press.

Lee, Everett S., Ann Ratner Miller, Carol P. Brainerd, and Richard E. Easterlin. 1957. *Population Redistribution and Economic Growth in the United States, 1870–1950.* Vol. 7. Methodological Considerations and Reference Tables. Philadelphia: American Philosophical Society.

Low, D. A., ed. 1977. *Congress and the Raj.* London: Heinemann.

Lynn, Herbert. 1955. *The Dream of Success.* Boston: Little, Brown.

McAdam, Doug. 1982. *Political Process and the Development of Black Insurgency, 1930–1970.* Chicago: University of Chicago Press.

McCubbins, Mathew, Roger Noll, and Barry Weingast. 1987. "Administrative Procedures as Instruments of Political Control." *Journal of Law, Economics, and Organization* 3:243–77.

———. 1989. "Structure and Process, Politics and Policy: Administrative Arrangements and the Political Control of Agencies." *Virginia Law Review* 75:431–82.

McCubbins, Mathew, and Terry Sullivan, eds. 1987. *Congress: Structure and Policy.* New York: Cambridge University Press.

McLane, John R. 1977. *Indian Nationalism and the Early Congress.* Princeton: Princeton University Press.

McLeod, Duncan J. 1983. "Toward Caste." In *Slavery and Freedom in the Age of the American Revolution,* ed. Ira Berlin and Ronald Hoffman. Urbana: University of Illinois Press.

Manor, James. 1977. *Political Change in an Indian State: Mysore, 1917–1955.* New Delhi: Manohar Publishing.

Mayhew, David. 1974. *Congress: The Electoral Connection.* New Haven: Yale University Press.

Mehta, Haroobhai, and Hasmukh Patel, eds. 1985. *Dynamics of Reservation Policy.* New Delhi: Patriot Publishers.

Moore, R. J. 1974. *The Crisis of Indian Unity, 1917–1940.* London: Oxford University Press.

Myrdal, Gunnar. 1944. *An American Dilemma.* New York: Harper and Row.

North, Douglass C. 1981. *Structure and Change in Economic History.* New York: W. W. Norton.

Norton, Anne. 1986. *Alternative Americas: A Reading of Antebellum Political Culture.* Chicago: University of Chicago Press.

O'Halloran, Sharyn. 1994. *Politics, Process, and American Trade Policy.* Ann Arbor: University of Michigan Press.

O'Neill, Timothy. 1985. *Bakke and the Politics of Equality.* Middletown: Wesleyan University Press.

Orfield, Gary. 1969. *The Reconstruction of Southern Education.* New York: Wiley.

Page, Benjamin I., and Robert Y. Shapiro. 1992. *The Rational Public.* Chicago: University of Chicago Press.

Paige, Jeffery M. 1975. *Agrarian Revolution.* New York: Free Press.

Pocock, J. G. A. 1975. *The Machiavellian Moment: Florentine Political Thought and the Atlantic Republican Tradition.* Princeton: Princeton University Press.

Pole, J. R. 1978. *The Pursuit of Equality in American History.* Berkeley and Los Angeles: University of California Press.

Preer, Jean L. 1982. *Lawyers v. Educators: Black Colleges and Desegregation in Public Higher Education.* Westport, Conn.: Greenwood Press.

Pressman, Jeffrey L., and Aaron B. Wildavsky. 1984. *Implementation.* 3d ed. Berkeley and Los Angeles: University of California Pres.

Przeworski, Adam, and Henry Teune. 1982. *The Logic of Comparative Social Inquiry.* Malabar, Fla.: Robert E. Krieger.

Quadagno, Jill. 1988. *The Transformation of Old Age Security.* Chicago: University of Chicago Press.

Ragin, Charles. 1987. *The Comparative Method.* Berkeley and Los Angeles: University of California Press.

Rasmusen, Eric. 1989. *Games and Information: An Introduction to Game Theory.* New York: Basil Blackwell.

Raychaudhuri, Tapan, and Irfan Habib. 1982. *The Cambridge Economic History of India.* Vol. 1. Delhi: Cambridge University Press.

Riker, William. 1986. *The Art of Political Manipulation.* New Haven: Yale University Press.

Robinson, Francis. 1974. *Separatism among Indian Muslims: The Politics of the*

United Provinces' Muslims, 1860–1923. Cambridge: Cambridge University Press.

Rosenbluth, Frances. 1989. *Financial Politics in Contemporary Japan.* Ithaca, N.Y.: Cornell University Press.

Rosenthal, Howard. 1990. "The Setter Model." In *Advances in the Spatial Theory of Voting,* ed. James M. Enelow and Melvin J. Hinich. New York: Cambridge University Press.

Rubinson, Richard. 1986. "Class Formation, Politics, and Institutions: Schooling in the United States." *American Journal of Sociology* 92:519–48.

Ruchames, Louis. 1953. *Race, Jobs, and Politics: The Story of FEPC.* New York: Columbia University Press.

Rudolph, Lloyd I., and Susanne H. Rudolph. 1967. *The Modernity of Tradition: Political Development in India.* Chicago: University of Chicago Press.

———. 1987. *In Pursuit of Lakshmi: The Political Economy of the Indian State.* Chicago: University of Chicago Press.

Schuman, Howard, Charlotte Steeh, and Lawrence Bobo. 1985. *Racial Attitudes in America.* Cambridge: Harvard University Press.

Schwartz, Bernard. 1988. *Behind Bakke: Affirmative Action and the Supreme Court.* New York: New York University Press.

Seal, Anil. 1971. *The Emergence of Indian Nationalism,* London: Cambridge University Press.

Shefter, Martin. 1977. "Party and Patronage: Germany, England, and Italy." *Politics and Society* 7:403–51.

Shepsle, Kenneth, and Barry R. Weingast. 1981. "Structure-Induced Equilibrium and Legislative Choice." *Public Choice* 37:509–19.

Sindler, Allan F. 1978. *Bakke, DeFunis, and Minority Admissions.* New York: Longman.

Sitkoff, Harvard. 1978. *A New Deal for Blacks.* New York: Oxford University Press.

Sivakumar, Chitra. 1982. *Education, Social Inequality, and Social Change in Karnataka.* Delhi: Hindustan Publishing.

Skocpol, Theda. 1979. *States and Social Revolutions.* New York: Cambridge University Press.

———, ed. 1984. *Vision and Method in Historical Sociology.* New York: Cambridge University Press.

———. 1994. *Protecting Soldiers and Mothers: The Political Origins of Social Policy in the United States.* Cambridge: Harvard University Press.

Skocpol, Theda, and G. John Ikenberry. 1983. "The Political Formation of the American Welfare State in Historical and Comparative Perspective." *Comparative Social Research* 6:87–147.

Skocpol, Theda, and Margaret Somers. 1980. "The Uses of Comparative History in Macrosocial Inquiry." *Comparative Studies in Society and History* 22:174–97.

Skowronek, Stephen. 1982. *Building a New American State: The Expansion of National Administrative Capacities, 1877–1920.* New York: Cambridge University Press.

Slessarev, Helen. 1988. "Racial Tensions and Institutional Support: Social Programs during a Period of Retrenchment." In *The Politics of Social Policy in the United States,* ed. Margaret Weir, Ann Orloff, and Theda Skocpol. Princeton: Princeton University Press.

Sovern, Michael. 1966. *Legal Restraints on Racial Discrimination in Employment.* New York: Twentieth Century Fund.

Srinivas, M. N. 1962. *Caste in Modern India and Other Essays.* Bombay: Asia Publishing House.

———. 1986. "On Living in a Revolution." In *India 2000: The Next Fifteen Years,* ed. James R. Roach. Riverdale, Md.: Riverdale Co.

Steeh, Charlotte, and Maria Krysan. 1996. "Poll Trends: Affirmative Action (and Race)." *Public Opinion Quarterly.*

Steele, Shelby. 1991. *The Content of Our Character.* New York: HarperCollins.

Steinmo, Sven, Kathleen Thelen, and Frank Longstreth, eds. 1992. *Structuring Politics: Historical Institutionalism in Comparative Analysis.* New York: Cambridge University Press.

Stokes, Eric. 1959. *The English Utilitarians and India.* London: Oxford University Press.

Sundquist, James L. 1968. *Politics and Policy: The Eisenhower, Kennedy, and Johnson Years.* Washington, D.C.: Brookings Institution.

Tendulkar, D. G. 1952. *Mahatma: Life of Mohandas Karamchand Gandhi.* 3 vols. Bombay: Vithalbhai K. Jhaveri and D. G. Tendulkar.

Tocqueville, Alexis de. 1969. *Democracy in America.* New York: Anchor.

Tsebelis, George. 1990. *Nested Games: Rational Choice in Comparative Politics.* Berkeley and Los Angeles: University of California Press.

Tucker, Richard P. 1972. *Ranade and the Roots of Indian Nationalism.* Midway reprint. Chicago: University of Chicago Press.

Tushnet, Mark V. 1987. *The NAACP's Legal Strategy against Segregated Education, 1925–1950.* Chapel Hill: University of North Carolina Press.

Tyack, David, Thomas James, and Aaron Benavot. 1987. *Law and the Shaping of Public Education.* Madison: University of Wisconsin Press.

Weiner, Myron. 1967. *Party Building in a New Nation.* Chicago: University of Chicago Press.

Weingast, Barry R., and William Marshall. 1988. "The Industrial Organization of Congress." *Journal of Political Economy* 96:132–63.

Weir, Margaret. 1992. *Politics and Jobs: The Boundaries of Employment Policy in the United States.* Princeton: Princeton University Press.

Weir, Margaret, and Theda Skocpol. 1985. "State Structures and the Possibilities for 'Keynesian' Responses to the Great Depression in Sweden, Britain, and the United States." In *Bringing the State Back In,* ed. Peter Evans, Dietrich Rueschemeyer, and Theda Skocpol. New York: Cambridge University Press.

Whalen, Charles, and Barbara Whalen. 1985. *The Longest Debate: A Legislative History of the 1964 Civil Rights Act.* New York: New American Library.

Wood, Gordon S. 1969. *The Creation of the American Republic, 1776–1787.* Chapel Hill: University of North Carolina Press.

———. 1991. *The Radicalism of the American Revolution.* New York: Vintage Books.

Woodward, C. Vann. 1974. *The Strange Career of Jim Crow.* 3d ed. New York: Oxford University Press.

Yagnik, Achyut, and Anil Bhatt. 1984. "The Anti-Dalit Agitation in Gujarat." *South Asia Bulletin* 4:45–60.

Zelliot, Eleanor. 1969. "Dr. Ambedkar and the Mahar Movement." Ph.D. diss., University of Pennsylvania.

Index